Strategic Management and the Circular Economy

In recent years, the Circular Economy (CE) has gained worldwide attention as an effective alternative economic system to the current take-make-waste model of production and consumption. As more and more firms begin to recognize the potential of this novel approach, the CE quickly moves from theory to practice and the demand for a coherent and structured strategic approach – one that companies can rely upon when commencing their circular journey – grows accordingly. *Strategic Management and the Circular Economy* aims to bridge the theory-practice gap by putting forward a detailed step-by-step process for analysis, formulation, and planning of CE strategies.

Starting from a solid framework of easy-to-grasp constructs (key principles, business objectives and areas of intervention), the authors guide the reader through an understanding of how conventional tools for strategic management can be re-programed under a CE perspective. To assist learning and encourage circular thinking, the reader is constantly prompted with examples of how forward-looking companies across industries and geographies are already applying circular strategies to future-proof their operations, boost innovation, penetrate new markets and secure customer loyalty.

Dr Marcello Tonelli is the founder and Managing Director of WorlDynamics Pty Ltd, an organization that promotes sustainable development and green innovation. After obtaining his PhD degree in Business Strategy in 2009, Dr Tonelli worked with the Australian Centre of Entrepreneurship Research (ACE) in the fields of Social Innovation, Territorial Strategies, and Poverty Alleviation generating growing academic interest. He also practiced as a Certified Management Consultant and a Fellow of the Australian Institute of Management.

Nicoló Cristoni is a sustainability professional operating at the intersection of Environmental Stewardship, Sustainable Innovation and the protection of Human and Workers' Rights. He is specialized in planning and executing responsible sourcing programs for multinational brands that are increasingly Circular Economy-inspired. Nicolò also provides technical support to international human rights organizations.

Routledge Research in Strategic Management

This series explores, develops and critiques the numerous models and frameworks designed to assist in strategic decision making in internal and external environments. It publishes scholarly research in all methodologies and perspectives that comprise the discipline, and welcomes diverse multi-disciplinary research methods, including qualitative and quantitative studies, and conceptual and computational models. It also welcomes the practical application of the strategic management process to a business world inspired by new economic paradigms.

Strategic Management and the Circular Economy

Marcello Tonelli and Nicoló Cristoni

Routledge
Taylor & Francis Group

NEW YORK AND LONDON

First published 2019
by Routledge
52 Vanderbilt Avenue, New York, NY 10017

and by Routledge
2 Park Square, Milton Park, Abingdon, Oxon, OX14 4RN

Routledge is an imprint of the Taylor & Francis Group, an informa business

© 2019 Taylor & Francis

Library of Congress Cataloging-in-Publication Data
Names: Tonelli, Marcello (Economist), author. | Cristoni, Nicoláo Fabrizio, author.
Title: Strategic management and the circular economy / Marcello Tonelli and Nicolâo Cristoni.
Description: New York : Routledge, 2019. | Series: Routledge research in strategic management
Identifiers: LCCN 2018035273| ISBN 9781138103634 (hardback) | ISBN 9781315102641 (ebook)
Subjects: LCSH: Sustainable development. | Strategic planning.
Classification: LCC HC79.E5 T66326 2019 | DDC 658.4/012—dc23
LC record available at https://lccn.loc.gov/2018035273

ISBN: 978-1-138-10363-4 (hbk)
ISBN: 978-1-315-10264-1 (ebk)

Typeset in Sabon
by codeMantra

This book is dedicated to our awareness of interconnectedness and the hope for a better future. Special thanks to WorlDynamics Pty. Ltd. for providing the necessary resources [www.worldynamics.org]

"As mankind is overusing many natural ecosystems, new and rebalanced ways of doing business are needed. Moving towards a circular economy could offer a solution. Tonelli and Cristoni present a comprehensive framework to work on this solution from a strategic management perspective. This book is a must read for scholars and practitioners interested in actionable frameworks, business models, and strategic approaches to developing circular businesses".
Florian Lüdeke-Freund, Chair for Corporate Sustainability, ESCP Europe Business School – Berlin, GERMANY

"Over the last decades our awareness of the limits of the use of natural resources has become more and more embedded in evidence. However, only awareness cannot solve this. What we need is a course of action to turn this around. That´s what is offered in this book. The idea of the Circular Economy is both timely and rather straightforward, but its application comes together with many challenges and imperfections. The beauty of this book is that it embraces these difficulties in order to separate the rhetoric from substance. This proves to be very helpful in creating practical guidance for the application of the principles of the Circular Economy".
Andre Nijhof, Professor Sustainable Business and Stewardship at Nyenrode Business Universiteit – Enschede Area, THE NETHERLANDS

"Strategic Management and the Circular Economy opens with Victor Hugo's eponymous quote 'you can resist an invading army; you cannot resist an idea whose time has come'. With the increasing focus of neo-liberal governments on downsizing, the role of sustainability stewardship is increasingly moving towards the private sector. This book powerfully makes the case for enhanced sustainability management through the circular economy model in shaping the actions we need to take to preserve our own future. It presents easy to understand business models and strategies that will help to achieve the circular economy key principles of improved waste and resource sustainability in a world of finite resources and an ever-growing population".
Michele John, Associate Professor, Director Sustainable Engineering Group, Curtin – Perth, AUSTRALIA

"The Circular Economy is a potential key driver for sustainable development. The concept has recently gained widespread uptake in business, academia and policy. *Strategic Management and the Circular Economy* provides an engaging overview for academics and practitioners wanting to understand the concept of the Circular Economy, as well as potential strategic approaches to start the transition from a linear take-make-waste to a Circular Economy paradigm"
Nancy Bocken, Professor in Sustainable Business Management & Practice, Lund University (IIIEE) – Lund, SWEDEN

"Nowadays circular economy has become a top priority in the political agenda of most developed countries. Many initiatives have been put forward by governments to switch to a circular model, but there is still a poor understanding on how to support companies in adapting to the new economic system. This book provides a thorough analysis of how companies can effectively combine CE principles with business objectives and an exhaustive list of concrete examples from different countries and sectors is shared. All the information is presented from the realistic perspective that we cannot demand companies to radically change their business models and processes from one day to the next, and this aspect represents one of the most important added values of the book. The authors have succeeded in producing a helpful and clear guide for companies and policy makers, while keeping scientific rigour and solidity in their approach".
Michelle Perello, CEO Consulta Europa Projects and Innovation – Las Palmas de G.C., SPAIN

"Strategic Management and the Circular Economy (CE) has an implication for the academia, practitioners and policymakers alike as it offers theoretical approaches as well as practical examples. It starts by arguing why enterprises can no longer rely on the linear economic

paradigm, before explaining how circular economy as a strategic concept works. Through a series of in-depth and original discussions the book offers a rich contribution to companies, highlighting their interactions with stakeholders at various levels of society for the creation of a better future for us all".

Lara Johannsdottir, Professor, Environment and Natural Resources, School of Business, University of Iceland – Reykjavík, ICELAND

"This is an inclusive, informative and appealing book on the complicated subject of the circular economy and strategic management. The way the circular economy is explained to replace the produce-use-dispose approach and to bring this concept into reality through strategic processes, policies, business models, and technologies is amazing. The book has not only highlighted the fruits of the circular economy, as repeatedly done in earlier books but rather practically demonstrated how one nation or society can implement the concept of circularity in its day-to-day activities and so boost its socio-economic and cultural development. Undoubtedly, this book is a must-read for all professions including academics, managers, engineers, scientists, researchers, policy and decision makers. I am very confident this book will have a positive and constructive impact in our understanding and learning of how to move ahead with this sustainable economic approach, in which waste becomes a valuable resource".

Abdul-Sattar Nizami, Head of Solid Waste Management Unit, Center of Excellence in Environmental Studies at King Abdulaziz University – Jeddah, SAUDI ARABIA

"The book is an engaging and stimulating reading on the circular economy paradigm, which has gained momentum in recent years. On the one hand, it clearly and thoroughly explains how the adoption of a circular economy framework can have positive implications not only on the environment (e.g. saving scarce resources), which is what most people would expect, but also on society (e.g. meeting the growing needs of the middle-class) and on the economy (e.g. making industrial processes more cost-effective). On the other hand, the authors, while emphasizing the appeal and elegance of what could be described as a win-win approach, do not shy away from the complexities that the implementation of a circular economy model would entail. Indeed, after defining a circular economy theoretical framework, they set out a new and innovative methodology to allow practitioners to integrate such framework with more traditional strategic tools".

Matteo di Castelnuovo, Director of Master in Green Management, Energy and CSR, Universita' Bocconi – Milan, ITALY

Contents

List of Figures and Tables

Figures

Tables

Preface

The desire to write this book grows out of a conviction that belief systems have always sustained human action. Today, in a time when spiritual faiths are losing traction, we need to believe in something else to guide our lives. Without hope, I fear that life loses much of its purpose and actions become meaningless. So, if the distinctive knowledge of our time – which sets us apart from previous millennia of human history – is based on the certainty of anthropogenic activities irreversibly damaging the Earth's ecosystems at an uncontrolled pace, and on the dreadful consequences of this new reality for any living organism, we also need to have hope (i.e. a believe system, faith, etc.) based on something equally tangible and "*real*". The Circular Economy (CE) is a pragmatic approach that can take us away from the downward spiral of natural exploitation we are witnessing and fear. What I feel makes CE so realistic and rational, compared to other sustainability concepts, are its economic foundations based on reducing costs, identifying new opportunities, and maximizing efficiency. These objectives are the same in any company (or public institution) out there, regardless of whether this is about to enter a new market (start-up), seeks to increase profits and expand its market share (large corporation quoted on a stock exchange), or simply aims to survive in a rapidly evolving industry (family-based firm).

I am confident that as more and more companies hesitantly look at the transformation happening in their industries, this book will help them take the initial steps in a transition from linearity to circularity. By proving compelling and irrefutable evidence of the damages caused by the current economic model, readers are invited to look at the world economy in a new way and encouraged to leave behind outdated conceptions of the nature and purpose of a company. While the message is relatively simple, I also wanted the book to acknowledge the complexities of CE strategic decision-making and the infinite possibilities that exist, given that every company is a different reality needed to be studied independently to properly identify, analyse, formulate, and implement a fitting CE strategy. But how is that done? Little has been said thus far about the strategic investigation of circular decisions in a firm. This book argues that a methodology based on proven strategic management tools and concepts (Idea tree, VRIE framework, Five Forces model, SWOT matrix, PEST analysis, market positioning maps, gap analysis, etc.), calibrated according to principles of circularity, can be of major help to managers.

In writing this manuscript, we tried to address the needs of companies across the globe. With regard to firms operating in developed nations, the message is to "start with what you got", as it is very unlikely for the totality of a company's activities to be completely detached from circular principles, but defining what's usable, scalable, and how to act are some of the questions that need to be answered before seriously evaluating an investment in circular practices to disentangle production processes from environmental pressures. Firms based in emerging economies will also find the book insightful for it can be leveraged to leapfrog highly polluting industrial practices and reach a competitive position in the global market.

Marcello Tonelli
June 2018
Las Palmas de Gran Canaria

Acknowledgements

To my partner Ilaria for all your support and encouragement, and to my father, Giorgio, for enabling my pursuit of this work.

– M.T.

To my wife Mezhgan and my parents for their unparalleled love and enduring support.

– N.C.

Part I

An Overview

"You can resist an invading army; you cannot resist an idea whose time has come". Victor Hugo's notorious quote is what possibly best encapsulates the message carried by the first part of this book: the Circular Economy (CE) being the idea, the current production system – or take-make-waste linear model – being what needs to be replaced. This simple assumption is further elaborated in Chapters 1 and 2, with the former establishing the reasons why the human enterprise can no longer rely on its traditional economic paradigm, and the latter presenting the solid rationale behind what has been framed as an alternative system that "opens up ways to reconcile the outlook for growth and economic participation with that of environmental prudence and equity" (Ellen MacArthur Foundation 2014).

Arguably, the primary reason for the growing interest around the CE is its capacity to integrate environmental protection, social development, and economic prosperity all within a single, coherent, and actionable framework for sustainable development. Looking back, no other alternative approach has in fact ever acknowledged that economic growth does not necessarily require a corresponding increase in environmental pressure.

The time for a CE to blossom seems to have come. But why now? A number of diverse enabling factors, linked to regulatory, technological, and social trends, are facilitating its argumentation and acceptance. What remains to be seen are the ways in which private organizations (the engine of today's globalized civilization) will strategically embed circular principles into their growth plans to future-fit operations and be ready to grasp new opportunities. The rest of this book lays out the authors' view on the topic.

1 The Challenges of the Produce-Use-Dispose Model

1.1 Introduction

It has been estimated that between 1900 and 2000, global GDP has grown 20 times. Since the advent of the Second Industrial Revolution in 1880, and most notably after the end of Second World War, humanity has in fact experienced an unprecedented and steady growth in material wealth. Throughout the 20th century, the global economy has been radically re-shaped by the rapid industrialization of many regions of the world, boosted by the introduction of newer and more efficient production technologies, ever-lower labour costs, the creation of economies of scale, and the progressive globalization of markets. This extraordinary period of economic expansion has eventually culminated in a mass production of goods and services across all industries, delivering not only widespread material prosperity and higher-than-ever per capita disposable income, but also multiple tangible benefits in different key sectors of the human enterprise – e.g. better healthcare and longer lives, easy and reliable access to electricity, faster and safer transport, etc. The nine socio-economic trends reported later can be used to represent what the scientific community calls the "Great Acceleration", i.e. the booming period that ran from 1950 until today (Figure 1.1).

What is now generally defined as "human development" has not come without a cost though. The industrial model standing at the roots of our current standards of living has been based around a linear system of production or take-make-waste paradigm, where natural resources are extracted from the Earth; then processed in manufacturing plants, where they become usable objects; items are then used; and finally get either incinerated or discarded as waste in landfills.

Each of these four steps causes a great deal of damage to natural ecosystems. Because of the amount of resources used on a worldwide scale and the industrial processes involved, ecosystems get heavily polluted (air and water), deprived of key substances (soil), or irreversibly modified (forests). Today, we extract and consume roughly 95% more raw materials than we did in 1880 and the numbers keep rising. The aggregate global material extraction rate of 35 billion tonnes recorded in 1980 nearly doubled in three decades to the current 65+ billion tonnes per

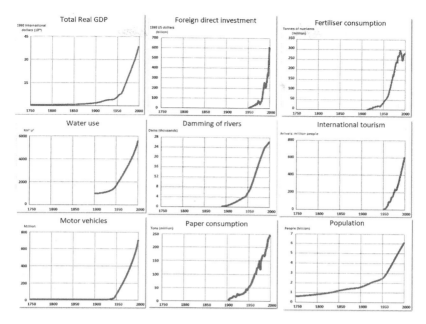

Figure 1.1 The Great Acceleration.[1]

year (Giljum et al. 2014). What is more, most assets end up being thrown away within just a few months from the time of purchase, resulting in waste generation levels exceeding 1.3 billion tonnes per year and projected to reach 2+ billion tonnes by 2025 (The World Bank 2012b). The situation becomes even more dramatic when considering that the linear economic model does not account for any effective regenerative actions.[2] As a result, particularly after 1950, global economic activities have amplified the environmental footprint of the human enterprise, affecting the Earth system structure and functioning on multiple levels. The set of diagrams below illustrate some of the most notable damages caused, including deforestation and biodiversity loss, ocean acidification, and carbon dioxide emissions (Figure 1.2).

The positive correlation between human development and environmental degradation is evident. And although today we make more efficient use of natural resources – with 50% more economic value being extracted from a tonne of raw materials compared to just 30 years ago (OECD 2012) – a radical shift, away from the core pillars of modern development practices, is required to break the link between economic prosperity and the loss of natural ecosystems. Hence, whilst natural reserves could theoretically supply the linear model for a while longer and, in some instances, even see it scaled up to developing countries over the short term, proponents of an industrial system change are getting

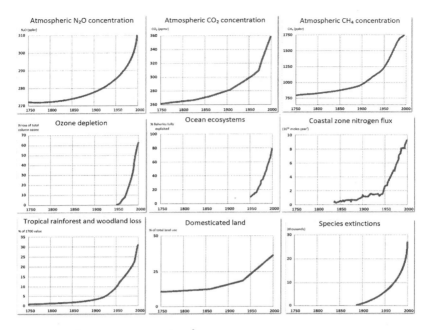

Figure 1.2 The Great Destruction.[3]

louder and evidence that the linear model has reached its tipping point is mounting. At least four trends are currently warning humanity of where it stands and of future dangers:

- natural thresholds are being exceeded;
- there is scarcity of raw materials;
- the middle class with their demands is growing;
- structural inefficiencies of the current economic model are worsening.

1.2 Exceeding Planetary Natural Thresholds

For the last 11 years, the World Economic Forum (WEF 2017) has been publishing a yearly "Global Risk Report" outlining the main dangers facing society and humanity. These risks are grouped into five broad categories (Economic, Environmental, Geopolitical, Societal, and Technological) and ranked according to their likelihood and impact. By looking at the top five risks identified each year since 2007, there is a clear trend moving away from economic threats (the clear majority over the period 2007–2010) towards environmentally related threats: "major natural disasters", "failure of climate-change mitigation and adaptation", and "extreme weather events" above all others (Table 1.1).

Table 1.1 The Evolution of Global Risks [4]

Legend: ENVIRONMENTAL | ECONOMIC

TOP 5 GLOBAL RISKS IN TERMS OF LIKELIHOOD

	2007	2008	2009	2010	2011	2012	2013	2014	2015	2016	2017
1st	TECHNOLOGICAL	Asset price collapse	Asset price collapse	Asset price collapse	Storms and cyclones	SOCIETAL	SOCIETAL	SOCIETAL	GEOPOLITICAL	SOCIETAL	Extreme weather events
2nd	SOCIETAL	GEOPOLITICAL	Slowing Chinese economy	Slowing Chinese economy	Flooding	Chronic fiscal imbalances	Chronic fiscal imbalances	Extreme weather events	Extreme weather events	Extreme weather events	SOCIETAL
3rd	Oil price shock	GEOPOLITICAL	SOCIETAL	SOCIETAL	GEOPOLITICAL	Rising greenhouse gas emissions	Rising greenhouse gas emissions	Unemployment and underemployment	GEOPOLITICAL	Failure of climate-change mitigation and adaptation	Major natural disasters
4th	China economic hard landing	Oil and gas price spike	GEOPOLITICAL	Fiscal crisis	Biodiversity loss	TECHNOLOGICAL	Water supply crisis	Climate change	GEOPOLITICAL	GEOPOLITICAL	GEOPOLITICAL
5th	Asset price collapse	SOCIETAL	Retrenchment from globalization	GEOPOLITICAL	Climate change	Water supply crisis	SOCIETAL	TECHNOLOGICAL	High structural unemployment and underemployment	Major natural disasters	TECHNOLOGICAL

TOP 5 GLOBAL RISKS IN TERMS OF IMPACT

Legend: ENVIRONMENTAL | ECONOMIC

	2007	2008	2009	2010	2011	2012	2013	2014	2015	2016	2017
1st	Asset price collapse	Asset price collapse	Asset price collapse	Asset price collapse	Fiscal crises	Major systemic financial failure	Major systemic financial failure	Fiscal crises	SOCIETAL	Failure of climate-change mitigation and adaptation	GEOPOLITICAL
2nd	GEOPOLITICAL	GEOPOLITICAL	Retrenchment from globalization	Retrenchment from globalization	Climate change	Water supply crisis	Water supply crisis	Climate change	SOCIETAL	GEOPOLITICAL	Extreme weather events
3rd	GEOPOLITICAL	Slowing Chinese economy	Oil and gas price spike	Oil and gas price spike	GEOPOLITICAL	SOCIETAL	Chronic fiscal crises	Water supply crisis	GEOPOLITICAL	SOCIETAL	SOCIETAL
4th	SOCIETAL	Oil and gas price spike	SOCIETAL	SOCIETAL	Asset price collapse	Chronic fiscal imbalances	GEOPOLITICAL	Unemployment and underemployment	GEOPOLITICAL	SOCIETAL	Major natural disasters
5th	Oil prices shock	SOCIETAL	Fiscal crises	Fiscal crises	Extreme energy price volatility	Extreme volatility in energy and agriculture prices	Failure of climate-change mitigation and adaptation	TECHNOLOGICAL	Failure of climate-change mitigation and adaptation	Severe energy price shock	Failure of climate-change mitigation and adaptation

The shift in focus is firmly grounded in recent scientific discoveries (Rockström et al. 2009; Wijkman and Rockström 2012; Hughes et al. 2013; Steffen et al. 2015) alerting of the nexus between man-made activities and a progressive, irreversible change in the dynamics of the Earth system (i.e. the functioning of natural ecosystems typical of the last 11,000 years, throughout the Holocene geological epoch). Researchers have in fact collected evidence that our current path of development – with its intense use of chemicals, heavy reliance on fossil fuels, and ever-greater demand for virgin land – is on a collision course with the stability of the natural system. In 2009 and then in 2015, a team led by Johan Rockström at the Stockholm Resilience Centre was able to isolate and assess the state of nine key biophysical processes that regulate the stability of the Earth system and to delimit a safe operating space for humanity to keep our planet within its current hospitable conditions – i.e. mild average climate, abundant water and vegetation cover, and occasional natural disasters (Rockström et al. 2009; Steffen et al. 2015). Their study led them to publish the "Planetary Boundaries" (PB) framework, which received worldwide recognition as a coherent guide to global environmental sustainability management and development. The correct measurement of environmental sustainability is not always a straightforward exercise, but a substantial number of indices and indicators are already available and new ones continue to be defined (Cook et al. 2017). What follows is an account of the likely consequences that surpassing each PB will have on the business sector.

1.2.1 Boundary: Climate Change

Status: Safe limit surpassed and worsening. Today, the atmospheric concentration of carbon dioxide is already beyond the established safe limit (390 ppm CO_2 against 350 ppm CO_2), and keeps rising. Because of it, as per the latest (fifth) report of the Intergovernmental Panel on Climate Change (IPCC), the global average temperature of combined land and ocean surface has already warmed by 0.85°C since pre-industrial levels (IPCC 2013).

Major impacts and industries most likely to be affected: As temperatures continue to rise, multiple extreme weather and climate events such as heat waves, heavy precipitation, droughts, cyclones, and high sea levels will inevitably be more frequent and marked by greater intensity. The primary ways in which these occurrences will have an impact on businesses are as follows:

- More and tougher legislative regulatory regimes: Laws and regulations aimed at curbing greenhouse gases (GHGs) emissions can affect firms on various levels, from imposing new taxes or costs, to limiting or banning specific activities or products (Tietenberg and Lewis 2015). Globally, climate change laws have seen a significant increase since 2009 (Ellen MacArthur Foundation 2015b), with new cap-and-trade schemes becoming operational in China (since December 2017) and part of North America (since January 2018), and Sweden legally committing itself to become carbon-neutral by 2045. Carbon-intensive activities like oil and gas extraction; the production of iron, steel, aluminium, and paper; and civil aviation service are inexorably the main target of these new policies.

- Impacts on physical manufacturing plants: Sectors like fashion, sportswear, toys, and automotive, all heavily relying on complex and elaborated supply chains, will predictably be the most exposed to business continuity uncertainty due to the growing risk of natural disasters hitting primary manufacturing hubs in countries like Cambodia, Thailand, Vietnam, the Philippines, and Bangladesh. As an example, the Thailand flood in 2011 caused Toyota a loss of 150,000 vehicles in output. Of course, it is not just manufacturing sites that will suffer. The risk extends to firms owning properties in climate-sensitive areas like coastal regions (e.g. hotel chains) or to those growing products that depend on favourable climate conditions (e.g. food producers). A case in point is the 2013 profit cut experienced by the world's leading agricultural trader Cargill, whose operations had been severely hit by a massive drought affecting the U.S. that year[5];

- Damages to "intangible" assets and shift in customer preferences: In the coming decades, as more natural disasters will occur because of the warming climate, carbon-intensive companies will inevitably run the risk of weakening their image and losing market share. These companies might also be the subject of customer actions like boycotts, protests, and legal actions.[6] In July 2017, for example, three coastal communities in California filed complaints against Shell, Exxon, and other oil giants in an attempt to seek monetary compensation for the costs incurred to adapt to sea level rise.

1.2.2 Boundary: Loss of Biosphere Integrity

<u>Status:</u> Safe limit surpassed and worsening. Today's rate of 100–1,000 extinctions per million species-years (E/MSY) is well beyond the planetary boundary set at 10 (with an aspirational goal of ca. 1 E/MSY).

<u>Major impacts and industries most likely to be affected:</u> The loss of biodiversity is bound to affect the correct functioning of natural ecosystems, and consequently the services they provide to humanity (provisioning, regulating, supporting, and cultural). Industries like tourism and agriculture will be some of the most affected.

1.2.3 Boundary: Changes to Biogeochemical Flows – Nitrogen and Phosphorus

Status: Safe limit surpassed and worsening. Man-made release of nitrogen and phosphorus into the natural environment, primarily due to industrial and agricultural fixation, is currently exceeding the amount produced by all the Earth's terrestrial processes combined[7] (Stockholm Resilience Centre 2017).

Major impacts and industries most likely to be affected: The primary impact of excessive nutrient pollution relates to water as these elements are eventually washed into rivers and seas. Aquatic ecosystems suffer greatly when they are overloaded with nitrogen and/or phosphorus intakes, and as a result, the population of marine species decreases sharply and abruptly (e.g. the massive dead zone in the Gulf of Mexico has been primarily caused by nutrient runoff into the Mississippi River).[8] Fishing operations are clearly highly sensitive to this issue. As the effects of nutrient pollution worsen, primary producers of nitrogen and phosphorus operating in sectors like agriculture, power generation, and transport (EPA 2017) will likely face regulatory constraints, shifting customer preferences, and boycotting campaigns from environmental NGOs.

1.2.4 Boundary: Freshwater Use

Status: Within limit (boundary set at 4,000 km^3 water use per year, current consumption: 2,600 km^3). However, global water withdrawals have tripled over the last 50 years (UNEP 2013) and continue to rise.[9]

Major impacts and industries most likely to be affected: Under a business-as-usual scenario, competition for water will intensify in many regions of the world, both among businesses and between the public and private sectors. Inevitably, water-intensive operations, typical of industries like food and beverage, pulp and paper, and textile and steel production, will be the most exposed to water shortages and higher costs of water. Additionally, firms operating in these industries will most likely feel growing pressure to obtain or renew their licences to operate, especially in resource-scarce areas. In 2014 for example, Coca-Cola was forced to shut down bottling plant operations in northern India due to enduring protests.[10]

1.2.5 Boundary: Land Use Change

Status: Safe limit of no less than 75% biome intactness[11] surpassed and worsening (62%).

Major impacts and industries most likely to be affected: Converting vegetation areas – primarily forests – to cropland affects climate and water flows, further worsening the consequences of climate change and water shortages for industries like fashion, food and beverage, and pulp and paper. Additionally, agricultural companies might soon be facing limitations on access to land, as governments tighten regulations to control the escalating crisis.

1.2.6 Boundary: Release of Novel Entities

Status: The kinds of substances falling under this boundary are those characterized by high toxicity levels and long-term permanency in the environment, like synthetic organic pollutants and heavy metal compounds.[12] The current status is unknown.

Major impacts and industries most likely to be affected: Novel entities are particularly abundant in sectors like agriculture (in the form of Genetically Modified Organisms or GMO), medicine, electronics (nanomaterials), and consumer goods (micro-plastics). The main risks faced by firms operating in these industries are the adoption by governments of specific regulations aimed at curbing the use of dangerous substances. A recent example is the EU Directive 2015/863 on the Restriction of Hazardous Substances (RoHS), which specifies maximum levels for ten dangerous substances utilized in the manufacturing of electronic products traded within the European Union. Moreover, as pollution from toxic substances increases exponentially the risks to environmental and human health alike, public opinion will inevitably ask for greater transparency over the practices of firms, including those of suppliers. Environmental NGOs have already started to act in this direction by targeting heavy polluting industries with campaigns specifically designed at phasing out dangerous substances. For example, the Detox initiative led by Greenpeace challenges big firms of the fashion industry to eradicate hazardous chemicals across their entire supply chains.

1.2.7 Boundary: Atmospheric Aerosol Loading

Status: Not known.

Major impacts and industries most likely to be affected: Man-made atmospheric aerosols are caused by the burning of tropical forests as well as coal and oil.[13] Once again, in the coming decades, we can envision governments taking steps to limit, when not ban altogether, some of these activities.

1.2.8 Boundary: Ocean Acidification due to Fossil Fuel CO_2

Status: Within limit (set at ≥80% of the pre-industrial aragonite saturation state of mean surface ocean) but on the brink of being exceeded (≥84%), with present pace of oceans acidification being the fastest ever recorded in the last 65 million years (Stockholm Resilience Centre 2017).

Major impacts and industries most likely to be affected: The oceans, like forests, are a primary carbon sink. However, if too much carbon dioxide is emitted[14] in the air, and subsequently absorbed by oceanic waters, this leads to an over-acidification of the oceans, which, in turn, can lead to drastic changes in the functioning of the marine ecosystem as a whole (Stockholm Resilience Centre 2017). As a result, it is anticipated that global fishery, fish processing, and food industries will be strongly affected.

1.2.9 Boundary: Loss of Stratospheric Ozone due to Chlorofluorocarbons (CFCs)

Status: Within limit and improving, only transgressed over Antarctica in Austral spring (Steffen et al. 2015). CFCs are substances that have the direct effect of depleting the ozone layer. In 1987, by adopting the Montreal Protocol, the global community took firm and universal action to phase out all major ozone-depleting substances. Since then, the use of CFCs has radically diminished and to date, the Montreal Protocol remains the most successful global environmental agreement ever enforced.

Major impacts and industries most likely to be affected: When the Montreal Protocol entered into action, CFCs were still widely used in refrigeration and air-conditioning, solvents and cleaning products, propellants in medicinal aerosols, and as blowing agents for foams. As a result, companies whose products embedded ozone-depleting agents were forced to innovate if they wanted to keep operating. This is a telling example of how regulatory constraints following an environmental agreement can heavily impact the private sector.

1.3 Scarcity of Raw Materials and Price Volatility

The turn of the century has been marked by a rapid and steep increase in the price of both hard and soft commodities,[15] followed by a period of high volatility that has continued up until today (The World Bank 2017). Between 2000 and 2010, the World Bank estimated an astonishing 300% increase in the price of oil and gas, +200% in metal prices (e.g. gold and nickel), and +60% for agricultural commodities.[16]

The abrupt and persistent uncertainty affecting commodities' prices is the result of global socio-economic forces that have altered the market dynamics that favoured the generally low costs typical of the mid-80s up until the year 2000. Over just a decade, we have basically witnessed the emergence of new economies that have, all together, significantly increased the demand for raw materials, energy, and primary agricultural produce. The rapid expansion of Chinese cities and its effect on the supply–demand balance of the steel market is a telling example of the disequilibrium that resulted when a new, fast-growing economy entered the commodities arena.

But the increasing need to feed the development of emerging economies is not the only reason behind soaring commodity prices. There are at least five more causes that contribute to the complexity of the problem and therefore its uncertainty.

- **Monopoly over reserves/deposits:** At a country level, the supply chain of Rare Earth Elements (REEs) is a case in point. REEs are 17 chemical elements sharing comparable properties and therefore located in the same geological deposits. Their applications are manifolds, particularly in the high-tech sector, from computer hard drives to cameras and telescope lenses, and from the catalytic converter of cars and aircraft engines to televisions and computer screens. Worldwide, China has by far the largest reserves of REEs – more than 90% of total output (Morrison et al. 2012) – and a sizeable proportion of these deposits are leveraged to meet the country's internal needs. In fact, since the turn of the century, the country has been limiting the amount of supplies to be exported by means of tariffs and trade restrictions on grounds of environmental concerns and mounting internal demand (Morrison et al. 2012). To further strengthen the centralized control over REEs, non-Chinese firms are not allowed to start mining operations in China unless they enter into local partnerships, which are, in turn, closely monitored by the government. As a result, China's total exports of REEs fell by over 70% in the last decade, and prices soared accordingly (up to 400%). As long as the country holds on to its strategy to undersupply the demand for REEs to the rest of the world, analysts predict that the landscape is not set to change, at least in the near future.[17]

  Monopoly can also be exercised at the firm level. Take lithium for example, a key component of rechargeable lithium-ion batteries used in home electronics but also appreciated in many other industries, including medicine and construction. Its production has long been in the hands of just three companies (SQM, FMC, and Albemarle), together accounting for 90% of the world's yearly extraction.[18] Looking ahead, as the demand for lithium is projected to skyrocket following the expected large-scale introduction of electric vehicles in mature economies, uncertainties about global availability and prices might follow accordingly.

- **Political instability, war, and conflicts affecting resource-rich countries:** African nations, like Rwanda and the Democratic Republic of Congo (DRC), have a long history of violence and conflicts associated with the extraction of some minerals, particularly tantalum, tin, and tungsten (also referred as the "3Ts"). Nowadays, the

DRC contribution to the world's supply of tantalum nears 20% (Papp 2014), but the severe political instability affecting the country brings great uncertainty over DRC's ability to secure operations in its mines.

- **Issues associated with exploration and extraction activities:** With the most accessible sites having already reached exploration maturity (Cook 2004), increased operational costs and lack of proper funding are the critical factors preventing the adoption of large-scale new exploratory and extraction plans, rising uncertainty in the metals and energy markets. On top of the poor commitment from mining companies to invest in long-term extraction strategies is the increased difficulty to obtain a licence to operate. After the incidents that occurred in the last few years – e.g. the Mariana mining dam disaster, which in November 2015 caused in Brazil the death of 17 people and released 50 million tons of iron ore and toxic waste into the Doce River in just one day[19] – securing approvals for new mining sites has become increasingly difficult, if not impossible in some countries. In April 2017, El Salvador's Legislative Assembly voted for a complete ban on mining activities concerning gold and other metals. The increased attention and scrutiny from environmental NGOs and human rights organizations have further exacerbated the situation, especially in those circumstances where new operations are proposed in territories occupied by indigenous people. Industry experts have calculated that the economic losses caused by operational delays attributable to civil society unrest amount to 20 million dollars per week.[20]

- **Supply chain disruptions due to labour-related issues:** Disruptions in the supply chain of raw materials can occur frequently and abruptly when mines and processing plants are located in countries experiencing political and social unrest due to poor labour conditions and often neglected workers' rights. Since 2016, labour unrest at copper mines in Indonesia, Peru, and Chile have produced stoppages to a steady supply to the world, causing instability in the market as well as planning problems for companies using copper in their supply chains.[21] Labour-related issues can be sparked by many reasons such as job cuts, low wages, poor health and safety measures, or the pending renewal of a Collective Bargaining Agreement (CBA). To complicate matters further, many industries are characterized by long and elaborated supply chains, making it almost impossible for the focal company (the final brand) to have control over its entire suite of suppliers. For example, automotive US giant Ford stated in its 2013–2014 Sustainability Report that raw materials can pass through up to ten suppliers prior to eventually entering the manufacturing process.[22]

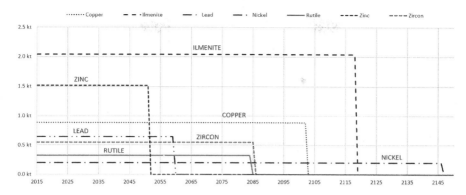

Figure 1.3 Forecasted Depletion of Mineral Resources.

- **Projected scarcity:** While global material resource use in 2030 is expected to be twice that of 2010 (EEA 2015), the limited supply of many key resources is now recognized and forecasted to be depleted within a relatively short period of time, under the current business-as-usual scenario. At current extraction rates, deposits of gold and silver will run out in the next 30 years, iron ore in 70, and black coal in 90. The lifespan of other minerals is illustrated above (Figure 1.3).

  This projection puts additional pressure on businesses which will soon need to be looking for alternative and cost-effective solutions to secure sufficient flows of raw materials for their manufacturing plants. For example, zinc is one of the elements whose reserves are projected to run out in just over 30 years and the steel industry makes great use of zinc by means of the galvanization process (i.e. the procedure of applying a protective layer of zinc to steel) in order to avoid corrosion, hence prolonging the life of assets like cars, buildings, and bridges.

The sum of risks that can disrupt a steady supply of raw materials is increasingly perceived as a critical factor, not just for the survival of businesses but also for society at large. From 2010 for example, the European Union has been publishing and regularly updating a list of key resources that are both vitally important for the EU economy and of high risk for supply chain disruptions.[23] This list is being used to devise strategies aimed at securing reliable and constant flows of critical raw materials.

1.4 Rising Middle-Class Population

The last 15 years have seen several countries rapidly and ferociously climbing up the ladder of economic growth. First, it was the BRIC (Brazil, Russia, India, China), then the MINT (Mexico, Indonesia,

Nigeria, Turkey), and then the CIVETS (Colombia, Indonesia, Vietnam, Egypt, Turkey and South Africa). And even if the economic performance of some has lately fallen short of expectations (e.g. Brazil), the overall market expansion of most of these populous countries (China and India above all others) has suddenly boosted their middle class – i.e. households spending between $10 and $100 per day, with access to higher education, respectable jobs, and ownership of assets. In BRIC countries alone, the size of the middle class has doubled since the year 2000,[24] and continues to rise at breakneck speed. A deeper analysis of some of these rapidly developing countries is provided below:

- Much has been said and written about China's impressive economic performance after the country embarked on its journey towards industrialization at the turn of the century. With a per capita GDP increase of more than 700% from 1998 to 2016,[25] millions of Chinese have been lifted out of poverty and today access middle-class benefits. Projections show that by 2022, 76% of China's urban population will have acquired such status (Barton et al. 2013).
- India, with the size of its middle class doubling from 300 million in 2004 to 600 million in 2012 (Breene 2016), is another clear example of a developing country quickly turning into a solid emerging economy. And the trend is set to continue, with forecasts predicting that by 2027, India's middle class will have exceeded that of the United States, Europe, and even China (Kharas 2010).
- Overall, the size of the middle class in Latin America has grown 50% during the first decade of the 21st century, more than ever before in the history of the continent.[26] Mexico has been at the forefront of this trend; its middle class being the fastest-growing segment of the population in the last 17 years. Looking ahead, another 3.8 million Mexicans are expected to reach middle-class status by 2030.[27]
- Turkey is a country that has experienced significant industrial development by progressively capitalizing on its strategic location set between three continents and harnessing its strong logistics capabilities. Over the last decade, Turkey has become a vital manufacturing hub for the global market – textile, agroprocessing, chemicals, and automotive plants account today for one-fourth of total GDP (which tripled from 2000 to 2012)[28] and represent a main driver for future economic growth[29] – meaning new and higher-paid jobs are created, thus boosting middle-class purchasing power.

In the short to medium term, the worldwide expansion of the middle class is bound to continue. Assuming the next decades will see similar economic growth to what characterized the last 20 years, experts from the Organisation for Economic Co-operation and Development (OECD) predict that the size of middle-income households will reach five billion by 2030, compared to the current three billion. Asia will be the epicentre of this massive expansion with 1.5 billion people between China and India alone. Besides Asia, densely populated countries like Brazil, Mexico, Pakistan, and Nigeria could also account for middle classes larger than 100 million people over the next decades.[30]

Today, the human enterprise is already borrowing from future generations half of their yearly global renewable natural resources – a phenomenon called "ecological overshoot" – gradually approaching the point where there will be no resources left for human use and consumption. Clearly, the take-make-waste economic model stands at the root of this problem, with the global environmental footprint deepening as more and more people have disposable income to spend on items and assets that are designed for short life cycles, manufactured using virgin resources, and inadequately disposed of in landfills. For example, the appetite for technological devices like smartphones and laptops recently took off in densely populated developing countries, as did the sourcing needs for the virgin materials required to manufacture them. The spending power of the global middle class increased by 12.5% annually between 2005 and 2015[31] and consumption demand for new goods and services has been estimated to grow from 4.5 USD trillion in 2009 to close to 44 USD trillion by 2030 in Asia alone.[32] The challenge of how to effectively decouple economic growth from resource consumption and environmental pollution is paramount. Not surprisingly, this dilemma has been central to a 2016 report prepared for UNEP (United Nations Environmental Programme) by the working group on global material flows of the International Resource Panel (IRP), addressing the links that connect middle-class escalation, global material use, and environmental degradation (IRP 2016). The report cites global per capita income growth as the primary cause (even more important than population growth) of the rampant levels of material use experienced worldwide since the year 2000. The study also sheds light on the global impact of single national economies, by ranking countries according to their annual material footprint – the yearly amount of material needed to meet internal demand. It is interesting and alarming to note that even rapidly developing economies are not yet close to resource consumption levels seen in the most industrialized nations. China and Brazil, for example, have a material footprint of 14 and 13 tonnes per capita, respectively, while Europe and the U.S.A. reach 20 and 25 tonnes each (UNEP 2016), suggesting that further increases in global material demand are to be expected along with associated environmental problems and conflicts over land use and resource exploitation.

1.5 Structural Inefficiencies of the Current Economic Model

The current industrial system has fundamentally evolved around two erroneous assumptions regarding the relationship that exists between the natural environment and the human enterprise: the limitless availability of resources on the one hand, and the capacity of the environment to act as an endless "waste sink" on the other. In this context, development has been driven by the optimization of sourcing, manufacturing, and trade processes with the only aim of increasing sales volumes and thus the bottom line of firms operating in the various markets, with no regards for environmental impacts. Resource depletion and environmental pollution have mainly been viewed as unavoidable consequences of the economic growth behind the industrialization and wealth creation of any nation. In sharp contrast with the gradual recognition of the inadequacies of this economic model, the last few decades have also witnessed a tendency towards "short-termism of business", i.e. a radical shift away from long-term strategies to focus on short-term profit in order to meet the quarterly expectations of shareholders and the stock market. The profit-maximization imperative that has monopolized corporate strategy led to a number of structural inefficiencies and waste-generating practices along the value chain that can be summarized as follows:

- Over-exploitation of resources at the manufacturing level: The WWF has found that global demand already exceeds the capacity of natural ecosystems to regenerate their resources and absorb wastes. Every year since 2012, we have in fact borrowed the equivalent of 1.5 Earth's renewable resources from the future (WWF 2016). One of the reasons behind this theft to future generations is the extensive list of products that require a disproportionate amount of resources to produce them. The overuse of water in some industries such as fashion, food, and metals is central to this problem, considering that for example, it takes 8,000+ litres of water to produce a pair of jeans,[33] and 2,500+ litres to grow enough cotton to make a t-shirt.[34]

- Underutilization of products. Recent studies, such as those conducted by the Ellen MacArthur Foundation (2015a), have analysed the utilization rates of some of the assets central to modern life – cars, buildings, and home appliances – and found that the majority of these suffer from chronic underutilization:

    - European cars are parked 90+ % of their time.
    - In Europe, there are 10+ million empty houses.
    - 60% of European offices are not used, not even during working hours.
    - In U.S. hospitals, the average utilization of clinical mobile devices is 42%.[35]

- Short lifespan of assets. In addition to being seldom utilized, many products are today marked by short life cycles. One of the primary reasons is the need for manufacturers to achieve fast replacement rates in saturated markets through "planned obsolescence". A 2016 briefing of the European Parliament defined the term as "the intentional production of goods and services with short economic lives, stimulating consumers to repeat purchases too frequently".[36] The document also puts forward a series of difficulties faced by consumers when dealing with assets produced according to planned obsolesce principles:

-   Barriers to repair (product characteristics preventing repair, high repair costs, and unavailability of spare parts).
-   Programmed failure (parts breaking down after limited usage).
-   Ad hoc marketing strategies inciting quick replacement of existing assets deemed old-fashioned.

Investigations conducted in Germany and the Netherlands between 2000 and 2005 reported evidence of a decrease up to 20% in the first-life duration of certain consumer electronics and home appliances (Bakker et al. 2014). Acknowledging the serious environmental issues linked to this problem, governments are now adopting specific laws punishing firms found to be pursuing planned obsolescence principles. For example, the 2015 "French Act on the energy transition for green growth" introduced the crime of a producer intentionally leveraging techniques to reduce the lifespan of a product, mandating severe economic fines and up to two years of imprisonment for managers.[37]

•   Disposal of assets reaching their end-of-life. Most products and their components manufactured after 1950 have ended up in landfills or incinerated, as the take-make-waste paradigm places very little attention on re-introducing end-of-use assets back into the economy. In the last few decades, the environmental problems associated with the disposal of an ever-increasing amount of waste have led some countries and regions to adopt stringent measures aimed at fostering recycling (e.g. the EU Action Plan for the CE).[38] However, despite some exceptions (e.g. Austria 63%, UK 62%, and Singapore 59%),[39] global recycling rates are still very low due to the inferior performance by some of the highest waste-generating nations (e.g. the U.S. recycles just 34% of its waste and Europe 40%), and the lack of a formal waste disposal and recycling structure in developing and densely populated regions. The waste problem is particularly felt in economic sectors like electronics and fashion, whose products are produced in large quantities, have a short lifespan, and cannot be recycled easily. The UNEP expected 50+ million tonnes of electronic waste (e-waste) to be generated in 2017 (UNEP 2015), with rates nearing 90% disposed illegally. The common practice is to ship assets to Africa's poorest countries, where the e-waste is then dumped into unauthorized landfills on the outskirts of major cities (e.g. Agbogbloshie in Ghana houses the world's largest digital dumping ground). There, toxic substances are then gradually released into the ground.

As for the fashion industry, much of the problem originates from the success of so-called fast fashion brands, whose cheap clothes are usually worn by consumers for a very limited time and then thrown away. In the U.S. alone, the volume of clothes discarded each year has doubled – from 7 to 14 million – in less than 20 years.[40]

Case Study: Focus on the Automotive Industry

The automotive industry is deeply rooted in the linear economic paradigm, with firms operating in this sector characterized by severe environmental impacts and major structural inefficiencies.[41] Sky-high fixed costs, overcapacity, and the presence of a few large incumbents controlling the market have made it nearly impossible for new players to enter. As a result, the industry has suffered from technological lock-in and a chronic lack of stimuli for breakthrough (green) innovation. What is more, new markets are very limited given the high motorization rate already achieved in most developed as well as developing countries, making the fine-tuning of planned obsolescence principles almost a necessity. To be profitable, carmakers need to achieve faster-than-ever replacement rates, which means radically short product lifespan and low-quality components (Table 1.2).

Table 1.2 The Limits of the Automotive Industry

Status Quo	Impacts and Inefficiencies
Few Original Equipment Manufacturers (OEMs) controlling the market	Technological lock-in
Old and massive manufacturing plants	High-energy requirements
	Short product lifespan
Saturated markets, especially in western economies	Low-quality components
	Fast replacement rates

When it comes to the environmental impacts of cars, the first and foremost issue that comes to mind is air pollution with its consequences for the deterioration of natural ecosystems and human well-being. Air pollution is in fact associated with a multitude of health problems, to the point that a 2014 report from the UNEP defined it as the world's worst environmental health risk. In Europe alone, emissions from vehicles expose 90% of city residents to harmful air pollution levels. Apart from locally polluting the air, the automotive industry also plays a significant role to global warming – both in terms of direct CO_2 emissions at the use stage and during the different phases of the production and assembly of cars. In fact, studies show that making a new car creates as much carbon pollution as driving it.[42] For this reason and in an attempt to curb the negative impacts caused by petroleum engines, new laws and pioneering measures are being adopted globally:

- The Directive 2014/94/UE of the European Union requires member states to increase the number of charging stations for electric vehicles by the end of 2020.
- In July 2017, France newly appointed environmental minister announced plans to ban all petrol and diesel vehicles by 2040. In doing so, poorer households will be given a voucher to spend on clean automobiles.
- Norway is currently discussing to prohibit the sale of fossil fuel cars by 2025.
- In December 2016, Paris, Madrid, Athens, and Mexico City announced plans to ban the use of diesel vehicles in their city centres by 2025.
- Helsinki has launched a programme to make private cars irrelevant by implementing a comprehensive mobility-on-demand system.
- Vienna is developing a prototype for an integrated mobility smartphone platform that integrates diverse mobility offerings.

In addition to its impacts on air quality and global warming, the automotive industry is also responsible for additional environmental threats, particularly with respect to natural resource depletion and hazardous chemicals' pollution. Car production involves the substantial use of materials like steel, plastics, glass, and paints that must be created before they are ready for assembly. In terms of hazardous chemicals, the end of a car life means that many harmful substances like mercury, lead, cadmium, and hexavalent chromium can accumulate in the environment, hence posing serious health risks to life. A recent report jointly created by Michigan-based Ecology Centre and New York-based Environmental Defence found that the use of lead in cars represents the largest source of lead pollution across all industries.

1.6 Conclusions

The evidence presented in this chapter makes a strong case for the global economy to rapidly shift towards more sustainable approaches of production and consumption. The linear economic model is in fact clearly not fit for the macro-trends emerged with the turn of the century (e.g. scarcity and price volatility of raw materials, rise of the middle class, and tougher regulatory environmental frameworks). In addition, negative economic consequences are only the surface of a much larger and permanent problem. Recent scientific discoveries have brought to light an alarming truth: our current path of development is on a collision course with the stability of the fundamental ecological systems that make our planet liveable and that have allowed civilization to thrive up to modern times. As comprehensively detailed in the beginning of this chapter, the consequences of surpassing these PB will be manifold for businesses across virtually all industries (e.g. damages to tangible and intangible assets, increased compliance costs, reduced licence to operate, etc.). Starting with Chapter 2, this book will describe and analyse one of the most promising approaches to sustainable development emerged in recent times, the CE.

Notes

1 Source: adapted from Will Steffen, Regina Angelina Sanderson, Peter D. Tyson, Jill Jäger, Pamela A. Matson, Berrien Moore III, Frank Oldfield et al. 2006. *Global Change and the Earth System: A Planet Under Pressure*. Springer Science & Business Media.

2 Recent studies on the recycling levels of solid waste *attest these being* of a rather moderate size compared to the amount of materials processed by the global economy (Haas et al. 2015) *and* those disposed of in other ways e.g. incinerated or landfilled (Tisserant et al. 2017).

3 Source: adapted from Will Steffen, Regina Angelina Sanderson, Peter D. Tyson, Jill Jäger, Pamela A. Matson, Berrien Moore III, Frank Oldfield et al. 2006. *Global Change and the Earth System: A Planet under Pressure*. Springer Science & Business Media.

4 Source: adapted from World Wildlife Fund (WWF). 2016. "Living Planet Report 2016". http://awsassets.panda.org/downloads/lpr_living_planet_report_2016.pdf.

5 Gregory Meyer. 2013. "Cargill Profits Wilted by US Drought". *Financial Times*. Posted on April 9, 2013. www.ft.com/content/8a4b7ef8-a114-11e2-bae1-00144feabdc0.

6 As explained in the following video by WorlDynamics: https://youtu.be/kF1ysDSrC_I.

7 For further information on the environmental cycle of nitrogen and the impacts from man-made activities, see: https://youtu.be/h5nSAfYKwxo.

8 Stockholm Resilience Centre. n.d. "The Nine Planetary Boundaries". Accessed July 1, 2017. www.stockholmresilience.org/research/planetary-boundaries/planetary-boundaries/about-the-research/the-nine-planetary-boundaries.html.

9 For further information on the environmental cycle of water and the impacts from man-made activities, see: https://youtu.be/Ukwhn4Blac8.

10 "Indian Officials Order Coca-Cola Plant to Close for Using Too Much Water". *The Guardian*, June 18, 2014. www.theguardian.com/environment/2014/jun/18/indian-officals-coca-cola-plant-water-mehdiganj.

11 A biome is a distinct ecological region characterized by its climate, major biological community and dominant vegetation. Terrestrial biomes include: grassland, tundra, desert, tropical rainforest, and deciduous and coniferous forests (www.informea.org/en/terms/biome).

12 Stockholm Resilience Centre. n.d. "The Nine Planetary Boundaries". Accessed July 1, 2017. www.stockholmresilience.org/research/planetary-boundaries/planetary-boundaries/about-the-research/the-nine-planetary-boundaries.html.

13 Sustainicum. n.d. "Planetary Boundaries Handouts". Accessed on July 4, 2017. www.sustainicum.at/files/projects/358/en/handouts/PlanBound_handout_the9Boundaries.pdf.

14 For further information on the environmental cycle of carbon and the impacts from man-made activities, see: www.youtube.com/watch?v=jnchKN oRjeM&feature=youtu.be.

15 Hard commodities are those for which some sort of extractive or mining work is required like oil or metals, while soft commodities are those coming from livestock or agriculture.

16 The World Bank. 2016. "Commodity Markets Outlook. April 2016. Special Focus: Resource Development in an Era of Cheap Commodities". Accessed on July 10, 2017. http://pubdocs.worldbank.org/en/520771461694380642/ CMO-April-2016-Special-Focus.pdf.

17 Sina Ebnesajjad. 2016. "Rare Earth Elements: The 21st century minerals and china, again!" *Elsevier*. Posted on November 15, 2016. https://chemical-materials.elsevier.com/new-materials-applications/rare-earth-elements-21st-century-minerals-china-again/.

18 Source: www.energyandcapital.com/articles/peak-lithium/5460.

19 Office of the United Nations High Commissioner for Human Rights (OHCHR). n.d. "Brazilian Mine Disaster: "This Is Not the Time for Defensive Posturing" – UN Rights Experts". Accessed on July 25, 2017. www.ohchr.org/ EN/NewsEvents/Pages/DisplayNews.aspx?NewsID=16803&LangID=E.

20 Kate Kunkel. 2016. "Mining: Are We There Yet?" *Valve Magazine*. Posted on October 25, 2016. www.valvemagazine.com/web-only/categories/end-user-industries/7957-mining-are-we-there-yet.html.

21 Staff Reuters. 2017. "Factbox: Disruptions, Labor Negotiations at Copper Mines". *Thomson Reuters*. Posted on February 21, 2017. www.reuters.com/ article/us-copper-disruptions-factbox-idUSKBN1601ER.

22 Ford. 2014. "2013–2014 Sustainability Report". Accessed on July 27, 2017. http://static.globalreporting.org/report-pdfs/2014/a6e84fbd07f989b5 78fa3a477965d46e.pdf.

23 European Commission. 2017. "Critical Raw Materials". Last Modified on September 13, 2017. https://ec.europa.eu/growth/sectors/raw-materials/ specific-interest/critical_en.

24 Homi Kharas. 2016. "How a Growing Global Middle Class Could Save the World's Economy". *The Pew Charitable Trusts*. Posted on July 5, 2016. http://trend.pewtrusts.org/en/archive/trend-summer-2016/how-a-growing-middle-class-could-save-the-worlds-economy.

25 The World Bank. n.d. "GDP per capita". Accessed on August 3, 2017. http:// data.worldbank.org/indicator/NY.GDP.PCAP.CD?locations=CN.

26 The World Bank. 2012a. "Mexican Middle Class Grows Over Past Decade". Posted on November 13, 2012. www.worldbank.org/en/news/ feature/2012/11/13/mexico-middle-class-grows-over-past-decade.

27 Sarah Boumphrey. 2015. "Mexico: It's All about the Middle Class". *Euromonitor International*. Posted on October 12, 2015. http://blog.euromonitor. com/2015/10/mexico-its-all-about-the-middle-class.html.

28 Turkey Data Monitor. n.d. "GDP Growth". Accessed on August 10, 2017. www.turkeydatamonitor.com/gallery_chartlist_eng.html.

29 Investment Support and Promotion Agency of Turkey. 2014. "The Manufacturing Industry in Turkey". Accessed on August 6, 2017. www.invest. gov.tr/en-US/infocenter/publications/Documents/MANUFACTURING. INDUSTRY.pdf.

30 Homi Kharas. 2016. "How a Growing Global Middle Class Could Save the World's Economy". The Pew Charitable Trusts. Posted on July 5, 2016. http://trend.pewtrusts.org/en/archive/trend-summer-2016/how-a-growing-middle-class-could-save-the-worlds-economy.

31 Homi Kharas. 2016. "How a Growing Global Middle Class Could Save the World's Economy". The Pew Charitable Trusts. Posted on July 5, 2016. http://trend.pewtrusts.org/en/archive/trend-summer-2016/how-a-growing-middle-class-could-save-the-worlds-economy.

32 International Policy Centre for Inclusive Growth. 2013. "Poverty in Focus No. 26 -October 2013". Accessed on August 27, 2017. www.ipc-undp.org/pub/IPCPovertyInFocus26.pdf.

33 The following video by WorlDynamics assesses the textile industry from a CE perspective, identifying and quantifying its major environmental impacts https://youtu.be/65zR2nU0sBU.

34 World Wildlife Fund (WWF). 2013. "The Impact of a Cotton T-Shirt". Posted on January 16, 2013. www.worldwildlife.org/stories/the-impact-of-a-cotton-t-shirt.

35 Ruslan Horblyuk, Kristopher Kaneta, Gary L. McMillen, Christopher Mullins, Thomas M. O'Brien, and Ankita Roy. 2012. "Out of Control. How Clinical Asset Proliferation and Low Utilization Are Draining Healthcare Budgets". *GE Healthcare.* Accessed on September 13, 2017. http://partners.gehealthcare.com/Out_Of_Control_Cost_Analysis-WP-01%2012_r2.pdf.

36 Jana Valant. 2016. "Planned Obsolescence: Exploring the Issue". *European Parliament.* May 2016. www.europarl.europa.eu/RegData/etudes/BRIE/2016/581999/EPRS_BRI%282016%29581999_EN.pdf.

37 French Ministry of Environment, Energy and The Sea. 2016. Law no. 2015-992 on Energy Transition for Green Growth (Energy Transition Law). www.legifrance.gouv.fr/ affichTexte.do?cidTexte=JORFTEXT0000 31044385&categorieLien=id.

38 More info at: http://ec.europa.eu/environment/circular-economy/index_en .htm.

39 Planet Aid. n.d. "Recycling Rates Around the World". Accessed on September 13, 2017. http://files.www.planetaid.org/blog/recycling-rates-around-the world/recycling_rates_around_the_world_Full_Size.jpg.

40 Alden Wicker. 2016. "Fast Fashion is Creating an Environmental Crisis". *Newsweek.* Posted on September 1, 2016. www.newsweek.com/2016/09/09/old-clothes-fashion-waste-crisis-494824.html.

41 As explained in the following WorlDynamics' video: https://youtu.be/xC_h8QLo1Iw.

42 Mike Berners-Lee, and Duncan Clark. 2010. "What's the Carbon Footprint of … a New Car?" *The Guardian.* Posted on September 23, 2010. www.theguardian.com/environment/green-living-blog/2010/sep/23/carbon-footprint-new-car.

Bibliography

Bakker, Conny, Feng Wang, Jaco Huisman, and Marcel den Hollander, 2014. "Products that Go Round: Exploring Product Life Extension through Design." *Journal of Cleaner Production* 69: 10–16.

Barton, Dominic, Yougang Chen, and Amy Jin. 2013. "Mapping China's Middle Class." *McKinsey Quarterly.* Posted on June 2013. www.mckinsey.com/industries/retail/our-insights/mapping-chinas-middle-class.

Berners-Lee, Mike, and Duncan Clark. 2010. "What's the Carbon Footprint of… A New Car?" *The Guardian.* Posted on September 23, 2010. www.theguardian.com/environment/green-living-blog/2010/sep/23/carbon-foot print-new-car.

Boumphrey, Sarah. 2015. "Mexico: It's All about the Middle Class." *Euromonitor International*. Posted on October 12, 2015. http://blog.euromonitor.com/2015/10/mexico-its-all-about-the-middle-class.html.

Breene, Keith. 2016. "6 Surprising Facts about India's Exploding Middle Class." *World Economic Forum*. Posted on November 7, 2016. www.weforum.org/agenda/2016/11/6-surprising-facts-about-india-s-exploding-middle-class/.

Cook, Brent. 2004. "Base Metals: Running on Empty." *Casey Research*. Accessed on July 15, 2017. www.caseyresearch.com/articles/base-metals-running-empty.

Cook, David, Nína Maria Saviolidis, Brynhildur Davíðsdóttir, Lára Jóhannsdóttir, and Snjólfur Ólafsson. 2017. "Measuring Countries' Environmental Sustainability Performance—The Development of a Nation-Specific Indicator Set." *Ecological Indicators* 74: 463–78.

Ebnesajjad, Sina. 2016. "Rare Earth Elements: The 21st Century Minerals and China, Again!" *Elsevier*. Posted on November 15, 2016. https://chemical-materials.elsevier.com/new-materials-applications/rare-earth-elements-21st-century-minerals-china-again/.

Ellen MacArthur Foundation. 2014. "Towards the Circular Economy Vol. 3: Accelerating the scale-up across global supply chains." Accessed on September 3, 2016. https://www.ellenmacarthurfoundation.org/publications/towards-the-circular-economy-vol-3-accelerating-the-scale-up-across-global-supply-chains

Ellen MacArthur Foundation. 2015a. "Growth Within: A Circular Economy for a Competitive Europe." Accessed on September 5, 2017. www.ellenmacarthurfoundation.org/publications/growth-within-a-circular-economy-vision-for-a-competitive-europe.

Ellen MacArthur Foundation. 2015b. "Toward a Circular Economy: Business Rationale for an Accelerated Transition." www.ellenmacarthurfoundation.org/assets/downloads/TCE_Ellen-MacArthur-Foundation_9-Dec-2015.pdf.

Environmental Protection Agency (EPA). 2017. "Nutrient Pollution. Sources and Solutions." Last Modified on March 10, 2017. www.epa.gov/nutrientpollution/sources-and-solutions.

European Environmental Agency (EEA). 2015. "Intensified Global Competition for Resources." Last Modified on July 6, 2017. www.eea.europa.eu/soer-2015/global/competition.

European Commission. 2017. "Critical Raw Materials." Last Modified on September 13, 2017. https://ec.europa.eu/growth/sectors/raw-materials/specific-interest/critical_en.

Giljum, Stefan, Monika Dittrich, Mirko Lieber, and Stephan Lutter. 2014. "Global Patterns of Material Flows and Their Socio-Economic and Environmental Implications: A MFA Study on All Countries World-Wide from 1980 to 2009." *Resources* 2014, 3 (1): 319–39. doi:10.3390/resources3010319.

Haas, Willi, Fridolin Krausmann, Dominik Wiedenhofer, and Markus Heinz. 2015. "How Circular Is the Global Economy? An Assessment of Material Flows, Waste Production, and Recycling in the European Union and the World in 2005." *Journal of Industrial Ecology* 19 (5): 765–77. doi:10.1111/jiec.12244.

Horblyuk, Ruslan, Kristopher Kaneta, Gary L. McMillen, Christopher Mullins, Thomas M. O'Brien, and Ankita Roy. 2012. "Out of Control. How Clinical

Asset Proliferation and Low Utilization Are Draining Healthcare Budgets."
GE Healthcare. Accessed on September 13, 2017. http://partners.gehealth
care.com/Out_Of_Control_Cost_Analysis-WP-01%2012_r2.pdf.

Hughes, Terry P., Stephen Carpenter, Johan Rockström, Marten Scheffer,
and Brian Walker. 2013. "Multiscale Regime Shifts and Planetary Boundaries." *Trends in Ecology & Evolution* 28 (7): 389–95. doi:10.1016/j.
tree.2013.05.019.

Intergovernmental Panel on Climate Change (IPCC). 2013. "Climate Change
2013: The Physical Science Basis. Contribution of Working Group I to the
Fifth Assessment Report of the Intergovernmental Panel on Climate Change."
Cambridge University Press. www.ipcc.ch/pdf/assessment-report/ar5/wg1/
WG1AR5_SPM_FINAL.pdf.

International Policy Centre for Inclusive Growth. 2013. "Poverty in Focus No.
26-October 2013." Accessed on August 27, 2017. www.ipc-undp.org/pub/
IPCPovertyInFocus26.pdf.

International Resource Panel. 2016. "Global Material Flows and Resource
Productivity Assessment Report for the UNEP International Resource
Panel." Accessed on August 30, 2017. www.resourcepanel.org/reports/
global-material-flows-and-resource-productivity.

Investment Support and Promotion Agency of Turkey. 2014. "The Manufacturing Industry in Turkey." Accessed on August 6, 2017. www.invest.
gov.tr/en-US/infocenter/publications/Documents/MANUFACTURING.
INDUSTRY.pdf.

Kharas, Homi. 2010. "The Emerging Middle Class in Developing Countries."
Working Paper No. 285, OECD Development Centre. Accessed on August
10, 2017. www.oecd.org/dev/44457738.pdf.

Kharas, Homi. 2016. "How a Growing Global Middle Class Could Save the
World's Economy." *The Pew Charitable Trusts.* Posted on July 5, 2016.
http://trend.pewtrusts.org/en/archive/trend-summer-2016/how-a-growing-
middle-class-could-save-the-worlds-economy.

Kunkel, Kate. 2016. "Mining: Are We There Yet?" *Valve Magazine.* Posted on
October 25, 2016. www.valvemagazine.com/web-only/categories/end-user-
industries/7957-mining-are-we-there-yet.html.

Meyer, Gregory. 2013. "Cargill Profits Wilted by US Drought." *Financial Times*,
April 9, 2013. www.ft.com/content/8a4b7ef8-a114-11e2-bae1-00144feabdc0.

Morrison, Wayne. M., and Rachel Tang. 2012. "China's Rare Earth Industry
and Export Regime: Economic and Trade Implications for the United States."
*CRS Report for Congress Prepared for Members and Committees of Con-
gress.* Accessed on March 17, 2018. https://fas.org/sgp/crs/row/R42510.pdf.

Office of the United Nations High Commissioner for Human Rights (OHCHR).
n.d. "Brazilian Mine Disaster: 'This Is Not the Time for Defensive Posturing' –
UN Rights Experts." Accessed on July 25, 2017. www.ohchr.org/EN/News
Events/Pages/DisplayNews.aspx?NewsID=16803&Lang ID=E.

Papp, John F. 2014. "Conflict Minerals from the Democratic Republic of the
Congo—Global Tantalum Processing Plants, a Critical Part of the Tantalum
Supply Chain." *U.S. Geological Survey.* Accessed on July 12, 2017. https://
pubs.usgs.gov/fs/2014/3122/pdf/fs20143122.pdf.

Pezzini, Mario. n.d. "An Emerging Middle Class." *OECD Observer.* Accessed
on September 13, 2017. http://oecdobserver.org/news/fullstory.php/aid/3681/
An_emerging_middle_class.html.

Planet Aid. n.d. "Recycling Rates Around the World." Accessed on September 13, 2017. http://files.www.planetaid.org/blog/recycling-rates-around-theworld/ recycling_rates_around_the_world_Full_Size.jpg.

Rockström, Johan, Will Steffen, Kevin Noone, Åsa Persson, F. Stuart Chapin III, Eric Lambin, Timothy M. Lenton et al. 2009. "Planetary Boundaries: Exploring the Safe Operating Space for Humanity." *Ecology and Society* 14 (2) www.jstor.org/stable/26268316.

Reuters Staff. 2017. "Factbox: Disruptions, Labor Negotiations at Copper Mines." *Thomson Reuters*. Posted on February 21, 2017. www.reuters.com/ article/us-copper-disruptions-factbox-idUSKBN1601ER.

Steffen, Will, Regina Angelina Sanderson, Peter D. Tyson, Jill Jäger, Pamela A. Matson, Berrien Moore III, Frank Oldfield et al. 2006. *Global Change and the Earth System: A Planet under Pressure*. Springer Science & Business Media. www.igbp.net/download/18.56b5e28e137d8d8c09380001694/137638 3141875/SpringerIGBPSynthesisSteffenetal2004_web.pdf.

Steffen, Will, Katherine Richardson, Johan Rockström, Sarah E. Cornell, Ingo Fetzer, Elena M. Bennett, Reinette Biggs et al. 2015. "Planetary Boundaries: Guiding Human Development on a Changing Planet." *Science* 347 (6223): 1259855. http://science.sciencemag.org/content/347/6223/1259855.

Stockholm Resilience Centre. n.d. "The Nine Planetary Boundaries." Accessed on July 1, 2017. www.stockholmresilience.org/research/planetary-boundaries/ planetary-boundaries/about-the-research/the-nine-planetary-boundaries.html.

Sustainicum. n.d. "Planetary Boundaries Handouts." Accessed on July 4, 2017. www.sustainicum.at/files/projects/358/en/handouts/PlanBound_handout_ the9Boundaries.pdf.

The Organisation for Economic Co-operation and Development (OECD). 2012. "Material Resources, Productivity and the Environment. Key Findings." www. oecd.org/greengrowth/MATERIAL%20RESOURCES,%20PRODUCTIVITY %20AND%20THE%20ENVIRONMENT_key%20findings.pdf.

The World Bank. n.d. "GDP per capita." Accessed on August 3, 2017. http:// data.worldbank.org/indicator/NY.GDP.PCAP.CD?locations=CN.

The World Bank. 2012a. "Mexican Middle Class Grows Over Past Decade." Posted on November 13, 2012. www.worldbank.org/en/news/feature/2012/11 /13/mexico-middle-class-grows-over-past-decade.

The World Bank. 2012b. "What a Waste. A Global Review of Solid Waste Management." *Urban Development Series Knowledge Papers*. Accessed on January 08, 2018. https://siteresources.worldbank.org/INTURBANDEVEL OPMENT/Resources/336387-1334852610766/What_a_Waste2012_ Final.pdf.

The World Bank. 2016. "Commodity Markets Outlook. April 2016. Special Focus: Resource Development in an Era of Cheap Commodities." Accessed on July 10, 2017. http://pubdocs.worldbank.org/en/520771461694380642/ CMO-April-2016-Special-Focus.pdf.

The World Bank. 2017. "Commodity Markets Outlook. April 2017." Accessed on July 10, 2017. http://pubdocs.worldbank.org/en/174381493046968144/ CMO-April-2017-Full-Report.pdf.

Tietenberg, Tom and Lynne Lewis. 2016. *Environmental & Natural Resource Economics Tenth Edition*. New York, NY: Routledge.

Tisserant, Alexandre, Stefan Pauliuk, Stefano Merciai, Jannick Schmidt, Jacob Fry, Richard Wood, Arnold Tukker. 2017. "Solid Waste and the Circular

Economy: A Global Analysis of Waste Treatment and Waste Footprints." *Journal of Industrial Ecology* 21: 628–40. doi:10.1111/jiec.

Turkey Data Monitor. n.d. "GDP Growth." Accessed on August 10, 2017. www.turkeydatamonitor.com/gallery_chartlist_eng.html.

United Nations Environment Programme (UNEP). 2013. "GEO-5 for Business. Impacts of a Changing Environment on the Corporate Sector." www.unep.org/geo/sites/unep.org.geo/files/documents/geo5_for_business.pdf.

United Nations Environment Programme (UNEP). 2014. "Air Pollution: World's Worst Environmental Health Risk." Accessed on April 7, 2017. http://home.iitk.ac.in/~anubha/H6.pdf.

United Nations Environment Programme (UNEP). 2015. "Waste Crime – Waste Risks: Gaps in Meeting the Global Waste Challenge. A UNEP Rapid Response Assessment." Accessed on September 7, 2017. www.grida.no/publications/166.

United Nations Environment Programme (UNEP). 2016. "Global Material Flows and Resource Productivity. An Assessment Study of the UNEP International Resource Panel." www.resourcepanel.org/reports/global-material-flows-and-resource-productivity-database-link.

Valant, Jana. 2016. "Planned Obsolescence: Exploring the Issue." *European Parliament.* May 2016. www.europarl.europa.eu/RegData/etudes/BRIE/2016/581999/EPRS_BRI%282016%29581999_EN.pdf.

Wicker, Alden. 2016. "Fast Fashion Is Creating an Environmental Crisis." *Newsweek.* Posted on September 1, 2016. www.newsweek.com/2016/09/09/old-clothes-fashion-waste-crisis-494824.html.

Wijkman, Anders and Johan Rockström. 2012. *Bankrupting Nature. Denying Our Planetary Boundaries.* London: Routledge.

World Economic Forum. 2017. "The Global Risks Report 2017 12th Edition." www3.weforum.org/docs/GRR17_Report_web.pdf.

World Wildlife Fund (WWF). 2013. "The Impact of a Cotton T-Shirt." Posted on January 16, 2013. www.worldwildlife.org/stories/the-impact-of-a-cotton-t-shirt.

World Wildlife Fund (WWF). 2016. "Living Planet Report 2016." http://awsassets.panda.org/downloads/lpr_living_planet_report_2016.pdf.

2 An Introduction to the Circular Economy

2.1 Introduction

In the face of the many threats, challenges, and opportunities posed by the linear economic model, a new concept has recently emerged with strong impetus as the panacea for an economically successful and environmentally sustainable future. The Circular Economy (CE) is an alternative industrial model (Ellen MacArthur Foundation 2012, 2013 and 2014; Mendoza et al. 2017) where, by taking a holistic (Bonciu 2014) and systemic approach (Webster 2013), industrial processes are not seen as the inevitable cause of natural resource exploitation, environmental pollution, and waste generation, but rather, as a means to contribute to sustainable development (Kirchherr et al. 2017). While the focus is still on making business operations profitable, in a CE model, this is achieved by embracing a number of regenerative (Ellen MacArthur Foundation 2012; Prieto-Sandoval et al. 2016) and closed-loop strategies (Bocken et al. 2016) like switching to bio-based materials and green energy sources; designing for modularity and prolonged use; utilization rate maximization (e.g. sharing, re-use, etc.); refurbishment, remanufacturing, and components recovery.

The primary aim of these activities is to design out waste (Ellen MacArthur Foundation 2012) and maximize the (re-)utilization of materials (Ellen MacArthur Foundation 2015b) and products that would otherwise be quickly discarded, not used, or considered obsolete. To do so, the multidisciplinary (Lieder and Rashid 2016) CE framework builds upon innovative business models (Bocken et al. 2016) and novel approaches to product design, material management, and value retention that allow to continually circulate flows of products, components, and materials at their highest utility into production systems (Ellen MacArthur Foundation 2015a, 2015b, 2015c; Bocken et al. 2017a; den Hollander et al. 2017).

Amongst recent endeavours to define the CE, one of the most notorious is the work conducted at the Ellen MacArthur Foundation, according to which it is an "industrial system that is restorative or regenerative by intention and design" (Ellen MacArthur Foundation 2012, 7). Such a definition builds on three key pillars that together lay the foundations for creating a closed system, where materials are continually kept at their highest utility and with negligible environmental damage: preserving and enhancing natural capital, optimizing resource yields, and fostering system effectiveness by revealing and designing out negative externalities (Ellen MacArthur Foundation 2015a). Since its inception, the Ellen MacArthur Foundation has visually represented its interpretation of the CE model with the Butterfly Diagram,[1] which illustrates the continuous flow of materials through the so-called "value circle". Academics have also provided definitions for the CE, some mainly focusing on the aspect of closed loops (Geissdoerfer et al. 2017; Linder et al., 2017), while others on combining the 3R activities of reduce, re-use, and recycle (Ghisellini et al. 2014; Kirchherr et al. 2017). Another stream of research, while recognizing the necessity of establishing closed-loop flows of products and materials, has also emphasized the importance of slowing down resource loops, a business strategy that allows for the retention of product value for as long as possible (Bocken et al. 2017b), through, for example, designing for long-life products and product-life extension (Bocken et al. 2016).

As a concept, the CE has been instrumental in grouping a range of waste and resource management approaches by "drawing attention to their capacity of prolonging resource use as well as to the relationship between these strategies" (Blomsma and Brennan 2017, 6). As a holistic framework that joins multiple sustainability approaches together, the CE concerns all business processes (i.e. planning, resourcing, procurement, production, and reprocessing) (Murray et al. 2017) and human activities at large (Bonciu 2014). Given its all-inclusive and comprehensive stance, the CE model has been explicitly linked to sustainable development on multiple occasions, and more specifically to an economy that works in line with the socio-economic and environmental systems in which it is embedded, for the benefit of current and future generations (Brundtland 1987; Webster 2013; Kirchherr et al. 2017). Researchers have already identified a range of shared attributes that connect the CE model with the concept of sustainability,[2] like both having a global reach; both including intra- and intergenerational commitments and socio-environmental considerations; both focusing on design, innovation, breakthrough technology, and cooperation between stakeholders; both being multi-/interdisciplinary at their core; and both identifying the private sector as the key driver for change (Geissdoerfer et al. 2017).

Despite being highly innovative, the concept of a CE is just the most recent manifestation of an environmentally conscious mindset that has previously led to the formation and development of other important schools of thought like Cradle to Cradle, Biomimicry, Regenerative Design, Natural Capitalism, Blue Economy, Industrial Ecology, and Permaculture. Each of these movements called invariably for a drastic change in the way we manage the value generation of products: a strong emphasis is repeatedly placed on the need to build an economy where the value of any product and its components is protected, maintained, and exploited even after reaching end-of-life state.

- **Cradle to Cradle** is a sustainability design and management certification process first conceptualized by architect William McDonough and chemist Michael Braungart (2002) in their book "Cradle to Cradle: Remaking the Way We Make Things". This holistic approach to sustainability enables organizations to radically transform their processes so they can eventually get rid of any environmental externality. To achieve this, the certification process challenges businesses to concurrently focus on five primary sustainability actions:

  - Gradually phase out toxic substances from production processes and switch to environmentally friendly materials.[3]
  - Apply product's disassembly/recovery principles at the design stage.
  - Replace fossil fuel energy sources with renewables.
  - Implement measures to reduce water quality/quantity impacts.
  - Be ethically responsible towards internal/external stakeholders.

- **Biomimicry** is a school of thought that considers Nature's millenary wisdom – tangibly infused into evolutionary patterns, forms, and processes, as well as animals' characteristics and behaviours – as the source of design solutions for today's sustainable development challenges. The term gained global attention when scientist Janine Benyus (1997) published her book "Biomimicry: Innovation Inspired by Nature" and today, a wide range of solutions and ideas – from kingfisher-inspired bullet trains to green chemistry innovations – can be found across a variety of industries (Pawlyn 2011).

- **Industrial Ecology (or Symbiosis)** seeks to harness the potential synergies between two or more value-creating industrial systems, facilities, or companies, so that the by-products and waste flows originating from one entity are fed into the other as production inputs and raw materials (like the surplus of steam exiting an energy plant being supplied to a chemical facility or the by-products of an oil refinery plant being fed into sulphuric acid or plastics). To accomplish this, industrial ecology experts utilize advanced sustainability and waste management tools like Material Flows Analysis (MFA),[4] design for disassembly and green technologies. Large-scale Eco-Industrial Parks (EIPs) have been introduced in China (Zhang et al. 2010; Wen and Meng, 2015; Yu et al. 2015) to replicate the dynamics of already operational highly efficient industrial parks like Kalundborg (Denmark) and Burnside (Nova Scotia). In these locations, inter-firms' symbiosis involves businesses operating in all sorts of economic sectors like food, machinery, pulp and paper, textile and garment, wine refining, and biochemical (Yu et al. 2015).

- **Regenerative Design** is an innovative approach with a focus on devising processes that restore and improve both sources of energy and materials used, and the society and the environment at large. In the construction industry for example, the creation of regenerative cities envisions buildings that continue to burn fossil fuels, but at a rate that can be reabsorbed through "bio-sequestration" in soils and forests.[5] Living spaces can also be designed to produce more energy than is required, devoting what remains to grow vegetation and food for the local community and to protect ecosystems where animals can shelter and live (Nugent et al. 2016).

- **Natural Capitalism** is an approach to corporate sustainability that develops from the recognition that natural resources are finite and must therefore be soundly managed by businesses, if these are to prosper in the long term. As described in "Natural Capitalism: Creating the Next Industrial Revolution" (Hawken et al. 1999), the four key business actions of the approach involve: dramatically increasing the productivity of natural resources; shifting to biologically inspired production models; moving to solutions-based business models; and reinvesting in natural capital.

- **Blue Economy** is a solutions-based business model that promotes re-designing highly polluting industrial processes by: incorporating the value of natural capital into business activities; replacing processes that use rare resources and high energy with cleaner technologies; and harnessing the power of cascading systems, where the waste flows of one process become the input of another. At its core, the Blue Economy seeks to decouple economic activities from environmental degradation by leveraging open-source scientific solutions that make use of what is locally available to devise simpler and greener technologies. The successful application of the approach has been monitored and documented by Gunter Pauli in his three books (2010, 2015, and 2017).

- **Permaculture** is "a design system for creating sustainable human environments. A philosophy of working with, rather than against nature… and of looking at plants and animals in all their functions, rather than elements as a single-product system" (Mollison 1994, 1). To this end, permaculture offers a set of methods and design principles to establish sustainable agricultural and social systems. In 2002, the book "Permaculture: Principles and Pathways Beyond Sustainability" by David Holmgren identified the fundamental pillars of permaculture, with some of these closely relating to the CE principles of using renewable resources, producing zero waste, valuing diversity, and effectively interacting with natural patterns.

Since 2009, the Ellen MacArthur Foundation has played a vital role in grouping (both explicitly and not) all of these theories under a single overarching CE framework of principles and practical actions for both the public and business sectors. The foundation has in fact been publishing a series of highly informative books, reports, and technical papers[6] covering far and wide the main topics, challenges, and opportunities of a CE. By all accounts, the new paradigm has been warmly welcomed by governments, sustainable development institutions, the academia, and, perhaps most importantly, the corporate world as a win-win approach for sustainable development, capable to deliver not only large-scale environmental benefits but also significant efficiency gains, multiple economic advantages, and positive social implications. Below is a summary of some of the most important recent studies investigating the environmental, social, and economic reasons for switching to a circular industrial system (Table 2.1).

Table 2.1 Review of Main CE Studies

Title	Organization	Year	Key Findings
Towards the circular economy: Accelerating the scale-up across global supply chains	World Economic Forum; Ellen MacArthur Foundation; McKinsey & Co.	2014	In Europe, creating circular loops in manufacturing could yield net materials cost savings of up to US$ 630 billion
Delivering the circular economy: A toolkit for policymakers	Ellen MacArthur Foundation	2015c	Transitioning towards a circular economy system in five focus sectors (food and beverage, construction and real estate, machinery, plastic packaging, and hospitals) could mean for Denmark: • a 0.8%–1.4% boost in GDP; • plus 7,000/13,000 job equivalents; • a 3%–7% decrease in carbon footprint; • a 5%–50% reduction of consumption of selected resources by; • plus 3%–6% in net exports.
The circular economy and benefits for society: Swedish case study shows jobs and climate as clear winner	The Club of Rome	2015a	If comprehensively implemented in Sweden, the circular economy model can lead to: • an overall reduction of global greenhouse gases of 70%; • an increase in employment of 2%–3% of the labour force; and • a further improvement in the trade balance of >3% of the national GDP by 2030.

(Continued)

Title	Organization	Year	Key Findings
The circular economy and benefits for society. Jobs and climate clear winners in an economy based on renewable energy and resource efficiency. A study pertaining to Finland, France, the Netherlands, Spain and Sweden.	The Club of Rome	2015b	The circular economy model would bring significant benefits for the countries covered by the study in terms of: • carbon emissions (down by up to 70% in Sweden and Spain by 2030); and • employment creation (e.g. 500,000 more jobs in France, 400,000 in Spain, and 200,000 in The Netherlands)
Waste to wealth: The circular economy advantage	Accenture Strategy	2015	In the next 15 years, the circular economy has the potential to unleash 4.5 trillion worth of economic opportunities across the globe
The social benefits of a circular economy: Lessons from the UK	Green Alliance; WRAP	2015	In UK, the switch to circular economy operations can create more 20,000 jobs. The same is true for other EU countries.
Growth within: A circular economy vision for a competitive Europe	Ellen MacArthur Foundation; McKinsey Center for Business and Environment	2015a	Adopting large-scale circular solutions in the food, mobility, and built environment sectors could mean for Europe: • an increase in GDP of 6.7% by 2030; • a reduction by 32% by 2030 and 53% by 2050 of primary material consumption; and • 48% decrease of CO_2 emissions • by 2030 and 83% by 2050 (compared to 2012 levels)
Sustainable phosphorus use — evaluating past patterns to inform future management	The European Union	2016	Recycling waste from farming and mining could significantly improve the sustainable use of phosphorus (Chen and Graedel, 2016).
Implementing circular economy globally makes Paris targets achievable	Circle Economy; Ecofys	2016	CE measures targeting material efficiency can bridge the emission gap necessary to achieve the climate change objectives set in the 2016 Paris Agreement.

(Continued)

Title	Organization	Year	Key Findings
Automotive's latest model: Redefining competitiveness through the circular economy	Accenture Strategy	2016	By 2030, circular business models in the automotive sector could grow by 400–600 USD billion.
Less is more: Circular economy solutions to water shortages	ING Group	2017	By embracing circular economy solutions to water management, the regions of California, Ghana, Bangladesh, Northern India, The Netherlands, and United Arab Emirates can have 412 billion cubic metres of water each year, the equivalent to 11% of annual global water demand.

2.2 Biosphere and Technosphere Products

For a circular industrial model to be efficient and environmentally neutral, it is necessary for operations like take-back and return schemes, reusing, remanufacturing, refurbishing, and recycling to run smoothly regardless of the number of actors involved in the cycle. To this end, CE theorists argue (Ellen MacArthur Foundation 2012) that there shall be a clear distinction between materials that can be returned safely back to the biosphere (e.g. food, fibres, wood, etc.) and those that are not suited to get in contact with the natural world (e.g. chemicals, plastics, etc.). Accordingly, the formers are usually called "biosphere products", while the latter are defined as "technosphere products".

Biosphere Products are natural products (or materials) that can safely re-enter the natural ecosystem when their purpose is served. These products can either be 100% natural like food and wood, or man-made bio-based goods such as biodegradable bags or vegan cosmetics. In a CE model, these products are designed so that they, or the by-products generated during their consumption or use, have a positive impact on the natural environment even when they are disposed of, rather than polluting it. At the end of their lifespan, these resources can thus be wholly leveraged by other human processes in agriculture, aquaculture, renewable energy generation, or more simply be safely returned to the natural world. The German start-up Leaf Republic, for example, is specialized in producing eco-friendly disposable dishes and packaging through processed leaves that biodegrade in the environment in less than a month. On a broader level, the sportswear and fitness apparel sector is currently exploring solutions linked to the bioproducts trend, with some of the most notorious brands already promoting alternative collections deploying natural biodegradable materials. In 2013, the German manufacturer Puma launched a new pioneering line of apparel, shoes, and accessories – called Puma InCycle – that was entirely biodegradable (or recyclable). In early 2017, another leading German sportswear company, Adidas, followed by releasing a 100% biodegradable running sneaker[7] whose performance characteristics of lightness and toughness are – according to the firm – equivalent to their standard models. Another example has been Reebok, which, in April 2017, announced the use of an innovative corn-based material as an alternative to petroleum-based fabrics.[8]

Of course, biosphere materials are not limited to commercial applications and can be leveraged in many ways. A growing number of progressive cities around the world – e.g. Milan (Italy), San Francisco, and Seattle (U.S.A.) – have already implemented organic waste recovery schemes whereby food scraps and the likes are collected at households and then sent to dedicated composting facilities and anaerobic digestion plants to produce biogas and compost. In doing so, these municipalities not only produce energy at low cost, but also save waste disposal costs and prevent garbage from releasing greenhouse gases, as they would in landfills (Ellen MacArthur Foundation, 2017).

Technosphere Products are those that cannot re-enter the biosphere due to their toxicity for the environment. These products are everyday items like plastic packaging and glass bottles, or more complex objects like engines, home appliances, and cars. Today, such goods are primarily designed to serve their function as technical objects, with little or no emphasis placed on how to loop them back into production once broken or discarded. However, in a CE system, these products are valuable resources that shall be maintained, re-distributed, refurbished, disassembled, and recycled within the industrial system – i.e. the Technosphere (Figure 2.1). Materials such as plastic, paper, and glass are already being at the centre of massive recycling programmes at both local and regional levels, particularly in advanced economies.[9]

However, when it comes to more complex items, examples of technical assets re-entering the economic system are still few compared to the number of goods ending up in landfills. But there are some exceptions. At Renault's factory in Choisy-le-Roi plant, parts from old cars are removed and either re-used in manufacturing or as supplies for spare components. This plant produces no waste: every single component entering the facility is re-valorized in some way. At an industry level, petrochemical companies are known to be relying on the re-use and regeneration (Akcil et al., 2015) of catalysts used in several refining processes. As these assets are made up of costly metals – primarily platinum group metals (PGMs) – they are looped back to specialized sites, where metals are separated and re-used to manufacture new catalysts.

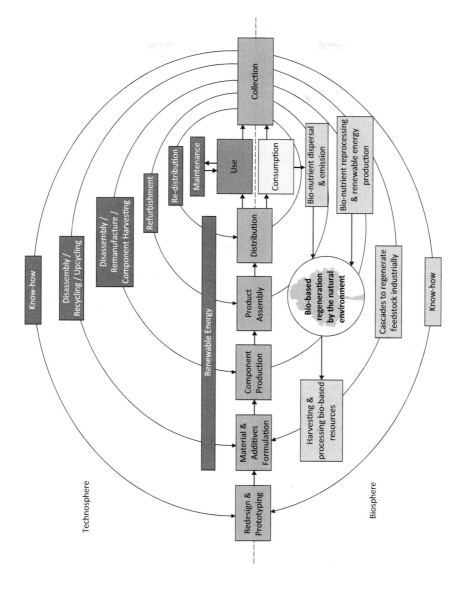

Figure 2.1 The Coexistence of Biosphere and Technosphere Products.[10]

2.3 Technological, Regulatory, and Social Factors

As we have seen, the CE is not a novel concept, for its underlying principles have been borrowed from a variety of previously existing sustainability approaches, some of which conceived a few decades ago. Why then, it is only in the recent three to five years that this alternative industrial model has gained exponential interest at all levels of society? Undoubtedly, the term "circular economy" has a powerful catch and the work of academia and nonprofit organizations has been intense. This, however, is only part of the answer, having the CE moved well beyond theoretical approaches, reaching governments' agendas as well as the strategic planning of some of the largest global multinationals. Arguably, behind the rapid emergence of CE stands a favourable alignment of global technological, regulatory, and social factors that have together contributed to make the CE proposition attractive, feasible, and, in most instances, highly lucrative.

Technological factors. Recent technological innovations – such as the Internet of Things (IoT), sensor and mobile technologies, digital sharing platforms, big data, 3D printing, and advanced recycling machinery – have favoured the establishment of key circular activities concerning the monitoring, collection, and re-processing of end-of-life assets. These innovations are helping forward-looking firms to: drastically reinvent the way they keep track of the levels of consumption, degradation, and re-usability of products; interact with the different actors along the supply chain to support reverse-loop strategies and practices; and engage with costumers well beyond the point of sale.

- In Western Australia for example, IoT technology is deployed by Caterpillar to predict damages and provide timely maintenance operations on its fleet of autonomous mining trucks.
- Through its Asset Recovery Programme, global technology company Ricoh leverages its proprietary trace and return system to collect and re-process pre-owned materials, like toner cartridges, with the aim of remarketing them.
- In the healthcare sector, technology company Cohealo utilizes a dedicated platform to optimize the utilization of medical equipment through asset sharing across facilities.

Regulatory factors. In response to the latest scientific findings (Rockström et al., 2009; Wijkman and Rockström, 2012; Hughes et al., 2013; Steffen et al., 2015), clearly pointing at a paradigm shift of the Earth system – and possibly from the mounting pressure of concerned citizens and environmental groups – public institutions have started to adopt policies and implement measures aimed at curbing man-made environmental impacts. Increasingly, these regulatory frameworks and sustainability initiatives are informed by principles of circularity that make it advantageous and/or easier for companies to implement green solutions throughout their operations:

- China Association of Circular Economy – CACE. In 2013, the Chinese government established a national, multi-industry organization with the aim to "building the resource recycling system covering the whole society, improving resource utilization, preventing pollutions at source, promoting recycling and low-carbon development, speeding up the building of eco-civilization, promoting transformation to a green economy".[11] Its 800+ members benefit from a variety of services like strategy and policy research, plans formulation, project assessment, and training.
- French Consumption Law with its Article L111–3, covering all items traded in France since 2015. In 2014, in an effort targeted to curb planned obsolescence and prolong the lifespan of products, the French government passed a specific regulation requiring manufacturers to disclose information about the availability of a product's spare parts.[12]
- EU CE Package. In late 2015, the European Commission adopted a set of measures to boost circular initiatives in its member states and covering the entire life cycle of goods – from design to consumption, and from waste management to the re-introduction of discarded resources.[13] The proposed plan, built around 54 legislative and non-legislative actions that the European Commission is currently crystallizing into concrete policies covering different economic activities and sectors, intended to close the life cycle loop through ambitious objectives for waste reduction, waste management, and recycling.
- Autosvolta. In 2016, the Municipality of Milan targeted owners of outdated and highly polluting vehicles by means of a dedicated smartphone application that calculated the car value and facilitated a request for its demolition, at zero cost, in one of the specialized facilities located around the city. In return, the municipality also offered the citizen a range of green incentives in the forms of vouchers and discounts for bike-sharing and electric car-sharing services.[14]
- Tax breaks on repair activities. As of January 2017, in Sweden the value-added tax (VAT) on repair activities concerning goods like clothes and bicycles was lowered by 13% (from 25% to 12%).[15]
- Advance London. In April 2017, the city of London launched a CE scheme for its Small and Medium Enterprises (SMEs).[16] CE consultants started offering free-of-charge support to SMEs wanting to explore and/or scale up circular business models. The programme is part of a broader set of measures adopted by London to achieve 65% recycling rate by 2030 and become a carbon-neutral city by 2050.

Social factors. Population growth and changes in customer preferences are constants that have historically marked the maturity and profitability of new business opportunities. Over the last few years, at least two social megatrends have contributed to making circular business models viable and profitable alternatives: an expansion of urban centres and a reduced attachment to ownership.

- Urbanization. Today, roughly four billion people – i.e. more than half of the world's population – live in urbanized areas, the epicentre of the human enterprise. Altogether, cities produce already 80% of the global GDP, make up 80% of global energy consumption, account for 75% of the world's natural resources, and produce about 1.3 billion tonnes of solid waste per year. These figures are evidently going to increase as the urbanization trend heightens. By 2030, the number of city dwellers is expected to reach five billion, 80% of them in developing countries; and at least 41 megacities worldwide are on track to become home to more than ten million people by 2030. Although the figures might seem alarming, this is good news for CE advocates, as high urbanization means lower operating costs associated with at least two important processes. First, asset sharing (cars, bikes, or houses) works best when a large number of users live in the same area, as this makes the sharing process faster and easier to be managed by the operator. Second, collecting, recycling, and treatment of end-of-use products are easier and more cost-effective when large volumes of discarded goods are in a few and nearby pickup points.[17]
- Customer acceptance of alternative business models. More and more people all over the world, but especially in western economies, are now familiarizing with "servitization".[18] A second notion that is attracting growing attention from customers is that of a "sharing economy".[19] Such business models have proved to be highly successful and rewarding in many industries like transportation, housing, chemicals, medical equipment, agriculture, and others. A survey by PricewaterhouseCoopers (2015) into the U.S. market showed 80+% of respondents agreeing that a sharing economy makes life easier, more affordable, and efficient.[20]

2.4 Conclusions

The aim of a CE is to enable human society transition towards a system of production and consumption that minimizes environmental externalities, thus preserving or re-establishing planetary boundaries. Because of the inherent economic challenges and environmental threats posed by the current economic system, this alternative paradigm has recently gained worldwide recognition and interest at all levels of society (e.g. business, government, citizens, etc.). While not easy to frame nor innovative in its essence, as it assembles and attempts to unify the thoughts of prior philosophies and approaches to environmental sustainability – like Cradle to Cradle, Biomimicry, Regenerative Design, Natural Capitalism, Blue Economy, Industrial Ecology, and Permaculture – the CE proposition appears increasingly appealing, feasible, and profitable because of the convergence of technological, regulatory, and social macro-trends that together are contributing to push for drastic and historic transformations in the way we do business.

Since 2009, this new vision of the economy, with its related business opportunities, has been successfully promulgated by the Ellen MacArthur Foundation. Various definitions of CE have followed, transferring the attention towards specific aspects of the proposition (e.g. combining the 3Rs or slowing down resource loops), but in its essence, the core of CE remains solidly grounded on: devising regenerative strategies and actions for creating a closed-loop production and consumption system. As we will begin to see in the next part of this book, adopting a CE model goes well beyond being environmentally friendly, for circular solutions hold the potential to boost the bottom line of those businesses that will strategically re-shape their operations and embed circularity at the heart of their future plans.

Notes

1 The diagram can be accessed here: www.ellenmacarthurfoundation.org/circular-economy/interactive-diagram.

2 In this book, the term sustainability is defined as a broad concept grounded in the interdependent and mutually reinforcing pillars of people, planet, and profit (Elkington's 1997 Trible Bottom Line approach).

3 Product ingredients are screened, and each substance gets assigned to one of three lists: X (most harmful substances or suspected to be so, e.g. asbestos, benzene, etc.); Gray (harmful substances not quite so urgent to get rid of and for which there is no viable alternative, e.g. cadmium); P (positive substances that are safe to use and for the environment).

4 The concept of MFA is discussed in greater detail in Chapter 12.

5 As explained in the following video by WorlDynamics https://youtu.be/8XYbqLbeiL8.

6 The reports and studies released by the Ellen MacArthur Foundation since 2012 can be accessed at: www.ellenmacarthurfoundation.org/publications. Among some of the most relevant are: "Towards the Circular Economy: Economic and Business Rationale for Accelerated Transition. Vol. 1". (2012); "Growth within: A Circular Economy Vision for a Competitive Europe. Ellen MacArthur Foundation" (2015); "Towards a Circular Economy: Business Rationale for an Accelerated Transition" (2015); "The New Plastics Economy: Catalysing Action" (2017).

7 These environmentally neutral shoes are made of a 100% natural fibre called Biosteel.

8 Reebok's "Cotton+Corn" initiative is the result of a collaboration between the company's innovation department – Reebok Future – and bio-based experts DuPont Tate and Lyle Bio Products.

9 For example, the Circular Economy Package adopted by the European Parliament in April 2018 set new targets for the recycling of municipal waste (55% by 2025, 60% by 2030, and 65% by 2035). In addition, the new measures target packaging materials (65% will have to be recycled by 2025, and 70% by 2030). This overall rate includes specific goals for certain materials like plastic (50% by 2025 and 55% by 2030), wood (25% by 2025 and 30% by 2030), glass (70% by 2025 and 75% by 2030), and paper and cardboard (75% by 2025 and 85% by 2030). Source: www.globalelr.com/2018/04/european-parliament-adopts-circular-economy-package/.

10 Source: adapted from www.epea.com/circular-economy.

11 China Association of Circular Economy (CACE). n.d. "Overview". Accessed on May 5, 2017. http://en.chinacace.org/about?tag=Overview.

12 Dynamix – Pollfree Policy Platform. 2015. "Circular Economy in France and Expectations about the EU Package". Accessed April 15, 2018. http://dynamix-project.eu/sites/default/files/event/attachment/Session2%20%20-%20chevassus.pdf.

13 European Commission. 2018. "Circular Economy. Implementation of the Circular Economy Action Plan". Last Updated on March 7, 2018. https://eur-lex.europa.eu/legal-content/EN/TXT/?uri=CELEX%3A52015DC0614.

14 Autosvolta https://autosvolta.it/progetto.

15 Apolitical. 2016. "Sweden Fights Wasteful Consumer Culture with Subsidised Repairs". Posted on September 29, 2016. https://apolitical.co/solution_article/sweden-tax-breaks-repairs-mend-per-bolund/.

16 London Waste and Recycling Board. n.d. "Advance London". Accessed on June 5, 2017. www.lwarb.gov.uk/what-we-do/advance-london/.

17 Global waste generation levels in cities are expected to increase to approximately 2.2 billion tonnes per year by 2025 (The World Bank, 2012).

18 Servitization refers to the novel concept allowing customers to enjoy the benefits of a product or service only when and for the time needed, without bearing the costs and stresses associated with ownership.

19 Sharing economy is an umbrella term used to define the peer-to-peer renting of assets through digital devices and platforms.

20 PricewaterhouseCoopers (PwC). 2015. "The Sharing Economy. Consumer Intelligence Series". Accessed on August 9, 2017. www.pwc.com/us/en/industry/entertainment-media/publications/consumer-intelligence-series/sharing-economy.html.

Bibliography

Accenture. 2016. "Automotive's Latest Model: Redefining Competitiveness Through the Circular Economy." Accessed on September 29, 2017. www.accenture.com/t20161216T034331__w__/us-en/_acnmedia/PDF-27/Accenture-POV-CE-Automotive.pdf.

Akcila, Ata, Francesco Vegliò, Francesco Ferella, Demet Okudana Mediha, and Aysenur Tuncuka. 2015. "A Review of Metal Recovery from Spent Petroleum Catalysts and Ash." *Waste Management* 45: 420–33. doi:10.1016/j.wasman.2015.07.007.

Benyus, Janine M. 1997. *Biomimicry: Innovation Inspired by Nature.* New York, NY: HarperCollins.

Bocken, Nancy M. P., Conny Bakker, Ingrid de Pauw, and Bram van der Grinten. 2016. "Product Design and Business Model Strategies for a Circular Economy." *Journal of Industrial and Production Engineering* 33 (5): 308–20. doi:10.1080/21681015.2016.1172124.

Bocken, Nancy M. P., Elsa A. Olivetti, Jonathan M. Cullen, José Potting, and Reid Lifset. 2017a. "Taking the Circularity to the Next Level: A Special Issue on the Circular Economy." *Journal of Industrial Ecology* 21: 476–82. doi:10.1111/jiec.12606.

Bocken, Nancy M. P., Paavo Ritala, and Pontus Huotar. 2017b. "The Circular Economy. Exploring the Introduction of the Concept among S&P 500 Firms." *Journal of Industrial Ecology Special Issue: Exploring the Circular Economy* 21 (3): 487–90. doi:10.1111/jiec.12605.

Bonciu, Florin. 2014. "The European Economy: From a Linear to a Circular Economy." *Romanian Journal of European Affairs* 14 (4): 78–91.

Blomsma, Fenna, and Geraldine Brennan. 2017. "The Emergence of Circular Economy: A New Framing Around Prolonging Resource Productivity." *Journal of Industrial Ecology* 21: 603–14. doi:10.1111/jiec.12603.

Brundtland Commission. 1987. *Our Common Future: Report of the World Commission on Environment and Development.* Oxford, UK: Oxford University Press.

Chen, Minpeng, and T. E. Graedel. 2016. "A Half-Century of Global Phosphorus Flows, Stocks, Production, Consumption, Recycling, and Environmental Impacts." *Global Environmental Change* 36: 139–52.

China Association of Circular Economy (CACE). n.d. "Overview." Accessed on May 5, 2017. http://en.chinacace.org/about?tag=Overview.

Circle Economy, and Ecofys. 2016. "Implementing Circular Economy Globally Makes Paris Targets Achievable." Accessed September 27, 2017. www.ecofys.com/files/files/circle-economy-ecofys-2016-circular-economy-white-paper.pdf.

den Hollander, Marcel C., Conny A. Bakker, and Erik Jan Hultink.. 2017. "Product Design in a Circular Economy: Development of a Typology of Key Concepts and Terms." *Journal of Industrial Ecology* 21: 517–25. doi:10.1111/jiec.12610.Dynamix – Pollfree Policy Platform. 2015. "Circular Economy in France and Expectations about the EU Package." Accessed April 15, 2018. http://dynamix-project.eu/sites/default/files/event/attachment/Session2%20%20-%20chevassus.pdf.

Elkington, John. 1998 "Accounting for the Triple Bottom Line." *Measuring Business Excellence* 2 (3): 18–22. doi:10.1108/eb025539.

Ellen MacArthur Foundation. 2012. "Towards the Circular Economy Vol. 1: An Economic and Business Rationale for an Accelerated Transition." Accessed on September 7, 2016. www.ellenmacarthurfoundation.org/assets/downloads/publications/Ellen-MacArthur-Foundation-Towards-the-Circular-Economy-vol.1.pdf.;

Ellen MacArthur Foundation. 2013. "Towards the Circular Economy Vol. 2; Opportunities for the consumer goods sector." Accessed on September 3, 2016. https://www.ellenmacarthurfoundation.org/publications/towards-the-circular-economy-vol-2-opportunities-for-the-consumer-goods-sector;

Ellen MacArthur Foundation. 2014. "Towards the Circular Economy Vol. 3; Accelerating the scale-up across global supply chains." Accessed on September 14, 2016. https://www.ellenmacarthurfoundation.org/publications/towards-the-circular-economy-vol-3-accelerating-the-scale-up-across-global-supply-chains;

Ellen MacArthur Foundation. 2015a. "Growth Within: A Circular Economy for a Competitive Europe." Accessed on September 5, 2017. www.ellenmacarthur

foundation.org/publications/growth-within-a-circular-economy-vision-for-a-competitive-europe.

Ellen MacArthur Foundation. 2015b. "Toward a Circular Economy: Business Rationale for an Accelerated Transition." www.ellenmacarthurfoundation. org/assets/downloads/TCE_Ellen-MacArthur-Foundation_9-Dec-2015.pdf.

Ellen MacArthur Foundation. 2015c. "Delivering the Circular Economy: A Toolkit for Policymakers." Accessed October 19, 2017. www.ellenmac arthurfoundation.org/assets/downloads/publications/EllenMacArthurFoun dation_PolicymakerToolkit.pdf.

Ellen MacArthur Foundation. 2017. "Urban Biocycled." Accessed on September 5, 2017. www.ellenmacarthurfoundation.org/assets/downloads/publications/ Urban-Biocycles_Ellen-MacArthurFoundation_30-3-2017.pdf.

Environmental Protection Encouragement Agency (EPEA). n.d. "Cradle to Cradle: Toolbox for a Circular Economy." Accessed on January 18, 2018. www. epea.com/circular-economy/.

European Commission. 2018. "Circular Economy. Implementation of the Circular Economy Action Plan." Last updated on March 7, 2018. https://eur-lex. europa.eu/legal-content/EN/TXT/?uri=CELEX%3A52015DC0614.

Geissdoerfer, Martin, Paulo Savageta, Nancy M.P. Bocken, and Erik Jan Hultink. 2017. "The Circular Economy — A New Sustainability Paradigm?" *Journal of Cleaner Production* 143: 757–68. doi:10.1016/j.jclepro.2016.12.048.

Ghisellini, Patrizia, Catia Cialani, and Sergio Ulgiati. 2016. "A Review on Circular Economy: The Expected Transition to a Balanced Interplay of Environmental and Economic Systems." *Journal of Cleaner Production* 114: 11–32. doi:10.1016/j.jclepro.2015.09.007.

Green Alliance. 2015. "The Social Benefits of a Circular Economy: Lessons from the UK." Accessed September 21, 2017. www.green-alliance.org. uk/resources/The%20social%20benefits%20of%20a%20circular%20 economy.pdf.

Hawken, Paul, Amory Lovins, and Hunter Lovins. 1999. *Natural Capitalism: The Next Industrial Revolution.* London, UK: Earthscan Publications.

Holmgren, David. 2002. *Permaculture: Principles and Pathways Beyond Sustainability.* Hepburn, Vic: Holmgren Design Services.

Hughes, Terry P., Stephen Carpenter, Johan Rockström, Marten Scheffer, and Brian Walker. 2013. "Multiscale Regime Shifts and Planetary Boundaries." *Trends in Ecology & Evolution* 28 (7): 389–95. doi:10.1016/j. tree.2013.05.019.

ING. 2017. "Less is More: Circular Economy Solutions to Water Shortages." Accessed September 23, 2017. www.ing.nl/media/ING_EBZ_circular-solutions-to-water-shortage_tcm162-121757.pdf.

Kirchherr, Reike, Denise Julian, and Marko Hekkert. 2017. "Conceptualizing the Circular Economy: An Analysis of 114 Definitions." *Resources, Conservation & Recycling* 127: 221–32. doi:10.1016/j.resconrec.2017.09.005.

Lacy, Peter, and Jakob Rutqvist. 2015. *Waste to Wealth. The Circular Economy Advantage.* New York, NY: Palgrave Macmillan.

Lieder, Michael, and Amir Rashid. 2016. "Towards Circular Economy Implementation: A Comprehensive Review in Context of Manufacturing Industry." *Journal of Cleaner Production* 115: 36–51. doi:10.1016/j.jclepro.2015. 12.042.

Linder, Marcus, Steven Sarasini, and Patricia van Loon. 2017. "A Metric for Quantifying Product-Level Circularity." *Journal of Industrial Ecology* 21: 545–58. doi:10.1111/jiec.12552.

McDonough, William, and Michael Braungart. 2002. *Cradle to Cradle: Remaking the Way We Make Things.* New York: North Point Press.

Mendoza, Joan Manuel F., Maria Sharmina, Alejandro Gallego-Schmid, Graeme Heyes, and Adisa Azapagic. 2017. "Integrating Backcasting and Eco-Design for the Circular Economy: The BECE Framework." *Journal of Industrial Ecology* 21: 526–44. doi:10.1111/jiec.12590.

Mollison, Bill C. 1994. *Introduction to Permaculture.* Tasmania, Australia: Tagari.

Murray, Alan, Keith Skene, and Kathryn Haynes. 2017. "The Circular Economy: An Interdisciplinary Exploration of the Concept and Application in a Global Context." *Journal of Business Ethics* 140 (3): 369–80. doi:10.1007/s10551-015-2693-2.

Nugent, Sarah, Anna Packard, Erica Brabon, and Stephanie Vierra. 2016. "Living, Regenerative, and Adaptive Buildings." *Whole Building Design Guide.* Updated on: May 8, 2016. www.wbdg.org/resources/living-regenerative-and-adaptive-building.

Pauli, Gunter. 2010. *The Blue Economy: 10 Years – 100 Innovations – 100 Million Jobs.* Taos, New Mexico: Paradigm Publications.

Pauli, Gunter. 2015. *The Blue Economy, Version 2.0: 200 Projects Implemented US$ 4 Billion Invested 3 Million Jobs Created.* Academic Foundation.

Pauli, Gunter. 2017. *The Blue Economy, Version 3.0: The Marriage of Science, Innovation and Entrepreneurship Creates a New Business Model That Transforms Society.* XLIBRIS

Pawlyn, Michael. 2011. *Biomimicry in Architecture.* RIBA Publishing.

PricewaterhouseCoopers (PwC). 2015. "The Sharing Economy. Consumer Intelligence Series." Accessed on August 9, 2017. www.pwc.com/us/en/industry/entertainment-media/publications/consumer-intelligence-series/sharing-economy.html.

Prieto-Sandoval, Vanessa, Carmen Garcia, and Marta Goenaga. 2016. "Circular Economy: An Economic and Industrial Model to Achieve the Sustainability of Society." Proceedings of the 22nd Annual International Sustainable Development Research Society Conference. *Rethinking Sustainability Models and Practices: Challenges for the New and Old World Contexts*, 2(July): 504–20.

Rockström, Johan, Will Steffen, Kevin Noone, Åsa Persson, F. Stuart Chapin III, Eric Lambin, and Timothy M. Lenton. 2009. "Planetary Boundaries: Exploring the Safe Operating Space for Humanity." *Ecology and Society* 14 (2) www.jstor.org/stable/26268316.

Steffen, Will, Regina Sanderson, Peter Tyson, Jill Jäger, Pamela Matson, Berrien Moore III, and Frank Oldfield. 2004. "Global Change and the Earth System: A Planet under Pressure" *Series: Global Change - The IGBP Series.* Accessed on July 18, 2017. www.igbp.net/download/18.56b5e28e137d8 d8c09380001694/1376383141875/SpringerIGBPSynthesisSteffenetal2004_web.pdf.

The Club of Rome. 2015a. "The Circular Economy and Benefits for Society: Swedish Case Study Shows Jobs and Climate as Clear Winner." Accessed

October 19, 2017. http://wijkman.se/wp-content/uploads/2015/05/The-Circular-Economy-and-Benefits-for-Society.pdf.

The Club of Rome. 2015b. "The Circular Economy and Benefits for Society. Jobs and Climate Clear Winners in an Economy Based on Renewable Energy and Resource Efficiency. A Study Pertaining to Finland, France, the Netherlands, Spain and Sweden." Accessed September 19, 2017. www.clubofrome.org/2016/03/07/a-new-club-of-rome-study-on-the-circular-economy-and-benefits-for-society/.

The World Bank. 2012. "What a Waste. A Global Review of Solid Waste Management." *Urban Development Series Knowledge Papers*. https://siteresources.worldbank.org/INTURBANDEVELOPMENT/Resources/336387-1334852610766/What_a_Waste2012_Final.pdf.

Webster, Ken. 2013. "What Might We Say about a Circular Economy? Some Temptations to Avoid If Possible." *World Futures: The Journal of New Paradigm Research* 69 (7–8): 542–54. doi:10.1080/02604027.2013.835977.

Wen, Zongguo, and Xiaoyan Meng. 2015. "Quantitative Assessment of Industrial Symbiosis for the Promotion of Circular Economy: A Case Study of the Printed Circuit Boards Industry in China's Suzhou New District." *Journal of Cleaner Production* 90: 211–19. doi:10.1016/j.jclepro.2014.03.041.

World Economic Forum (WEF). 2014. "Towards the Circular Economy: Accelerating the Scale-up Across Global Supply Chains." Accessed October 17, 2017. www3.weforum.org/docs/WEF_ENV_TowardsCircularEconomy_Report_2014.pdf.

Wijkman, Anders, and Johan Rockström. 2012. *Bankrupting Nature. Denying Our Planetary Boundaries*. London: Routledge.

Yu, Fei, Feng Han, and Zhaojie Cui. 2015. "Evolution of Industrial Symbiosis in an Eco-Industrial Park in China." *Journal of Cleaner Production* 87: 339–47. doi:10.1016/j.jclepro.2014.10.058.

Zhang, Ling, Zengwei Yuan, Jun Bi, Bing Zhang, and Liu Beibei. 2010. "Eco-Industrial Parks: National Pilot Practices in China." *Journal of Cleaner Production* 18: 504–509. doi:10.1016/j.jclepro.2009.11.018.

Part II

Circular Economy Strategy

Setting the Stage

The CE is a very elegantly simple and straightforward concept and, at the same time, a rather complex melting pot of different principles, green approaches, innovative business models, and disruptive technologies. For this reason, Part II of this book is dedicated to unpacking the CE notion into a detailed explanation of its building blocks, then summarized (in terms of principles, business objectives, and areas of intervention) in the comprehensive "CE Framework for Circularity in Business Strategy".

As the experiences of CE pioneers show, there is no one-size-fits-all solution for CE adoption in the private sector. The complexity of the CE paradigm needs to be acknowledged before investigating its many facets and approaches. Nevertheless, an exploration of how selected technologies have enabled circular practices and a review of successfully implemented CE business models are extremely valuable as a first step in a transition journey towards circularity.

This part of the book is thus of a rather informative nature, providing the reader with a considerable amount of information and cases.

3 A CE Framework for Action

3.1 Introduction

In recent years, the CE has rapidly evolved from theory to practice, with several companies across industries embracing circular solutions. And as more and more firms begin to recognize the potential benefits of circularity, demand for a coherent and simple framework for action – one that all companies can rely upon when commencing their transition – is rising. Many SMEs in fact still perceive CE as something not applicable to them or too costly and risky to implement (Cristoni and Tonelli 2018), despite the wealth of opportunities that exist when a company has clarity over what circular actions fit its unique profile and strategies. Indeed, the CE is a vast concept that covers a conspicuous number of innovative processes and business models touching all stages of the value chain, with no one-size-fits-all solution. Dematerialization, input materials optimization and circular feedstock, environmental performance maximization, renewable energy adoption, solid waste and water management and re-use, and servitization are just some of the many leverages a firm can use to exploit the economic opportunities of the CE.

Given the degree of complexity in CE decision-making, the strategic map below was designed to help practitioners explore the most appropriate circular strategies for their organizations (Figure 3.1). The framework assembles the ideas of several important studies (Ellen MacArthur Foundation 2012; Ellen MacArthur Foundation 2013; Bakker et al. 2014; Ellen MacArthur Foundation 2014; Lovins and Braungart 2014; Ellen MacArthur Foundation 2015b; Ellen MacArthur Foundation 2015c; Ellen MacArthur Foundation 2015d; EEA, 2016; Lacy and Rutqvist 2015; U.S. Chamber of Commerce Foundation 2015; Lovins et al. 2016) and outlines in sequence from left to right: high-level guiding CE principles, the philosophical pillars of circular thinking; CE objectives that can lead to new business opportunities; and finally, areas of intervention for operationalizing the circular opportunities identified (Cristoni and Tonelli 2018). These areas will, in turn, be leveraged for the implementation of one, or more, of the circular business models presented in Chapter 5.

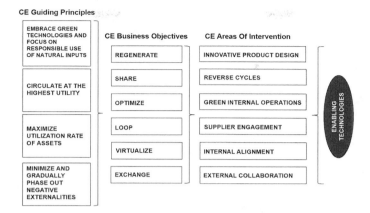

Figure 3.1 Framework for Circularity in Business Strategy.

3.2 EMS vs CE

Before delving into a detailed analysis of the CE framework, it is necessary to spend some time on Environmental Management Systems (EMSs) and their connections with CE principles. EMS is in fact an established and arguably overarching concept that already includes several CE considerations within itself. Today, it is one of the primary tools for organizations to systematically address environmental risks, make sure environmental regulations are met, and strive for a continuous improvement of overall environmental performance through the adoption of dedicated policies, procedures, environmental risk analyses, internal audits, management meetings, etc. In doing so, some would argue that environmental protection is brought by EMS to a strategic level (Winkler 2011).

Its usefulness in helping identify and achieve the new CE goals and objectives set by an organization is still debated, especially in the context of SMEs (Rizos et al. 2015). In large organizations, however, it would seem that the existence of a formalized EMS can indeed facilitate the introduction of CE-oriented practices like waste minimization, product re-design through LCA approaches, and the use of bio-based feedstock (Winkler 2011). Such an assumption has been recently confirmed by a study conducted by the European Commission to investigate whether the EU EMS approach (also called EMAS: Eco-Management and Audit Scheme) is actually fit for fostering CE practices. The findings suggest that EMAS-certified organizations can more easily transition towards a CE model for they already systematically measure, control, and manage resource consumption and environmental impacts (EC 2017).

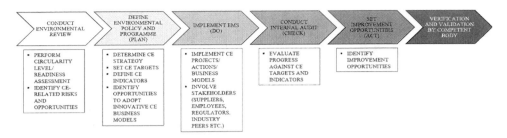

Figure 3.2 The PDCA Model.[1]

As illustrated above, the Plan-Do-Check-Act approach proposed by EMAS is suited to welcome circularity at various stages (Figure 3.2).

Besides EMAS, another internationally standardized process for EMS is the ISO 14001. With its 2015 revision, the standard has introduced several elements – like life cycle thinking, context and risk, business strategy, stakeholder engagement, and communication – that prompt organizations towards a more holistic and strategic approach to environmental management, while favouring the integration of CE principles in already existing ISO-certified EMS (IEMA 2017). On the one hand, companies are encouraged to be more meticulous, in their environmental risk assessments by considering the whole life cycle impacts of their products and services and by including the needs and expectations of their key stakeholders like consumers, policymakers, the local community, and NGOs. On the other hand, environmental management must now be more flexible to deal with an ever-changing environment where issues like resource scarcity and climate change need to be fully integrated into the strategic environmental plans of the organization. An EMS needs to align with the core organizational processes and strategic decision-making of the organization, ultimately fitting with the drivers that guide the company's business strategy (IEMA 2017). In such a new context of enhanced focus on strategic thinking, external collaboration, and top-management involvement, the adoption of CE considerations within an existing EMS is clearly favoured.

Notwithstanding these recent attempts to integrate CE considerations within the existing ISO 14001 EMS, in September 2017, the International Organization for Standardization (ISO) began developing ISO 14009, a dedicated standard for organizations to adopt CE considerations at a product level in a systemic way to redesign products and components with the aim of improving material circulation.[2] These new developments clearly show that the evolution of EMSs is being progressively influenced by the worldwide success of the CE. Conversely, EMAS and ISO 14001 today can count on a global coverage reaching most industries, and as such can play a vital role in fostering the transition towards a worldwide CE model.

3.3 CE Guiding Principles

The CE is at its core, a model where products, components, energy, and materials continually flow re-entering the production cycle thereby minimizing the impact of the firm's operations on the environment. This simple explanation can be further broken down into four, more practical, principles:

- **Embrace green technologies and focus on a responsible use of natural inputs.** This principle concentrates on the company's inputs: the energy it uses to feed its machineries, offices, etc., and the raw materials sourced to manufacture goods and provide services. When entering a CE, businesses are encouraged to switch to renewable energy sources (solar, wind, composting, anaerobic digestion, etc.) and reduce to a minimum the need for virgin raw materials.
- **Maximize utilization rate of assets.** The focus here is on product's usage: once in the market, assets need to be exploited fully by maximizing their utilization rates. This requirement can be achieved through innovative solutions linked to asset sharing and servitization.
- **Circulate goods, product components, and materials at the highest utility.** The emphasis is on the company's capabilities to set up circular flows of materials and products. Today, recycling is the primary way for materials to re-enter production loops. However, re-use, repair, re-manufacturing, and refurbishing are more effective methods for keeping the value of products at its highest during every stage of the life cycle.
- **Minimize and gradually phase out negative externalities.** The last principle builds on the efforts of thoroughly applying the previous three to gradually achieve zero negative environmental externalities (e.g. water and air pollution, soil degradation, release of chemicals and toxins, etc.).

These four principles are a response to the environmental and socio-economic limits of the linear production system introduced in the first chapter and represent the philosophical pillars of a more resource-efficient, environmentally neutral, and economically sound alternative for growth.

3.4 CE Business Objectives

How shall a company interpret the broad CE principles and translate them into practical action? The six business objectives identified by the Ellen MacArthur Foundation (2015c) answer the question.[3] While they can be prioritized and tackled individually, they have been thought so that each one corroborates and perfects the performance of the others, creating a sort of natural snowballing effect.[4]

Regenerate includes all efforts to minimize the environmental impacts of operations while – when possible – helping restore natural ecosystems. This objective can be achieved by: switching to renewable energy; sourcing bio-based materials (composed, wholly or substantially by biological products or renewable agricultural materials); and phasing out toxic production inputs. Examples in practice include:

- Interface. A collaboration between Interface Inc. and the Zoological Society of London, called Net-Works™, was forged to tackle the growing problem of discarded fishing nets in some of the world's poorest coastal communities. By establishing a community-based supply chain for discarded nets, Net-Works aimed to improve the livelihood of local fishermen while providing Interface with an innovative source of recycled materials for its carpet tiles.
- Commonland Foundation. This Amsterdam-based organization works to develop sound business cases around specific environmental restoration projects. Through its holistic approach for large-scale landscape restoration, the foundation helps the setting up of multidisciplinary teams of investors, companies, and entrepreneurs to forge long-term partnerships benefitting land users, farmers, local communities, and the businesses willing to invest in the project. The foundation currently manages projects in Spain, South Africa, Australia, and The Netherlands.
- Heathrow Airport. With its new "Heathrow 2.0" strategy, the London airport aims to become a role model in terms of sustainable development and environmental stewardship. Its strategy for "a world worth travelling" includes bold environmental objectives like powering the airport operations with 100% renewable energy and operate carbon-neutral fixed assets by 2050.

Share focuses on maximizing a product usage through sharing platforms and servitization business models. Repair and re-use are crucial activities, as well finding new markets for unsold inventory stocks. Examples in practice include:

- ASOS is one of the fastest growing retailers in the UK. Through its online marketplace, the company has placed the re-use of clothing at the heart of its corporate strategy.
- Patagonia. In 2013, the U.S. outdoor clothing firm joined forces with multinational e-commerce giant eBay to set up a dedicated website promoting pre-owned Patagonia items.

Optimize. The fine-tuning of an organization environmental performance can occur on multiple levels: supply chain – where a great deal of waste and economic losses are generated – company operations, and product. Today's advancements in technology (e.g. IoT, sensor and digital solutions, and big data) can be harnessed to foster efficiency at proprietary or supplier facilities. As for product performance, this can be at times utterly re-invented via sounder design practices (e.g. green, modular, and for disassembly). Examples in practice include:

- Levi Strauss & Co. In 2014, the clothing manufacturer pioneered a programme for financially rewarding suppliers that would score best on a range of sustainability metrics, including those related to environmental performance. The programme was established by partnering with the International Finance Corporation (IFC)[5] – a branch of the World Bank Group.
- H&M. The fast-fashion company monitors suppliers' sustainability performance through a dedicated assessment programme called SIPP (Sustainable Impact Partnership Programme). Through this assessment, the brand makes sure suppliers abide to the company's core sustainability requirements, and further support them to continually improve performance.

Loop means keeping products, components, and materials within the production system for as long as possible. Looping can occur at various stages of a life product, each one with a different degree of efficacy in preserving the remaining value of what is re-entered into the production system: practices of re-use are more efficient than refurbishing/re-manufacturing, but the preservation of value in these two activities is higher than in recycling. Looping can therefore be operationalized by a firm in many ways: by establishing take-back schemes for discarded products and further implementing re-manufacturing, refurbishing, or recycling processes; by harnessing anaerobic digestion processes; and by finding circular solutions for the company's water demand. Examples in practice include:

- Disney World. At Orlando's Disney Park, food waste is collected across the hotels, bars, and restaurants of the complex and then sent to an anaerobic digestion plant nearby, operated by Harvest Power, an organics management company. Here, most of the food scraps are converted into biogas, which is then combusted to generate electricity. What does not become biogas is turned into valuable fertilizer and then sold in local markets. The plant can process up to 12,000 tons of organic waste annually producing 5.4 megawatts of combined heat and power.[6]
- The Dutch start-up Green Recycled Organics Holland (GRO-Holland) uses coffee residue as a growth substrate for oyster mushrooms. The company teamed up with local food chains (e.g. Deli XL and La Place) to create a closed-loop system whereby coffee waste is collected by

GRO-Holland to grow oyster mushrooms which are then sold back to the restaurants. According to company management, GRO-Holland can grow 2,000 kilos of oyster mushrooms per week.[7]

Virtualize. The virtualization of products and services, enabled by technological innovation and higher customers' acceptance, has already transformed many industries and markets, e.g. books, music, travel booking, and education (e.g. Coursera, WebEx, etc.). Pioneers of the virtualization of things can concurrently reduce their environmental footprint while enjoying multiple first-mover advantages. Examples in practice include:

- In early 2016, The Independent became the first fully digital UK newspaper. In the months that followed this strategic move, the newspaper enjoyed a substantial growth (up to 46% year-on-year).[8]

Exchange. Today, the pace of technological innovation is extremely high and diversified. A focus on circularity implies a firm attention towards green technologies and exchange means staying at the edge of the technological revolution by replacing outdated materials, machines, and devices with superior, environmentally friendly solutions. Examples in practice include:

- Favini is an Italian-based firm operating in the market of fine paper solutions. Among its products stands "Shiro", a paper made using renewable non-tree biomass and recycled waste.
- At the Oak Ridge National Laboratory (U.S.A.), research works have succeeded in leveraging 3D printing technology[9] to manufacture a fully "printed" Shelby Cobra. The vehicle was showcased at the 2015 North American International Auto Show in Detroit.
- Material scientists at ETH Zurich have created force-resistant polymers – used in the production of bulletproof jackets and tow lines – sourcing natural inputs like peanut oil and extra-virgin olive oil. Normally, these polymers are instead prepared using inflammable and toxic solvents.[10]

3.5 CE Areas of Intervention

Having established the four CE guiding principles and the six business objectives, we now look at the six key areas of intervention, i.e. where a company needs to intervene in order to make the transition possible. As there is no one-size-fits-all mode of intervention, each of these different areas is likely to be addressed differently depending on the context. Also, it is inevitable that some areas will be out of scope for some businesses, while others will be overlapping during the implementation phase.

3.5.1 Innovative Product Design

Innovative, groundbreaking design principles stand at the roots of the CE system. With the realization that the intrinsic value of today's products is not being properly exploited and that customers demand greener solutions that lower the pressure on the natural environment, innovative approaches to product design are rapidly emerging as valid alternatives to old-fashioned ideas. There are at least three broad approaches to circular design that a firm can pursue: green design, design for durability, and design for reverse cycles.

A **Green design** is an umbrella term comprising different approaches to product design that seek a reduction in environmental and health impacts associated with product manufacturing. Because of its broad definition, green design can occur at various levels and lead to the following:

- Reduce or replace highly toxic substances. Phasing out toxic substances is the key to a CE as they cause harm to both the natural environment and the human health. The toxicity of inputs can be determined by reviewing international guidelines like the EU REACH Regulation,[11] EU RoHS Directive,[12] SIN List from the International Chemical Secretariat,[13] and the Cradle to Cradle Banned List of Chemicals.[14] Today, a considerable number of bio-based substitutes and Internet-dedicated portals exist, thereby making it easier for companies to address toxicity of their products. Companies in the fashion industry, for example, can log on "Fashion Positive"[15] and access the digital portfolio of C2C certified yarns, fabrics, dyes, thread, and other items. C2C certification assures superior product environmental performance and material health. In Italy, a similar database – Sustainability Lab[16] – lists brands producing eco-materials and products for the fashion and textile industry. Another way for companies to address material toxicity is by forging partnerships with research centres and technology innovation hubs. Outdoor clothing and sustainability-champion brand Patagonia, for instance, started in February 2017 a new research programme with Swiss chemical manufacturer HeiQ to develop water-repellent textiles that are perfluorinated chemicals (PFCs)-free. PFCs are in fact known to have toxic effects on both the environment and the human health.
  Flooring and carpet tiles is another dynamic sector for green design innovation, with major players like Tarkett, Desso, and Interface racing each other to develop the best toxic-free product. Tarkett has been a pioneer in devising sustainable substitutes to phthalate plasticizers in its vinyl flooring. The company already utilizes phthalate-free plasticizers at all its sites in the U.S. and

European vinyl production sites, and plans to get all its plants across the world do the same by 2020.[17] Interface, on the other side, wiped out perfluorinated chemicals (PFC) from its face fibres in 2014.[18] Finally, Desso (that was acquired by Tarkett in October 2014) devised a new non-toxic carpet backing called "Desso EcoBase". Among the ingredients used for its production is chalk, a by-product of water purification processes. Desso is presently partnering with an association of Dutch water companies to source this valuable component.[19]

- Replace technical inputs with environmentally neutral biological alternatives that can be safely returned to the biosphere. An example of this is replacing plastic packaging with biodegradable substitutes, like those developed by Biopac, a UK manufacturer and supplier of eco-friendly compostable food packaging and catering disposables. In March 2018, McDonald's announced it will be trialling the use of biodegradable paper straws in some of its Britain restaurants as part of the company's sustainability strategy.[20]
- Reduce or replace natural inputs and/or scarce Earth resources, possibly by applying lightweighting or dematerialization[21] design principles. Both approaches aim at using as little resources as possible in the production of an item, thereby reducing its material intensity. To achieve this, designers look at ways to produce smaller and lighter products or replace goods with non-material substitutes (e.g. MP3 technology superseding CDs). Evidently, these design strategies work best when materials play a key role in the overall environmental impact of a product or when there is major transportation involved (e.g. heavier vehicles produce more emissions).

B   **Design for durability** is particularly important for the increasing number of businesses switching from selling products to offering services (i.e. servitization), as they need to devise goods that can last the longest possible and remain attractive to customers over time. On the contrary, short planned durability remains a serious environmental threat which represents the basis for industry or firm-specific strategies (e.g. light bulbs or fast fashion). According to Autodesk® Sustainability Workshop,[22] a digital education platform for professionals wishing to apply sustainability principles to engineering and design, the chief principles of design for durability are:

- Understanding the appropriate product lifetime, also by considering how repair and recycling fit within the overall product life cycle(s).
- Devise parts, components, and connections that are robust, wear-resistant, and durable by deploying high-quality materials and by reinforcing those parts that are most weak.

- Promote maintenance by striving to create products that can be easily maintained and preserved by providing clear instructions, tools, and spare parts and by offering low-cost repairing services.
- Stay ahead of the fashion curve by choosing classic/timeless designs and by enabling customers to make use of the products in different settings and occasions.

Modular design is an innovative strategy for product durability. Through modularity, designers can build a product using a block grid pattern, where each element of the design fits into the modules in defined patterns. A single fixed structure holds together the different, upgradable product components. In doing so, broken or out-of-fashion parts can easily be removed and substituted with newer versions. Modular design is being progressively leveraged in a variety of settings. Fairphone 2, possibly the most notorious modular good, entered the cell phone industry in December 2015 firmly distinguishing itself from any other smartphone on the market. Spare parts and newer components including the core, the camera, and the battery are available on the company website. The screen can be easily changed by the customer himself in less than a minute, and the remaining modules can be replaced using a screwdriver. A free repair guide is also available to support with such simple tasks. Other brands (e.g. Samsung) are now making a move towards modularity, which is rapidly becoming appealing to other sectors as well, from headphones (sold by German Street) to entire buildings. Dutch sustainability consultancy Turntoo partnered with construction company BAM to erect the town hall in Brummen: a unique circular, temporary, and reconstructable building. Globally, modular housing is a trend on the rise, with California-based Blue Homes offering 100% modular prefab home solutions and Meka Modulars developing and selling modular living and work spaces since 2009. But modular living environments are not limited to physical structures and can also extend to animals and plants: Modularfarms.co, for example, is a Canadian website promoting an innovative farm system with exchangeable modules that is scalable, interconnected, and can host growing operations of any size.

C   **Design for reverse cycles**. According to linear thinking, products are devised – at times purposively – to last for a very limited time. Additionally, no emphasis at all is placed on how the intrinsic value of an outdated or discarded good can be harnessed and kept within the economic system. In this way, the value creation process is abruptly interrupted with the destruction of the item through incineration or its disposal in landfills (Figure 3.3).

On the other hand, a circular mentality allows us to see the advantages of making product recovery solutions accessible and more efficient. This means, for example, designing product components

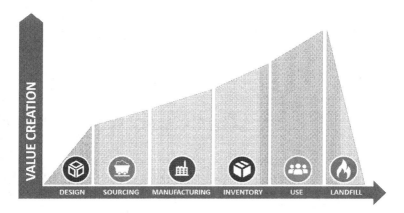

Figure 3.3 Creation and Destruction of Value through Linearity.

that can be dismantled and re-assembled more easily, which, in turn, has to do with minimizing the number of connections and using simple tools (Peiró et al. 2017), decreasing the overall number of a product's parts, simplifying its structure, and finally using materials that are more suitable for sorting and disassembly – such as ferromagnetic materials.[23] The "One Million Water Bottles Saved a Day" programme set up by HP and its partners, for example, was made possible by applying disassembly principles to product design. Ink cartridges returned to HP facilities now get disassembled and separated into different materials. The plastics are then processed and mixed with plastics from other sources to create the inputs for new cartridges. Another way to embrace design for reverse cycles is to develop products whose materials can be recycled more easily. Once again, Autodesk Sustainability Workshop provides key insights into the core pillars of design for recycling: reducing at a minimum the number of materials used, trying not to combine materials that cannot be separated easily, simplifying the removal of toxic and dangerous components, and choosing materials that are universally recyclable.

Applying these concepts might be rather challenging for large companies that have been operating in a linear fashion for decades and would rapidly need to acquire a wide range of new skills pertaining, for example, to a redefinition of customers' expectations and their perception of value, re-manufacturing processes, comprehensively assessing product wear by use, or analysing products' material and chemical properties (De los Rios and Charnley 2016). Thus, for some players, it is often recommended to seek the support of external consultants and experts in CE design rather than solely relying on in-house expertise. Through its "Design With Intent" programme, Waste Management (WM) in the U.S. offers dedicated services to help customers make sounder decisions when designing products. This is achieved by ensuring a positive second use cycle.[24] Similarly, Turntoo in The Netherlands supports businesses in devising pioneering circular design solutions as it was done for the conceptualization of the world's first Turnaround Terminal.[25]

3.5.2 Reverse Cycles

We have just learnt about the term as part of a conversation on innovative design but conceiving a product for reverse cycles is not the same as actually establishing and managing one or multiple flows of materials, components, and/or products from the moment they get damaged, broken, or discarded to their re-valorization and further re-introduction into the economic system through repair, re-use, refurbishing, re-manufacturing, or recycling. Thus, a company focusing on reverse cycles will be implementing actions aimed at collecting its used products and then establish effective post-value channels whereby items get processed according to the new function they will serve. The key circular activities linked to this specific area of intervention are presented below.

A **Repairing** is the practice of getting damaged or broken product's components back to a useful state. Instead of seeing repair programmes as a threat to bottom line profits, circular-oriented companies like Patagonia allow customers to get damaged goods repaired within 30 business days. The company has also teamed up with iFixit to provide an easy-to-follow online guide for self-repairing Patagonia items. CE firms focusing on repair activities are able to continue being profitable by exploiting their marketing and branding knowledge to increase market share and generate customer loyalty in the face of premium pricing (Bocken and Short 2015).

B **Re-using** is about giving a second life to a product, which invariably means finding a second market for it or using it for a different purpose (e.g. input to produce another item). Leveraging innovative trading platforms is a simple way for businesses to start tackling their excess inventory stocks and unused items. In the U.S., General Motors backed the creation of the "Reuse Opportunity Collaboratory Detroit (ROC Detroit)" programme in which one organization's unused materials and products are advertised on a dedicated database and traded according to the needs of other members. The programme helps Detroit businesses unlock the potential behind re-using: costs are reduced as cheaper feedstocks are available, disposal fees decreases, the overall impact of procurement on climate change lessens, and local development is fostered, as well as the reputation of member organizations. Similarly, tech start-up Globe-chain manages a digital marketplace for re-used unwanted items of every kind and targets businesses, individuals, charities, and schools. The platform has reached 10,000+ members and succeeded in giving a second life to more than one million tonnes of materials.[26]

C **Refurbishing**, as defined by the Ellen MacArthur Foundation, consists in "returning a product to good working condition by replacing or repairing major components that are faulty or close to failure and making cosmetic changes to update the appearance of a product, such as changing fabric or painting" (2015a, pp. 16). Because of the steps and costs involved, refurbishment is generally an activity best suited for complex goods and machinery. In the Netherlands, Philips runs a refurbishment facility where a variety of pre-owned healthcare systems – magnetic resonance imaging, interventional X-ray technologies, surgery, and computed tomography equipment – undergo a series of repair processes, renewed components, and latest software updates, before being resold with full warranty.[27] In the U.S., the same company conducts even further refurbishing operations.

D **Re-manufacturing** differs from refurbishing for it focuses on the disassembly of discarded assets and the re-valorization of their functioning parts. Reusable components are removed from the used product and assembled into a new one. Changes or improvements can also take place during this phase, and the full process is usually performed according to specific quality assurance criteria. Re-manufacturing activities are usually carried out in dedicated re-processing centres only after products have been inspected, triaged, tested, and graded (Diallo et al. 2016). Caterpillar's re-manufacturing programme, Reman, for example, is highly specialized in processing parts and components of engines, drivetrains, hydraulics, and undercarriages, assuring customers that its re-manufactured substitutes deliver the same performance of new products at a fraction of the costs.

E **Recycling** is the process of breaking down discarded products into their base materials and convert them into new products. Historically, recycling has been mainly associated with consumer and household materials like paper, glass, and plastic. More recently, the development of newer and more efficient technologies and the enhanced focus on re-capturing the residual value of products have contributed to expand recycling activities into previously unexplored settings, like chemicals and clinical waste. Veolia, for example, has developed a method to recover and recycle a spent chemical – KOH – which is a by-product of refinery processes and as a result normally disposed of as a hazardous waste.[28] As for the recycling of clinical waste, in 2016, Cardiff-based company Thermal Compaction Group (TCG) devised an innovative system – Sterimelt – allowing hospitals to recycle clinical sterilization wraps by turning surgical waste into briquettes that can then be used to manufacture new products.[29]

When leveraging reverse cycles as a preferred area of intervention, it is paramount to establish an effective customer engagement programme for the take-back of used products, particularly with respect to those products that consumers are not accustomed to recycling when they brake or become old-fashioned. There is a variety of strategies that companies can employ to trigger collaboration from their customers:

- **Educational activities.** For example, Coca-Cola Enterprise runs plastic re-processing facilities in the UK and France that act as education centres for visitors. Here, guests learn about the challenges of the CE and are encouraged to sort their waste properly. In North America, the "How2Recycle" programme spreads recyclability information to consumers via labels attached to all sorts of products, from beverages to toys. The labels also explain how to recycle the different packaging components. How2Recycle is presently backed by 60+ consumer brands among which stand Unilever, PepsiCo, Henkel, and Nestlé Waters North America.
- **Inspiring marketing campaigns**. As part of its global take-back and product recovery programme, fast-fashion Swedish giant H&M released in February 2017 a powerful video encouraging customers to return old clothes and textiles, of any brand and in any condition, to any H&M store across the globe so that they will be given a second life.[30]
- **Incentives to customers** in the form of money, discounts, or free products. In 2015, Ocado, the world's largest online-only grocery retailer, set up a "Bag Recycle Bonus Scheme" for customers to be rewarded with cash for any carrier bag they recycled.[31] In the U.S., some retailers are equipped with ecoATM kiosks that, when fed with a used device like a cell phone, MP3 player, or tablet, automatically recompense the user with cash equivalent to the item's current market value.

3.5.3 Green Internal Operations

When the environmental impact of a company is largely dependent on the performance of its own sites and internal operations, principles of circularity can be leveraged to gradually reduce environmental externalities like:

A   **Greenhouse gas emissions** often directly or indirectly (i.e. electricity) caused by the burning of fossil fuels. Google, for example, in 2016 announced that it would have acquired enough renewable energy to match 100% of its operations by the end of the following year.[32] Looking ahead, Google is now raising the bar of its sustainability commitment as it intends to power its operations on a region-specific, 24×7 basis with clean zero-carbon energy.[33]

B   **Water use and pollution.** Several alternatives allowing the re-use of both stormwater and greywater exist today: industrial re-use of reclaimed water derived from treated municipal effluent; individual on-site re-use systems and greywater re-use; LEED-driven on-site storage and use of rainwater and greywater through water harvesting;[34] and stormwater harvesting and use.

3.5.4 Supplier Engagement

The supply chain, accounting for approximately 80% of global trade and 60% of global production,[35] is where most opportunities exist to leverage circular solutions and re-invent processes. This is particularly true for sectors where environmental impacts occur mostly indirectly – i.e. caused by outsourced operations (Johannsdottir 2014). In industries like food and beverage, media, telecommunications, and retail, only a tiny fraction – less than 10% – of the overall environmental footprint depends on the internal operations of the final brand (Makower 2014).

Some forward-looking multinationals are already taking steps to support their suppliers in addressing environmental issues and introduce CE practices. Ford, for example, created the "Partnership for A Cleaner Environment" programme (PACE) to help business partners address energy, water, air pollution, and waste challenges, by providing a toolkit of practical solutions and best practices already internally tested at Ford's plants.[36] In the UK, following its commitment to eradicate food waste surplus in the country, grocery and merchandise multinational retailer Tesco announced in March 2017 the launch of "Food Waste Hotline", an online portal that business partners can use to report surplus stocks of food to Tesco Product teams and work with them to take appropriate actions.

It is important to note that acting at the supply chain level can also imply a broader re-structuring of both internal operations and relationships with business partners, most notably if reverse cycles for product recovery are established. To effectively invert flows of materials and/or goods, companies might be required to expand the boundaries and scope of their sourcing activities, going well beyond business-as-usual. This could mean:

A   **Growing the company's current role in the supply chain** by starting new activities, like the refurbish facilities set up by Philips in the U.S. and The Netherlands. But firms can also expand more aggressively further downstream – i.e. circular vertical integration. Italian companies Fantoni and Ri-Legno, for instance, are specialized in designing and building furniture from recycled wood they directly collect as waste or by-products of other carpentry-related activities. Fantoni alone recovers 200,000+ tons of discarded wood and 300,000+ tons of by-products such as sawdust, bark, chips, shavings, slabs, and edgings from other manufacturers across the territory.[37]

B   **Forging new partnerships with suppliers** to explore circular solutions jointly. Via its "Circular Community" project, global brewer Carlsberg has teamed up with supply chain partners to investigate ways to eliminate waste from its production processes. Through a strengthened collaboration between Carlsberg's designers and key suppliers, the firm began testing its 100% biodegradable and bio-based beer bottle (called Green Fibre Bottle) in late 2018.[38] Similarly, Walmart U.S. has engaged with several suppliers operating in different sectors to drive life-extension programmes. One example of this is its partnership with Pioneer Products, whose role is to collect icing buckets used in Walmart store delis and other difficult-to-recycle mixed plastics; these are then processed and the resulting resin is used to manufacture 45-gallon trash cans that are sold on Walmart shelves. Another example of CE collaboration initiated by Walmart is that with manufacturer Technimark, which turns old clothes' hangers collected from Walmart U.S. locations into retail hangers sold on its shelves.[39]

But partnering with suppliers to create new ventures can also lead to re-invent traditional business relationships altogether, moving away from rigid transaction-based exchanges between buyer and supplier. Jaguar's Realcar project is a case in point. The British brand started in 2007 a far-sighted project to achieve manufacturing the main body of its XE Model with up to 75% recycled aluminium. To do so, the company established a new relationship with Novelis, a global leader in aluminium recycling, in which traditional boundaries between buyer and supplier became blurred: while Novelis provided Jaguar with body panels from recycled aluminium, these were produced in part with the post-production aluminium scrap Novelis acquired directly from Jaguar. In doing so, Jaguar's waste aluminium has been diverted from the wider aluminium recycling system to become the core element of Realcar closed-loop supply chain.[40] This case confirms two main phenomena occurring with the establishment of a CE supply chain: a shift towards a material-centric perspective that aims to keep products and components in the production system for as long as possible, and the commencement of a network-centric model, where multiple players co-operate for the re-valorization of assets (Jonker and Faber 2017).

Because of the benefits linked to proximity (e.g. greater and faster supply of wasted materials and products, lower transport costs, etc.), it would seem that the greatest potential for developing CE supply chains is to be found at a regional and local level (WEF 2014).

As the adoption of circular principles is likely to have a profound impact across all of a company's operations, the whole network of existing suppliers should be analysed carefully through the lens of the intended circular strategy. For example, the abilities to use recycled materials or minimizing resource inputs – as well as negative outputs – could be a way to screen and rate suppliers. Arguably, big brands, with vast and complex supply chains, would benefit greatly from having an ongoing and automated screening process by incorporating CE elements into central platforms and databases. One of the most sophisticated tools of this kind is SEDEX Advance, the largest collaborative platform in the world to store, share, and report on suppliers' sustainability performance and metrics. SEDEX Advance is used by a network of more than 40,000 vendors and buyers around the world, with supplier data covering health and safety, labour, environment, and business ethics. Information more focused on CE would evidently fit well into similar frameworks. In those instances where the awareness of CE turns out to be poor across the majority of suppliers, a company could decide to bridge this gap by launching training programmes or setting up platforms where suppliers can interact and share best practices.

3.5.5 Internal Alignment

In addition to working closely with suppliers, any company embracing CE principles would need to manage the widespread implications this will carry across functions such as R&D, product design, procurement, accounting, marketing, sales, and operations. A change in culture touching all levels of the organization is to be centred around some key aspects:

A   **Buy-in from executives and senior stakeholders**. When a CE project is initiated by the sustainability or CSR department of an organization, early approval from top management is vital, not least to secure the necessary funding as well as internal support for the entire duration of the project.

B   **Getting managers and employees on board** by motivating them to embrace change. Communication about both structural adjustments in the company and the many benefits (financial and environmental, long and short terms, etc.) deriving from the new circular strategy will have to be frequent and complete. Between 2014 and 2015, Unilever launched several training programmes[41] to help selected management teams familiarize with CE principles and to inform them of the existing projects within the company that already embraced circular thinking.

C   **Strong cross-departmental alignment** over the new strategic principles is also key, especially among design, marketing, sales, and operations. Those are in fact the departments where most disruption is generally anticipated, as: products will be designed to last longer and be shared between users; sales people will need to be instructed on how to manage the transition towards servitization; and marketing will be asked to find ways to effectively communicate all of those changes to the public. Perhaps most importantly, teams specialized in CE operations like disassembly, refurbishment, and re-manufacturing will need to coordinate with designers so that products can be devised for easy dismantling and further processing of reusable components.

3.5.6 *External Collaboration*

As most organizations are still at the beginning of their circular journeys, collaboration with external stakeholders can bring multiple benefits, especially in industries where CE implementation is particularly difficult (e.g. due to complex and dispersed supply chains or heavy reliance on virgin materials). Moreover, transitioning towards a new circular business model is likely to impact the organization well beyond its traditional boundaries and current operations. Hence, for many firms, implementing a circular strategy will inevitably mean collaborating with a complex web of old and new stakeholders – as opposed to managing standard transactions in a linear fashion. There is a variety of categories of partners that CE-oriented organizations can approach:

A   **Industry partner associations** can act as enablers for sharing best practice and mutual support. For example, Tarmac Aerosafe[42] is a joint venture created to apply circular principles in the aviation industry. The organization dismantles aircrafts and processes the remaining components for re-use. In 2014, five years after it was created, the company had already dealt with more than 200 aircrafts.

B   **NGOs and other not-for-profit organizations** might also support businesses in applying circular principles to their operations. As part of Interface's Net-Works project is a network of NGOs, based in the Philippines and Cameroon, that encourage local fishermen to collect old fish nets from the bottom of the oceans. The nets are then shipped to Interface sites in the U.S. where they become a recycled source of nylon for carpet tile production.

C   **Policymakers** at all levels (international, national, regional, and local) can act as catalysts for change by supporting businesses towards circularity. The Singapore Packaging Agreement (SPA), for example, is a joint initiative by government, industry, and NGOs to reduce packaging waste. The programme provides flexibility for companies in various sectors (e.g. food and beverage, personal care, and electronics) to adopt cost-effective and resource-efficient solutions, like lightweight product packaging or machineries that produce less wastage during production.[43] As far as cities are concerned, in January 2017, the city of London launched a dedicated programme – Advance London – that focuses on helping circular businesses expand and improve their competitiveness.

D   **Research centres and universities** are valuable partners to engage when a business needs to devise technical solutions for the implementation of circular operations. In April 2017, H&M partnered up with the leading research institute on sustainability science in Sweden, the Stockholm Resilience Centre, to roll out a three-year programme aimed at setting up a new circular industrial model for textile processing and clothing manufacturing.

E   **Specialized Niche Organizations** operating in material recycling, waste management, or resource efficiency can be valuable for those businesses that still lack the full set of capabilities required to take full advantage of a CE strategy and/or satisfactorily address a negative environmental externality. International Synergies runs a free business network to help with knowledge and ideas on how to address resource efficiency challenges.[44] Parley is another example of niche organization that facilitated global brands joining together, in its Ocean Plastic Programme, to tackle marine plastic pollution. Thanks to this collaboration, in May 2017, Adidas was able to release three new editions of its UltraBoost shoe made of plastic debris collected from ocean depths.

In order to foster innovation through the adoption of groundbreaking CE concepts, some firms have moved beyond traditional collaborative practices by seeking out new business partners in innovative ways. Setting up global challenges and award competitions is an example. In 2015, H&M Conscious Foundation (the philanthropic arm of the Stockholm-based clothing retailer) launched its first Global Change Award to advance green, groundbreaking ideas aimed at closing loops in the fashion industry. But innovation can also come from establishing experimental labs for product innovation, like "Le Square". Located in central Paris, Renault's Open Innovation Lab was created to boost the sharing of ideas between the firm's researchers and a mix of external stakeholders including start-ups, local authorities, the local community, universities, and investors.

Ideally, the six areas of intervention (innovative product design, reverse cycles, green internal operations, supplier engagement, internal alignment, and external collaboration) would be addressed collectively to carefully identify all relevant aspects and opportunities for the proper implementation of a CE strategy. Today, Jaguar's Realcar is one of the most successful examples of a company thoroughly working on

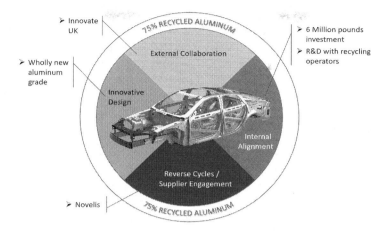

Figure 3.4 Jaguar's Realcar Strategy.

the six domains (Figure 3.4). Indeed, at least five out of six areas were leveraged by Jaguar throughout its CE project.[45] At the roots of the whole idea stood an intense phase of R&D, necessary to identify the correct aluminium grade to be used for the manufacturing of the new XE Model (1. Innovative Product Design). During that process, the company benefited from the technical advice of Innovate UK, a specialized agency providing support and funds to pioneering businesses in search of innovative solutions (2. External Collaboration). As far as the aluminium goes, recycled scrap was re-introduced in the value chain thanks to a partnership with supplier Novelis, a world leader in aluminium recycling and processing (3. Reverse Cycles). The relationship developed with Novelis exceeded standard supplier-dealing activities as the two companies cooperated in a closed-loop economic system, where both were supplier and buyer (4. Supplier Engagement). Finally, the whole project was possible thanks to Jaguar's internal alignment at least at two distinct levels of management. Firstly, the board gave its green light to invest in a multimillion new press line and a scrap system to support it. At the operational level, the R&D department worked closely with recycling operators to identify material solutions that would allow reverse cycles to run smoothly and efficiently (5. Internal Alignment).

3.6 Conclusions

The CE is a comprehensive concept that includes a wide range of very different activities (e.g. designing toxic-free products, implementing take-back schemes, re-using production by-products, transitioning towards the servitization of products, etc.), whose shared underlying reason to be conceived is for companies to progressively abandon the production system they have always relied upon, in favour of a new closed-loop model. Most of the times, a company will require new resources and capabilities at all levels of the organization to make a transition and it will be difficult to decide what to focus on. For this reason, the "Framework for Circularity in Business Strategy" presented in this chapter represents a high-level comprehensive guide for businesses to navigate through CE-related concepts. The framework draws on the work of others (primarily the reports released by the Ellen MacArthur Foundation since 2012) to combine CE guiding principles, business objectives, and areas for intervention. As highlighted with Jaguar's Realcar example, when a company strategically acts upon multiple areas of intervention simultaneously, and couples it with the adoption of effective technologies for closing the loop, the transition towards a novel CE-oriented business model can take place smoothly. Building on this insight, the following chapters will further investigate the role of CE-enabling technologies (Chapter 4) and the typology of CE business models (Chapter 5), with the aim of offering a detailed account of all the elements that need to be mastered prior to approaching the CE from a strategic perspective.

Notes

1 Source: adapted from European Commission (EC). 2017. "Moving Towards a Circular Economy with Emas. Best Practices to Implement Circular Economy Strategies (With Case Study Examples)". Luxembourg: Publications Office of the European Union.

2 This standard, expected to be officially released in late 2020, will provide guidelines "for reducing the use of materials, strengthening the recovery of materials, improving the assembly / disassembly of product and components in order to enhance material recovery and to reuse components". https://committee.iso.org/sites/tc207sc1/home/projects/ongoing/iso-14009.html.

3 The Ellen MacArthur Foundation lists the six business objectives as "activities". However, in this book, we are presenting a CE strategic framework followed by a step-by-step process to CE definition and realization. Under this perspective, it is this last stage that will define the activities to be implemented.

4 The six business objectives are explored in the following WorlDynamics' video: www.youtube.com/watch?v=50gCByhYXD0&feature=youtu.be.

5 Starting in 2010, the IFC run a programme, called Global Trade Supplier Finance (GTSF), providing short-term finance to emerging market suppliers and small- and medium-sized exporters, helping them address supply chain finance shortfalls.

6 Green Builder Staff. 2017. "Walt Disney World Using Biogas Technology for Food Waste". Posted on March 27, 2016. www.greenbuildermedia.com/energy-solutions/walt-disney-world-food-waste-biogas-technology.

7 Food Valley Society. 2016. "From Coffee Grounds to Vegetarian Oyster Mushroom Snack". Posted on April 1, 2016. www.foodvalleysociety.com/from-coffee-grounds-to-vegetarian-oyster-mushroom-snack/.

8 Freddy Mayhew. 2016. "Independent Readership Up 46 per cent While Mobile Offers Biggest Audience for Some". *PressGazette*. Posted on August 24, 2016. www.pressgazette.co.uk/independent-readership-up-46-per-cent-while-mobile-offers-biggest-audience-for-some/.

9 3D printing allows for the integration of advanced technologies with design principles centred around flexibility and modularity. In the next chapter, Section 4.3 discusses 3D printing among other key technologies for design and engineering.

10 The Economist. 2015. "No Tangled Web". Posted on December 19, 2015. www.economist.com/news/science-and-technology/21684112-greener-polymers-are-stronger-too-no-tangled-web.

11 European Parliament and the Council on the Registration, Evaluation, Authorisation and Restriction of Chemicals (REACH). 2006. Regulation (EC) No 1907/2006. https://echa.europa.eu/regulations/reach/legislation.

12 European Parliament and the Council. 2011. Directive 2011/65/EU. http://eur-lex.europa.eu/legal-content/EN/TXT/?uri=CELEX:32011L0065.

13 The SIN (Substitute it Now!) list is a database of chemicals likely to be banned or restricted in a near future. The chemicals on the SIN List have been identified by ChemSec as Substances of Very High Concern (SVHC) based on the criteria established by the EU chemicals regulation REACH (Source: http://chemsec.org/business-tool/sin-list/).

14 McDonough Braungart Design Chemistry, LLC. 2012. "Banned Lists of Chemicals". www.c2ccertified.org/resources/detail/cradle-to-cradle-certified-banned-list-of-chemicals.

15 The Fashion Positive portfolio of C2C materials can be accessed at: www.fashionpositive.org/fashionpositivematerials/.

16 The database created by Sustainability-Lab can be found at: http://www.sustainability-lab.net/en/groups/catalogo-tessuti-e-accessori.

17 Tarkett. 2014. "2013–2014 CSR/Sustainability Report". Accessed on June 5, 2017. www.tarkett.com/sites/default/files/TARKETT_2013-2014%20CSR-Sustainability%20Report_0.pdf.

18 Darius Helm. 2015. "State of Sustainability 2015: Manufacturers Adapt to Market Transformations". Accessed on June 5, 2017. www.floordaily.net/floorfocus/state-of-sustainability-2015-manufacturers-adapt-.

19 Desso. n.d. "Cradle to Cradle® Carpet Company Desso Launches New Circular Economy Material Stream". Accessed on June 5, 2017. www.desso.com/news-events/news-overview/2014/11/cradle-to-cradler-carpet-company-desso-launches-new-circular-economy-material-stream-of-up-to-20000-tonnes-of-chalk-from-local-water-companies/.

20 Adam Parsons. 2018. "McDonald's to Start Phasing out Plastic Straws from Its UK Restaurants". Sky News. Posted on March 28, 2018. https://news.sky.com/story/mcdonalds-to-start-phasing-out-plastic-straws-from-its-uk-restaurants-11306411.

21 The process of making better products using fewer materials. In some cases, digital technologies facilitate the migration from products to services, meaning no materials are used.

22 Autodesk. n.d. "Design for Durability. Quick Reference Guide". Accessed September 19, 2017. https://sustainabilityworkshop.autodesk.com/sites/default/files/core-page-files/dfdurability_quickreferenceguide_adsksustainabilityworkshop.pdf.

23 Autodesk. n.d. "Improving Product Lifetime". Accessed September 19, 2017. https://sustainabilityworkshop.autodesk.com/products/improving-product-lifetime.

24 Waste Management (WM). 2014. "Design with Intent: Sustainability in Product Design". Posted on January 17, 2014. http://mediaroom.wm.com/design-with-intent-sustainability-in-product-design/.

25 More info at: www.turnaroundterminal.com/.

26 Joel Iles. 2016. "Globechain Enable Re-use of One Million Tonnes of Unwanted Stuff". Posted on September 21, 2016. http://circulatenews.org/2016/09/globechain-enable-re-use-of-one-million-tonnes-of-unwanted-stuff/.

27 Philips. 2017. "Behind the Factory Doors". Posted on February 8, 2017. https://philips.exposure.co/behind-the-factory-doors.

28 Veolia. n.d. "Circular Economy Solutions for Processing & Manufacturing Koh". Accessed on June 8, 2017. www.veolianorthamerica.com/en/our-services/regeneration-services/koh-regeneration.

29 Thermal Compaction Group (TCG). n.d. "Environmental Sustainable". Accessed on June 28, 2017. http://www.tcg.ltd/.

30 The video can be accessed at: https://about.hm.com/en/media/news/general-2017/hm-bring-it-campaign.html.

31 Ocado Group. 2015. "Ocado Launches Bag Recycle Bonus Scheme". Posted on September 30, 2015. www.ocadogroup.com/news-and-media/news-centre/2015/20150930_bag_recycle_bonus.aspx.

32 Google. 2017. "Environmental Sustainability at Google". Accessed June 30, 2018. https://environment.google/projects/environmental-report-2017/.

33 Google. 2016. "Achieving Our 100% Renewable Energy Purchasing Goal and Going Beyond". Posted on December 2016. https://static.googleusercontent.com/media/www.google.com/en//green/pdf/achieving-100-renewable-energy-purchasing-goal.pdf.

34 The Leadership in Energy and Environmental Design (LEED) is the global reference standard in rating green buildings' design, operations, and construction.

35 International Trade Union Confederation. n.d. "Global Supply Chains = Exploitation". Accessed July 30, 2017. www.ituc-csi.org/supply-chains-resources-hub?lang=en.

36 Besides sharing with suppliers the leading practices implemented in its own manufacturing plants for reducing energy and water use, GHG and air emissions, and waste generation, Ford also encourages Tier 1 suppliers to cascade the information down the chain. https://corporate.ford.com/microsites/sustainability-report-2016-17/operations/supplier-impact.html.

37 Filiale Milano n.d. "Fantoni Partner per La Circular Economy Al Padiglione Italia Della Biennale". Accessed August 4, 2017. www.filialemilano.it/2016/06/04/fantoni-partner-per-la-circular-economy/.

38 Carlsberg Group. 2016. "Carlsberg Unveils New Green Fiber Bottle Design". Posted on September 28, 2016. https://carlsberggroup.com/newsroom/carlsberg-unveils-new-green-fiber-bottle-design/.

39 Walmart. 2015. "Global Responsibility Report". Accessed on May 5, 2017. https://cdn.corporate.walmart.com/f2/b0/5b8e63024998a74b5514e078a4fe/2015-global-responsibility-report.pdf.

40 The University of Cambridge Institute for Sustainability Leadership (CISL). 2016. "A Circular Economy Case Study. Collaboration for a Closed-Loop Value Chain". Accessed on February 8, 2017. www.cisl.cam.ac.uk/publications/publication-pdfs/cisl-closed-loop-case-study-web.pdf.

41 As an example, Unilever encourages its leaders to complete an executive education course run by Bradford University which includes circular economy thought leadership and practical business application.

42 Partnering organizations include AIRBUS Group, SUEZ environment Group, SNECMA/SAFRAN Group, and Equip'Aero Industrie.

43 Singapore Packaging Agreement. 2017. "SPA Awards 2017 Booklet". Accessed on March 28, 2017. www.nea.gov.sg/docs/default-source/energy-waste/recycling/spa/spa-awards-2017-booklet.pdf.
44 www.international-synergies.com/about-us/our-history/.
45 The University of Cambridge Institute for Sustainability Leadership (CISL). 2016. "A Circular Economy Case Study. Collaboration for a Closed-Loop Value Chain". Accessed on February 8, 2017. www.cisl.cam.ac.uk/publications/publication-pdfs/cisl-closed-loop-case-study-web.pdf.

Bibliography

Autodesk. n.d. "Design for Durability. Quick Reference Guide." Accessed on September 19, 2017. https://sustainabilityworkshop.autodesk.com/sites/default/files/core-page-files/dfdurability_quickreferenceguide_adsksustainability workshop.pdf.

Autodesk. n.d. "Improving Product Lifetime." Accessed on September 19, 2017. https://sustainabilityworkshop.autodesk.com/products/improving-product-lifetime.

Bakker, Conny, Marcel den Hollander, Ed van Hinte, and Yvo Zijlstra. 2014. *Products That Last: Product Design for Circular Business Models.* Delft, South Holland: TU Delft Library.

Bocken, Nancy M. P., and Short, S. W. 2016. "Towards a Sufficiency-Driven Business Model: Experiences and Opportunities." *Environmental Innovation and Societal Transitions* 18: 41–61. doi:10.1016/j.eist.2015.07.010.

Carlsberg Group. 2016. "Carlsberg Unveils New Green Fiber Bottle Design." Posted on September 28, 2016. https://carlsberggroup.com/newsroom/carlsberg-unveils-new-green-fiber-bottle-design/.

Cristoni, Nicolò, and Marcello Tonelli. 2018. "Perceptions of Firms Participating in a Circular Economy." *European Journal of Sustainable Development* 7 (4): 105–18. doi: 10.14207/ejsd.2018.v7n4p105

De los Rios, Irel Carolina, and Fiona J. Charnley. 2016. "Skills and Capabilities for a Sustainable and Circular Economy: The Changing Role of Design." *Journal of Cleaner Production* 160 (Sep): 109–22. doi:10.1016/j.jclepro.2016.10.130.

Desso. n.d. "Cradle to Cradle® Carpet Company Desso Launches New Circular Economy Material Stream." Accessed on June 5, 2017. www.desso.com/news-events/news-overview/2014/11/cradle-to-cradler-carpet-company-desso-launches-new-circular-economy-material-stream-of-up-to-20000-tonnes-of-chalk-from-local-water-companies/.

Diallo, Claver, Uday Venkatadri, Abdelhakim Khatab, and Sriram Bhakthavatchalam. 2016. "State of the Art Review of Quality, Reliability and Maintenance Issues in Closed-Loop Supply Chains with Remanufacturing." *International Journal of Production Research* 55 (5): 1277–96. doi:10.1080/00207543.2016.1200152.

Ellen MacArthur Foundation. 2012. "Towards the Circular Economy Vol. 1: An Economic and Business Rationale for an Accelerated Transition." Accessed on October 25, 2016. www.ellenmacarthurfoundation.org/publications/towards-the-circular-economy-vol-1-an-economic-and-business-rationale-for-an-accelerated-transition.

Ellen MacArthur Foundation. 2013. "Towards the Circular Economy Vol. 2: Opportunities for the Consumer Goods Sector." Accessed on October 30, 2016. www.ellenmacarthurfoundation.org/publications/towards-the-circular-economy-vol-2-opportunities-for-the-consumer-goods-sector.

Ellen MacArthur Foundation. 2014. "Towards the Circular Economy Vol. 3: Accelerating the Scale-up Across Global Supply Chains." Accessed on October 15, 2016. www.ellenmacarthurfoundation.org/publications/towards-the-circular-economy-vol-3-accelerating-the-scale-up-across-global-supply-chains.

Ellen MacArthur Foundation. 2015a. "Circularity Indicators. An Approach to Measuring Circularity. Methodology." Accessed on July 15, 2017. www.ellenmacarthurfoundation.org/assets/downloads/insight/Circularity-Indicators_Methodology_May2015.pdf.

Ellen MacArthur Foundation. 2015b. "Delivering the Circular Economy: A Toolkit for Policymakers." Accessed on September 15, 2017. www.ellenmacarthurfoundation.org/publications/delivering-the-circular-economy-a-toolkit-for-policymakers.

Ellen MacArthur Foundation. 2015c. "Growth Within: A Circular Economy for a Competitive Europe." Accessed on September 5, 2017. www.ellenmacarthurfoundation.org/publications/growth-within-a-circular-economy-vision-for-a-competitive-europe.

Ellen MacArthur Foundation. 2015d. "Toward a Circular Economy: Business Rationale for an Accelerated Transition." www.ellenmacarthurfoundation.org/assets/downloads/TCE_Ellen-MacArthur-Foundation_9-Dec-2015.pdf.

European Commission (EC). 2017. "Moving Towards a Circular Economy with EMAS. Best Practices to Implement Circular Economy Strategies (With Case Study Examples)." http://ec.europa.eu/environment/emas/pdf/other/report_EMAS_Circular_Economy.pdf

European Environmental Agency (EEA). 2016. "Circular Economy in Europe. Developing the Knowledge Base." EEA Report No 2/2016. www.eea.europa.eu/publications/circular-economy-in-europe.

European Parliament and the Council. 2006. Regulation (EC) No 1907/2006. https://echa.europa.eu/regulations/reach/legislation.

European Parliament and the Council. 2011. Directive 2011/65/EU. http://eur-lex.europa.eu/legal-content/EN/TXT/?uri=CELEX:32011L0065.

Filiale Milano n.d. "Fantoni Partner per La Circular Economy Al Padiglione Italia Della Biennale." Accessed on August 4, 2017. www.filialemilano.it/2016/06/04/fantoni-partner-per-la-circular-economy/.

Food Valley Society. 2016. "From Coffee Grounds to Vegetarian Oyster Mushroom Snack." Posted on April 1, 2016. www.foodvalleysociety.com/from-coffee-grounds-to-vegetarian-oyster-mushroom-snack/.

Google. 2016. "Achieving Our 100% Renewable Energy Purchasing Goal and Going Beyond." Posted on December 2016. https://static.googleusercontent.com/media/www.google.com/en/green/pdf/achieving-100-renewable-energy-purchasing-goal.pdf.

Green Builder Staff. 2017. "Walt Disney World Using Biogas Technology for Food Waste." Posted on March 27, 2016. www.greenbuildermedia.com/energy-solutions/walt-disney-world-food-waste-biogas-technology.

Helm, Darius. 2015. "State of Sustainability 2015: Manufacturers Adapt to Market Transformations." Accessed on June 5, 2017. www.floordaily.net/floorfocus/state-of-sustainability-2015-manufacturers-adapt.

Iles, Joel. 2016. "Globechain Enable Re-use of One Million Tonnes of Unwanted Stuff." Posted on September 21, 2016. http://circulatenews.org/2016/09/globechain-enable-re-use-of-one-million-tonnes-of-unwanted-stuff/.

Institute of Environmental Management & Assessment (IEMA). 2017. "Environmental Management Briefing: Driving Sustainable Resource Management through ISO 14001." Accessed on June 21, 2018. www.iema.net/policy/srm/.

International Organization for Standardization (ISO). n.d. "ISO 14009- Guidelines for Incorporating Redesign of Products and Components to Improve Material Circulation." Accessed on June 21, 2018. https://committee.iso.org/sites/tc207sc1/home/projects/ongoing/iso-14009.html.

International Trade Union Confederation. n.d. "Global Supply Chains = Exploitation" Accessed on July 30, 2017. www.ituc-csi.org/supply-chains-resources-hub?lang=en.

Johannsdottir, Lara. 2014. "Transforming the Linear Insurance Business Model to a Closed-Loop Insurance Model: A Case Study of Nordic Non-life Insurers." *Journal of Cleaner Production* 83: 341–55.

Jonker, Jan, and Niels Faber. 2017. "The Circular Economy - Developments, Concepts, and Research in Search for Corresponding Business Models." *Whitepaper*. Accessed on April 30, 2018. www.sumusitalia.it/wp-content/uploads/2017/09/WhitePaper-The-Circular-Economy_INT_ebook.pdf.

Lacy, Peter, and Jakob Rutqvist. 2015. *Waste to Wealth. The Circular Economy Advantage*. New York, NY: Palgrave Macmillan.

Lovins, Amory, and Michael Braungart. 2014. *A New Dynamic - Effective Business in a Circular Economy*. Isle of Wight: Ellen MacArthur Foundation Publishing.

Lovins, Hunter, Ellen Franconi, and Ken Webster. 2016. *A New Dynamic 2- Effective Systems in a Circular Economy*. Isle of Wight: Ellen MacArthur Foundation Publishing.

Makower, Joel. 2014 *State of Green Business Report*. www.greenbiz.com/research/report/2014/01/19/state-green-business-report-2014

Mayhew, Freddy. 2016. "Independent Readership up 46 per cent While Mobile Offers Biggest Audience for Some." *PressGazette*. Posted on August 24, 2016. www.pressgazette.co.uk/independent-readership-up-46-per-cent-while-mobile-offers-biggest-audience-for-some/.

McDonough Braungart Design Chemistry, LLC. 2012. "Banned Lists of Chemicals." www.c2ccertified.org/resources/detail/cradle-to-cradle-certified-banned-list-of-chemicals.

Ocado Group. 2015. "Ocado Launches Bag Recycle Bonus Scheme." Posted on September 30, 2015. www.ocadogroup.com/news-and-media/news-centre/2015/20150930_bag_recycle_bonus.aspx.

Parsons, Adam. 2018. "McDonald's to Start Phasing out Plastic Straws from Its UK Restaurants." Sky News. Posted on March 28, 2018. https://news.sky.com/story/mcdonalds-to-start-phasing-out-plastic-straws-from-its-uk-restaurants-11306411.

Peiró Laura, Fulvio Ardente, and Fabrice Mathieux. 2017. "Design for Disassembly Criteria in EU Product Policies for a More Circular Economy." *Journal of Industrial Ecology*. 21 (3): 731–41. doi:10.1111/jiec.12608.

Philips. 2017. "Behind the Factory Doors." Posted on February 8, 2017. https://philips.exposure.co/behind-the-factory-doors.

Rizos, Vasileios, Arno Behrens, Terri Kafyeke, Martin Hirschnitz-Garbers, and Anastasia Ioannou. 2015. "The Circular Economy: Barriers and Opportunities for SMEs." *CEPS Working Document* 412. www.ceps.eu/publications/circular-economy-barriers-and-opportunities-smes.

Tarkett. 2014. "2013–2014 CSR/Sustainability Report." Accessed on June 5, 2017. www.tarkett.com/sites/default/files/TARKETT_2013-2014%20CSR-Sustainability%20Report_0.pdf.

Thermal Compaction Group (TCG). n.d. "Environmental Sustainable." Accessed on June 28, 2017. www.tcg.ltd/.

The Economist. 2015. "No Tangled Web." Posted on December 19, 2015. www.economist.com/news/science-and-technology/21684112-greener-polymers-are-stronger-too-no-tangled-web.

The University of Cambridge Institute for Sustainability Leadership (CISL). 2016. "A Circular Economy Case Study. Collaboration for a Closed-Loop Value Chain." Accessed on February 8, 2017. www.cisl.cam.ac.uk/publications/publication-pdfs/cisl-closed-loop-case-study-web.pdf.

U.S. Chamber of Commerce Foundation. 2015. "Achieving a Circular Economy. How the Private Sector Is Reimagining the Future of Business." Accessed on February 5, 2017. www.uschamberfoundation.org/sites/default/files/Circular%20Economy%20Best%20Practices.pdf.

Veolia. n.d. "Circular Economy Solutions for Processing & Manufacturing Koh." Accessed on June 8, 2017. www.veolianorthamerica.com/en/our-services/regeneration-services/koh-regeneration.

Walmart. 2015. "Global Responsibility Report." Accessed on May 5, 2017. https://cdn.corporate.walmart.com/f2/b0/5b8e63024998a74b5514e078a4fe/2015-global-responsibility-report.pdf.

Waste Management (WM). 2014. "Design with Intent: Sustainability in Product Design." Posted on January 17, 2014. http://mediaroom.wm.com/design-with-intent-sustainability-in-product-design/.

Winkler, H. 2011. "Closed-Loop Production Systems—A Sustainable Supply Chain Approach." *CIRP Journal of Manufacturing Science and Technology* 4: 243–46. doi:10.1016/j.cirpj.2011.05.001.

World Economic Forum (WEF). 2014. "Towards the Circular Economy: Accelerating the Scale-up Across Global Supply Chains." Accessed on October 17, 2017. www3.weforum.org/docs/WEF_ENV_TowardsCircularEconomy_Report_2014.pdf.

4 CE-Enabling Technologies

4.1 Introduction

The Fourth Industrial Revolution, where disruptive technologies like the Internet of Things (IoT), 3D printing, and robotics are making the physical, digital, and biological dimensions (Schwab 2016) increasingly interconnected to each other, is rapidly becoming a reality, urging businesses to re-invent their operations if they are to keep pace with the wave of innovation hitting, to a different extent, all industries. As an example, it has been estimated that the number of connected devices will go from the current 10 billion up to 25–50 billion by 2020 (Ellen MacArthur Foundation 2016). Accordingly, forecasts estimate the IoT market to triple by 2020, reaching USD 1.7 trillion worth.[1] The Fourth Industrial Revolution is closely connected with the recent interest by the private sector for the CE. Disruptive innovations like big data, machine-to-machine connectivity, green chemistry, and advanced recycling systems are in fact opening new possibilities for businesses – like, for example, extending the control over items beyond point of sale up to product returns (Lieder 2017), creating closed-loop operations, instantly tracking the conditions of assets to minimize waste, maximizing the utilization of servitized products, or replacing polluting materials with bio-based alternatives. The wide range of CE-enabling technologies a firm can choose from when defining its business strategy can be broadly divided into *digital technologies* and *design and engineering technologies* (Table 4.1).

Table 4.1 Technologies for a CE

Digital Technologies	Design & Engineering Technologies
1. IoT	1. Green chemistry
2. Innovative traceability systems	2. Open source
3. Trace and return systems	3. 3D printing
4. Mobile technology	4. Advanced recycling tech.
5. Digital sharing platforms	
6. Digital substitutes	
7. Big data	

4.2 Digital Technologies

Digital technologies can allow for an enhanced control over assets both during the use phase and after the product is discarded, thus favouring CE strategies aiming, for example, at increasing utilization rates (see IoT, mobile and digital sharing platforms solutions, etc.) or prolonging the item's life through predictive maintenance and real-time information on the conditions of the asset. Some digital technologies like mobile and digital platforms rely heavily on the interaction between users. In this respect, the progressive narrowing of the digital divide represents a big opportunity for CE-oriented companies to enter new markets in developing countries, as their customer bases keep on growing. While, in fact, developed countries are accustomed to a widespread use of computers, cellular phones, and the Internet – and most people have had access to those technologies for decades – half of the global population has remained offline and still can't participate in the digital economy. However, the worldwide diffusion of digital technologies is increasing its speed and Internet users have doubled from 1.8 billion in 2010 up to 3.6 in 2016. The current 4.2 billion users represent just over 50% of the world population. Mobile-broadband subscriptions also have grown in similar fashion.[2] Looking at these statistics, it is safe to imagine the digital divide continuing to rapidly shrink and eventually disappear.

IoT. The IoT is the network of connected items and devices that interact through sensors, electronics, and dedicated software to collect, share, process, and interpret data that will eventually drive process improvements. In doing so, the IoT will thus progressively merge the physical world with the digital. The rapid expansion of IoT has been enabled by worldwide wireless network coverage – which makes data sharing and processing possible without human involvement – and developments in sensor technology that allows for an immediate exchange of multiple information (e.g. location, usability, deterioration, etc.) regarding a machine or other objects. This constant flow of information can then be harnessed to make descriptions, predictions, or prescriptions regarding the use of the good. German conglomerate Siemens, for example, has equipped its wind turbines with a suite of sensors that allow for a constant monitoring of the components most subject to damage and deterioration like generators, gears, and bearings. Siemens' Siplus CMS system for early detection of faults makes it possible to tackle predictable problems, hence providing operators with a cost-effective solution to prolong the lifetime of the asset.[3]

While the applications of IoT technology can definitely support decision-making to improve the functioning of complex processes, it is rarely implemented in such ways being IoT solutions deployed mainly to identify and correct anomalies rather than to drive decisions at the process level.[4] In a report, focused on data collection, the Ellen MacArthur Foundation (2016) found that, when looked through the lens of a CE, IoT technology can provide three different, but intertwined types of product-related information:

- <u>Knowledge of asset location</u>. Hello Tractor is an innovative Nigerian start-up that makes it possible for low-income farmers to rent cheap tractors for specific tasks like irrigation, ploughing, and fertilizer distribution. Each machine is equipped with sensors and a GPS so that by accessing the dedicated smartphone application, tractor owners are constantly updated about the assets' location. Owners also receive a message anytime the tractor is not where it was supposed to be.
- <u>Knowledge of asset availability</u>. This information is key for car sharing, for example. According to the data transmitted by sensors installed on the vehicles, operators can inform users – via dedicated smartphone applications – about what cars are ready to use and where.
- <u>Knowledge of asset (and/or its content) condition</u>. Since 2015, logistics giant A.P. Moller-Maersk Group has been utilizing AT&T IoT technology worldwide to track and monitor the temperature and working conditions of its refrigerated containers carrying perishable goods.[5] In the waste management sector, Enevo – a Finnish provider of waste and recycling services and analytics solutions[6] – installs wireless sensors on bins and other containers to measure waste fill levels and provide forecasting so that the client – either a business or a municipality – can choose the most appropriate waste management plan.

Apart from the evident decisions that these three types of information (location, availability, and condition) can facilitate, they can also be leveraged to attain more profound circular objectives, such as:

- <u>Increase the utilization of an asset or resource</u>, as in the case of car sharing. It has been calculated that, compared to privately owned cars, car sharing can increase the utilization rates of vehicles by up to 53%.[7]
- <u>Prolong the life of an asset</u>. In Western Australia, Caterpillar deployed IoT technology to predict damages and provide timely maintenance operations on its fleet of autonomous mining trucks. A suite of sensors attached to each machine makes it possible for Caterpillar operators to obtain real-time information on the conditions of some key components like filters and oil pressure.[8]
- <u>Reduce waste</u>. As per its "Food is Precious" initiative, IKEA has implemented an IoT solution at some of its restaurants and Swedish Food Markets that is helping the company dramatically reduce food

waste. Through a smart scale, IKEA kitchen staff can measure waste levels by food type and then make adjustments in menus and quantities.[9] A broader analysis of the food industry would also identify possible improvements further up the supply chain, where food products are shipped from one player to another, multiple times. California-based Zest Labs has, for example, developed a sensor-based, automated data capture and cloud-based real-time analytics technology capable of constantly monitoring the conditions of a pallet containing food. If any issues arise (like the ripening of fruit occurring too fast), a decision on how to respond can be taken promptly and effectively (e.g. the pallet being diverted from its scheduled destination and sent instead to the closest shop so that the products can be sold prior to becoming inedible).

- Reduce the use of natural resources hence help regenerating natural capital. IoT solutions are emerging rapidly in the agricultural industry, driving down consumption levels of water and fertilizers, and therefore costs. Through a combination of in-ground sensors and cloud analytics tools, Tel Aviv-based company CropX has managed to develop an innovative low-cost soil monitoring system that is aiding farmers to better understand the water needs of their fields: the system can increase crop yields while simultaneously cutting water usage by one-third. The company already serves 20 of the largest farms across the United States and has attracted investments from large sensor manufacturers like Bosch and Flex (formerly Flextronics). Similarly, Agrometius in the Netherlands informs farmers on the best crop management practices, with information coming from a network of connected devices including GPS, yield measurement systems, and soil sensors. IoT systems can also be deployed to reduce the demand for energy, both in the business and in the public sectors. Philips CityTouch is an end-to-end street lighting management system for cities that integrates connected devices and specialized services to utterly re-invent lighting operations. Essentially, through M2M technology,[10] stand-alone LED street lights are connected to each other and to a central dashboard whereby users can monitor light points and regulate light levels on demand.[11] In March 2016, Philips signed an agreement with Vodafone. Through a robust and reliable wireless connectivity, the partnership aims to boost the adoption of Philips' smart street lighting systems whereby city authorities can achieve substantial energy savings and ensure easier and more efficient maintenance operations.[12]

Innovative traceability systems are used by businesses to help trace the origins of products and eventually facilitate post-use operations like collection, sorting, and recycling. The Circular Content Management System (CCMS) is a cloud-based platform launched by Dutch Awareness to track and trace garments and their materials as they move from the point of manufacturing across the entire supply chain. Detailed information on the product's materials, the way it was manufactured, and the environmental impact associated with it are attached to the garment by means of a bar code that can be scanned by any operator or customer with a smartphone. The innovation is meant to boost reverse cycle operations in the garment industry.

Blockchain is another promising technology that could serve the function of providing real-time information about an item moving from one point of the value chain to the next. Blockchain, often associated with the birth to virtual currency Bitcoin, is essentially a process whereby transactions of any type are linked, registered, and verified on a decentralized ledger of a peer-to-peer network of computers. Hence, records are kept and secured without the need of a centralized authority overseeing the entire process, with benefits ranging from cost reduction, increased transparency, and more accurate tracking (Morrison and Sinha 2016). The technology is currently being tested to establish reliable platforms where products (e.g. slavery-free fish stocks or certified sustainable wood) can be monitored and correctly identified by all parties in the supply chain.

Trace and return systems increase cost-effectiveness in the collection and processing of discarded materials through, for example, asset identification and efficient material sorting machines. Through its asset recovery programme, global technology company Ricoh collects and re-processes supplies, parts, and components – like toner cartridges – with the aim of re-marketing them. The recovery of pre-owned materials is facilitated by the company's proprietary trace and return system, Ricoh Asset Management System (RAMS), which gives real-time information on each returned item through serial number codes linked to product components. The collected information is then sent to Ricoh staff, who can track and govern assets to be re-used and materials to be remitted to certified recycling partners. The system is already deployed in more than 20 sorting centres across Europe.

Mobile technology, including smartphone applications and social networks, enables digital, instant, quick, and low-cost access to data of any type, including usage of products and services. Most car sharing services operate via dedicated apps whereby users can gain immediate information about the location and conditions of vehicles (fuel level, overall state of the car, etc.). These apps are extremely user-friendly and easy to use, thus further favouring the diffusion of car sharing. Mobile technology can also provide customers with immediate and easy feedback systems to increase trust in online marketplaces for used goods. One such platform is Stuffstr, a mobile application that allows registered users to give their unwanted items a second life through recycling, renting, or donating.

In the agricultural sector, mobile technology has proven to be a successful ally for small farmers, who now can, through dedicated smartphone applications, enhance crop yields using fewer resources and more effectively protect fields from diseases and bad weather. The Grameen Foundation's Community Knowledge Worker (CKW) programme in Uganda, for example, has provided farmers with smartphone technology to help access information about weather, crop, and animal diseases. In 2016, the Rainforest Alliance piloted a similar project aiming at connecting farmers worldwide to exchange data on best agricultural management practices and commodity markets: smartphones were given to 25 small-scale producers responsible for involving locals to share information on a database. In April 2017, a "Farmer Training App" has been made available for free download by the Rainforest Alliance to its network of farmers in Africa, Asia, and Latin America. Via this app, rural farmers are now placed in a better position to adopt climate-smart agricultural best practices that will help increase yields with reduced resources and no additional land.[13]

Digital sharing platforms are essentially digital spaces enabling either businesses or individuals sharing and exchanging products. These can be of three main types:

- Platforms helping businesses prolonging the life cycle of their products. Optoro, for example, offers online solutions to optimize excess and returned inventory. The company relies on its proprietary data sets and real-time information to instantly determine whether inventory items shall be sold in the B2C or B2B markets, or rather returned to vendors, donated, or recycled. Optoro's service promises to facilitate re-use and maximize recovery of unsold items, cut both inventory and landfill costs, and also prevent environment-related liabilities. To further advance its business services, in 2016, the company signed agreements with UPS (global leader in logistics) and Groupon (the American worldwide e-commerce marketplace). The former was set to "help retailers and manufacturers simplify returns management and unlock the full value from their reverse logistics programs"[14] (Alan Gershenhorn – UPS Chief Commercial Officer). The latter aimed to find effective solutions to process returned and excess inventory, with the main objectives of reducing delivery time of returned assets, eliminating superfluous stages in the chain and eventually reducing waste.

  Downstream the waste generation process, New Hope Ecotech, a technology solution company headquartered in Brazil, is pioneering an innovative waste credit market that would help businesses address their waste management duties and concurrently benefit informal waste pickers. Manufacturers are linked to all the players performing waste management activities (recyclers, aggregators, and waste pickers) through a digital platform that tracks such activities and issues a "Reverse Logistic Certificate" to the waste producer. As a result, the business can prove to have fulfilled its legal obligation of recycling the product packaging, and money gets shared among all waste operators – who played a role in the chain – thanks to New Hope Ecotech technology.

- Platforms increasing the utilization rate of company assets. In the healthcare sector, Cohealo is a technology company that developed a platform for healthcare systems to optimize the utilization of medical equipment through asset sharing across facilities. Once the equipment has been registered onto the database, each user can locate and reserve it easily, with Cohealo taking care of the logistic operations needed to move the equipment from one medical centre to another. The company also provides analytics services so that management of multiple hospital facilities can make informed decisions on how to allocate assets more efficiently.

- Platforms creating second-hand markets where users offer to rent, lease, or exchange their products. Craigslist and eBay enable the trading of used products worldwide; Fashionhire encourages the rental of designer handbags; the Library of Things is a UK social enterprise allowing users to borrow any sort of stuff (e.g. carpet cleaners, barbecues, tents, etc.) at affordable prices – between 0.50 and 15 pounds depending on the item. When it comes to non-currency markets, platforms are set up to let users freely exchange (bartering, gifting, etc.) used products of any type like toys (Toyswap) or food items (Cropmobster).

Digital substitutes including cloud computing. This technology refers to the process of "dematerializing" the content of physical products into a digital format. Over the past decades, various industries like newspapers, music CDs, video entertainment (DVDs), and travel services have witnessed an almost complete shift towards digital alternatives. In the B2B market, the transition has recently accelerated thanks to cloud computing technology, "a model for enabling ubiquitous, convenient, on-demand network access to a shared pool of configurable computing resources (e.g., networks, servers, storage, applications, and services) that can be rapidly provisioned and released with minimal management effort or service provider interaction" (Mell and Grance 2011, p.2).

One of the most widely known cloud-based companies is Google, whose major services – from Gmail to Google Earth – are all delivered from the cloud. The main environmental sustainability advantage of cloud technology is a centralization of energy requirements in the hands of the one company operating the cloud computing data centres – as opposed to individual users – hence making the search for energy efficiency more vital for the business. Allowing for a better alignment between the interests of the service provider and those of its clients (i.e. pay-per-use), cloud computing also pushes the boundaries of server usage efficiency. IBM offers a wide range of cloud computing solutions spanning from Platform as a Service (PaaS) – where applications can be transferred to public or private clouds – to Infrastructure as a Service (IaaS) – which provides companies with computing resources including servers, networking, storage, and data centre space on a pay-per-use basis.[15]

But cloud computing can also assist businesses to make their circular operations more efficient. In January 2017, French-based utility company Suez Environnement joined efforts with cloud-based waste and recycling company Rubicon Global to speed up the digitalization of its Recycling & Recovery Division and improve collection activities across mainland Europe, particularly those concerned with small and dispersed quantities of waste.[16] In the public arena, the US Business Council for Sustainable Development (US BCSD), the World Business Council for Sustainable Development (WBCSD), and Corporate Eco Forum collaborated to establish a cloud-based platform – called Materials Marketplace – that helps identify company-to-company re-use opportunities and boost the exchange of underutilized materials. Currently, the platform has been adopted at the national level in the U.S.A. and Turkey, as well as at the local level by several U.S. cities and states, namely Austin, Ohio, Detroit, Southern California, and Tennessee.

Big data is a term for groups of data – both structured and unstructured – so large or complex that present challenges with regards to their capture, collection, analysis, sharing, storage, and transfer with traditional data processing applications. For big data to effectively inform (CE-oriented) decision-making through business intelligence techniques and decision support systems, advanced analytics techniques are required (Bressanelli et al. 2018). In the energy sector, American AutoGrid is using big data to assist leading companies which provide customers with access to clean, reasonably priced, and reliable power. To do so, the company leverages big data analytics to make sense of the countless information and data coming from equipment like smart meters, thermostats, and other connected devices to improve system operations, optimize supply and demand patterns, and curb power use. But big data can also be further leveraged to support users in reducing the energy consumption of their assets by providing ad hoc advice on how to optimize usage phase (Bressanelli et al. 2018). Looking ahead, big data is starting to be investigated by both academics (Dubey et al. 2016; Wang et al. 2016) and private sector organizations to make supply chains more efficient and gradually design out waste as well as economic losses.

4.3 Design and Engineering Technologies

Different from the digital technologies, where the focus is mostly on boosting CE practices at the use phase, design and engineering technologies assist practitioners in incorporating CE-oriented product strategies either at the beginning (design: green chemistry and open source) or at the end (post-use: advanced recycling technologies) of the value chain. Additionally, re-manufacturing is another dimension that can be reassessed with the adoption of 3D printing.

Green chemistry is a branch of chemistry that specializes in devising sustainable alternatives to chemical products and production processes known to be harmful to both the environment and human health. As the presence of hazardous substances spans across the entire life cycle of a chemical (i.e. design, manufacturing, and use), alternatives are expected to benefit every stage of development. Some of the fundamental pillars of green chemistry[17] fit seamlessly within the definition of a CE model, and particularly:

- Design chemicals whose toxic effects are negligible or non-existent.
- Design chemicals that, once their function is served, do not persist in the environment but rather go through degradation processes.
- Use renewable raw materials and feedstock.
- Minimize the energy requirements of chemical processes.

Recent discoveries in the field have emphasized the crucial role that green chemistry can play in advancing circular practices in the business environment. The interest from the business sector for bioplastics has skyrocketed over the last few years, due primarily to a mounting concern from NGOs and the public opinion over plastic pollution. Bioplastics is a broad term used to define plastic materials that are fully or partly developed from organic biomass (agricultural products, plants, or organic waste), instead of petroleum. Today, a growing number of specialized firms around the world offer bioplastic solutions that are either fully biodegradable or suitable for composting. In California, Full Cycle Bioplastics works alongside municipal compost facilities, farmers, food processors, and biorefineries to bring into their operations its close-loop bioplastic production process. The firm has in fact devised a novel process to convert organic waste into a compostable and marine degradable plastic called polyhydroxyalkanoate (PHA). But organic waste is just one possible source; bioplastics can also be generated from a combination of paper waste and agricultural waste, as the one developed by Pulp Works, a San Francisco-based company that has patented Karta-Pack™, a recyclable, compostable, and biodegradable alternative to the plastic blister pack. Yet, another approach is to purposively grow specific crops and vegetation that can be a source for bioplastic materials. Founded in

2006, Ecovative Design is a pioneering biomaterials company headquartered in New York that produces bioplastic using mushroom technology. Currently, the company is developing a biopolymer material 100% made of mycelium,[18] the vegetative part of a fungus.

Capture and re-utilization of CO_2 has been another area to show increased attention from the business sector. If looked through the lens of climate change, human-induced carbon dioxide is the number one public enemy, but there are firms that have actually managed to harness the qualities of CO_2. Indian company Carbon Clean Solutions Limited (CCSL) is one of them, having licenced a series of CO_2 capture and re-utilization methods that can convert the gas into chemicals (e.g. soda ash and urea), materials (e.g. green cement and polycarbonate), and fuels (e.g. biofuels and methanol). The company's chemical-solvent-based technology can be applied on different industrial gas streams and reduce the cost of CO_2 capture by 40%.[19] In North America, Newlight Technologies, another firm specialized in carbon capture and re-use, provides customers with a process that converts greenhouse gas emissions into a high-performance thermoplastic called AirCarbon. This groundbreaking material is Cradle to Cradle (C2C) certified and already in use today by many large brands to manufacture goods of various kinds. As an example, in 2016 the firm had a contract signed with IKEA for half of the total amount of AirCarbon produced at the Newlight's plant in the United States, and with the agreement of reaching one billion pounds' worth of supplies per year over time.[20]

Degradable packaging is arguably the third most important area of application for green chemistry. In September 2016, UK food company Snact began using a sustainable packaging developed by Israeli start-up Tipa that is 100% home compostable and biologically decomposes in six months. Other chemical discoveries, still at preliminary stages of commercialization, are also worth a mention. In February 2017, scientists at the University of California created a type of paper with some very unique characteristics: ink-free, printed by light, and re-writable up to 80 times as text can be easily eliminated using heat (Yin 2017). Chemists at McGill, a public research university in Montreal, devised an alternative green process to refine metals that uses organic molecules instead of toxic solvents or reagents (like chlorine and hydrochloric acid) and requires less energy than traditional methods.[21]

A 2015 report commissioned by the American Sustainable Business Council (ASBC) and the Green Chemistry & Commerce Council (GC3) concluded that green chemistry holds the potential to unlock substantial profit opportunities given the expanding market for harmless chemical products. Avoiding the use of toxic substances can also generate important cost savings linked to tougher legislations being adopted in many countries.[22]

Open source is a remote working system enabling people to collaborate with unidentified others anywhere in the world. Organizations and individuals can all autonomously contribute to the development of a certain product or service by tackling different parts of the project simultaneously. Many open-source principles – transparency, reparability, modularity, long-term perspectives, and open standards – are shared by the CE (Muirhead 2016). Today, synergies between the two approaches are being exploited by some organizations. OSVehicle, a company operating in the B2B market of electric vehicles, offers a ready-to-use hardware platform usable by car manufacturers as a starting point to build customized electric vehicles in half the time and one-sixth of the costs.[23] Along with the platform, the user can buy all the mechanical and electrical components needed for the vehicle to run. These elements are shipped for easy assembly at the customer's premises. Another example is Precious Plastic, an open-source programme that aims at tackling the global plastic pollution problem by enabling people to develop together machines to recycle plastic waste. So far, the Precious Plastic movement has created four technologies that are showcased on the organization's website:[24] a shredder machine, an extrusion machine, an injection machine, and a compression machine.

3D printing is the making of three-dimensional solid objects from a digital file by using additive processes. In an additive process, an object is created by laying down successive layers of material until the entire object is formed. 3D printing technology was originally developed in the 1980s; yet, its widespread adoption has been possible only recently thanks to open-source movements, which contributed to lower its costly industrial manufacturing applications. The technology has now matured to the point that in January 2017, a team of researchers at the Massachusetts Institute of Technology (MIT) was able to design and prototype one of the strongest, lightest materials known using porous, 3D forms of graphene (Chandler 2017). The additive manufacturing system of 3D printing is thought to use a circular approach for at least two reasons (Unruh 2015). First, it is suited to meet manufacturing needs using renewable energy (solar) and local (recycled) materials as inputs for production. As part of the World's Advanced Saving Project (WASP), Italian-based Centro Sviluppo Progetti (CSP) is aiming at creating an experimental ecovillage near the city of Bologna using an innovative solar-powered giant 3D printer that combines local resources (water, soil, and vegetable fibre) to build basic housing structures. Secondly, the additive process can originate from recycled products (thereby accomplishing the task of re-introducing pre-owned objects into the economic system). The Indian social enterprise Protoprint, for example, is creating a recycling system whereby the plastic waste (specifically high-density polyethylene, largely used for plastic bottles) collected by urban waste pickers (i.e. scavengers) is transformed into a marketable plastic filament suitable for 3D printing machines. To do so, the organization runs a low-cost filament production facility in Pune (Liang and Paddison 2016).

Advanced recycling technologies allow for the recovery and recycling of materials from complex waste – such as electronics and chemicals. As far as in-house recycling activities are concerned, some businesses are taking big steps in setting up state-of-the-art machinery and advanced sorting processes to speed up operations, increase efficiency, and generate new value. Apple is one clear example. According to its Environmental Responsibility Report of 2015, the company was able to recover more than 27,000 tons of valuable materials from its recycling activities, of which 10,000+ tons of steel, 6,000+ tons of plastic, close to 3 tons of silver, and nearly 1 ton of gold.[25] To further beef up its recycling activities, in 2016 the company announced that it would implement lines of disassembly robots – called Liam – capable of recycling a total capacity of over one million phones a year (Rujanavech et al. 2016). As of April 2017, Apple was operating two Liam disassembly lines that can recover up to 1,900 kg of aluminium, 7 kg of silver, and 0.3 kg of gold for every 100,000 iPhone devices they process.[26]

The sorting and disassembly of returned goods can prove a rather complex task, particularly if the item is made up of a variety of components and parts. To address this problem, the Japanese multinational imaging and electronics company Ricoh uses a unique sorting process, whereby collected items (copiers and printers) are evaluated and enter different recycling streams (re-manufacturing or disassembly) depending on their condition. In the clothing industry, Levi's joined efforts with technology firm Evrnu to develop a process that will regenerate used cotton clothes into high-quality jeans. The initiative is an effort to close the technology gap affecting the desire to convert worn cotton into a quality denim-like material. At the collection phase of recycled materials, TerraCycle has already become a valuable partner for many brands (e.g. P&G, Henkel, Suez, Office Depot, etc.) wishing to boost their recycling rates, particularly with respect to hard-to-recycle products. With operations in more than 20 countries and projects involving 60+ million people, TerraCycle's Zero Waste Boxes enable the recycling of practically any type of waste, from packaging materials to personal safety equipment.

4.4 Conclusions

A growing number of businesses across industries is starting to leverage a new generation of highly innovative and sometimes relatively cheap technologies to tackle the threats (e.g. resource price volatility and tougher regulatory environmental frameworks), and take advantage of the opportunities (e.g. urbanization), of the 21st century. In doing so, most of these forward-looking companies boost their bottom lines, while concurrently making operations, processes, and products more environmentally sustainable. Technologies like IoT and Big Data, for example, help firms attracting customers via improved marketing, as well as supporting CE activities like providing preventive and predictive maintenance, optimizing product utilization, and enhancing renovation and end-of-life recovery actions.

CE-enabling technologies are being leveraged by large incumbents and newcomers alike. The formers generally make use of these technologies to devise CE-oriented solutions for their products and processes, like Siemens' Siplus CMS system for early detection of faults (IoT), Ricoh's asset recovery programme (trace and return system), or the IoT solution implemented by A.P. Moller-Maersk Group to monitor the conditions of the food contained in its refrigerated containers. But they also use CE technologies more extensively to develop new business models that allow them to differentiate themselves in the market. Car sharing solutions adopted by Mercedes (Car2Go) and BMW (DriveNow), or the bio-based sneakers developed by Puma, Reebok, and Adidas are just a few examples. As for young firms, most often than not, CE technologies are harnessed to tackle the specific socio-environmental issue around which the organization is created. The case studies provided in this chapter include Nigeria-based Hello Tractor (tractor sharing among small farmers), Israeli CropX (smart irrigation systems for dry regions), Tipa (compostable packaging), and CCSL (CO_2 capture and re-utilization methods).

Clearly, identifying the right CE-enabling technology must be placed at the heart of a company CE strategic process. Therefore, performing an in-depth assessment of the different solutions available and monitoring their evolution is a very important activity that allows for a better understanding of the possibilities for growth, repositioning, Sustained Competitive Advantage, etc. A technological assessment is closely linked to the CE business model a company wishes to undertake, which is the content of the next chapter.

Notes

1 Reuters. 2015. "Internet of Things Market to Triple to $1.7 Trillion by 2020: IDC". Posted on June 2, 2015. www.reuters.com/article/us-idc-research-idUSKBN0OI1NO20150602.

2 International Communication Union (ITU). n.d. "ICT Facts and Figures 2017". Accessed on June 20, 2017. www.itu.int/en/ITU-D/Statistics/Pages/facts/default.aspx.

3 Siemens. n.d. "Creating the Most from Wind". Accessed on October 1, 2017 www.industry.siemens.com/verticals/global/en/wind-turbine/Documents/E20001-A110-P550-X-7600.pdf.

4 McKinsey&Company. 2015. "Unlocking the Potential of the Internet of Things". Posted on June 1015. www.mckinsey.com/business-functions/

digital-mckinsey/our-insights/the-internet-of-things-the-value-of-digitizing-the-physical-world.

5 AT&T. 2015. "Maersk Teams with AT&T to Track and Monitor Cold Shipping Containers". Posted on September 9, 2015. http://about.att.com/story/maersk_teams_with_att_to_track_cold_shipping_containers.html.

6 Analytics is the application of advanced data analysis techniques to extract value from large volumes of complex data (big data) generated by connected devices (IoT), in order to inform decision-making.

7 Accenture Strategy. 2016. "Car Sharing Service Outlook in China". Accessed on September 30, 2017. https://www.accenture.com/t20160701T062629_w_/cn-en/_acnmedia/PDF-24/Accenture-Insight-Car-Sharing-Service-China-v2.pdf

8 The company has recently partnered up with analytics firm Uptake to provide a predictive diagnostics platform for its customers as well.

9 LeanPath and Winnow are the partners supplying the smart food waste solution to IKEA. More information is available on their websites. "IKEA Saves One Million Meals Through Food Waste Initiative". Posted on March 13, 2018. https://newsroom.inter.ikea.com/News/ikea-saves-one-million-meals-through-food-waste-initiative/s/96d248e2-98cd-436a-846e-ceda216da74d.

10 Machine-to-Machine (or M2M) technology is here referred to as the process, carried out by a machine itself, to communicate directly with a remote application infrastructure for monitoring and control purposes.

11 Philips. N.d. "CityTouch Light Management System". Accessed on February 4, 2017. www.lighting.philips.com/main/systems/lighting-systems/citytouch#.

12 Vodafone. 2016. "Vodafone and Philips Join Forces for Connected Lighting and Smart City Services". Posted on March 14, 2016. www.vodafone.com/content/index/media/vodafone-group-releases/2016/philips-connected-lighting.html.

13 Rainforest Alliance. 2017. "Scaling up Sustainable Agriculture Through Technology: The Rainforest Alliance Launches Farmer Training App". Posted on April 4, 2017. www.rainforest-alliance.org/press-releases/farmer-training-app-launch.

14 UPS. 2016. "UPS and Optoro Form Strategic Alliance to Enhance Retail Reverse Logistics Services". Posted on December 12, 2016. https://pressroom.ups.com/pressroom/ContentDetailsViewer.page?ConceptType=PressReleases&id=1482265436045-955.

15 IBM. n.d. "What Is Cloud Computing?" Accessed on October 1, 2017. www.ibm.com/cloud-computing/what-is-cloud-computing.

16 Resource. 2017. "Suez Partners with 'Uber of waste' to Digitalise European Services". Posted on January 13, 2017. http://resource.co/article/suez-partners-uber-waste-digitalise-european-services-11607.

17 American Chemical Society. n.d. "12 Principles of Green Chemistry". Accessed on September 25, 2017. www.acs.org/content/acs/en/greenchemistry/what-is-green-chemistry/principles/12-principles-of-green-chemistry.html.

18 If placed in a mould, mycelium rapidly grows to the desired shape, until halted through heat exposure. The following video illustrates the use of these organic matters, found in rotting organisms like tree trunks and agricultural by-products, for wall insulation. https://youtu.be/8XYbqLbeiL8.

19 Carbon Clean Solution Limited. n.d. "Innovation". Accessed on September 25, 2017. www.carboncleansolutions.com/technology/innovation.

20 Newlight Technologies. n.d. "Newlight Signs 10 Billion Pound Production License with IKEA". Accessed on September 27, 2017. www.newlight.com/newlight-signs-10-billion-pound-production-license-with-ikea-2/.

21 McGill University. 2017. "A More Sustainable Way to Refine Metals". Published on June 7, 2017. www.mcgill.ca/newsroom/channels/news/more-sustainable-way-refine-metals-268517.
22 Trucost. n.d. "Making the Business & Economic Case for Safer Chemistry". Accessed on September 12, 2017. www.trucost.com/publication/making-business-economic-case-safer-chemistry/.
23 "Tabby Evo", the primary platform developed by OSVehicle and available for download on its website (www.osvehicle.com/product/tabby-evo/), provides plans and blueprints for creating electric vehicles of all types, including city cars, agricultural machines, and military and multi-utility vehicles.
24 https://preciousplastic.com/en/machines.html.
25 Source: https://images.apple.com/environment/pdf/Apple_Environmental_Responsibility_Report_2016.pdf.
26 Apple. 2017. "Environmental Responsibility Report. 2017 Progress Report, Covering Fiscal Year 2016". Accessed on October 20, 2017. https://images.apple.com/environment/pdf/Apple_Environmental_Responsibility_Report_2017.pdf.

Bibliography

Accenture Strategy. 2016. "Car Sharing Service Outlook in China." Accessed on September 30, 2017. www.accenture.com/t20160701T062629__w__/cn-en/_acnmedia/PDF-24/Accenture-Insight-Car-Sharing-Service-China-v2.pdf.

Americal Chemical Society. n.d. "12 Principles of Green Chemistry." Accessed on September 25, 2017. www.acs.org/content/acs/en/greenchemistry/what-is-green-chemistry/principles/12-principles-of-green-chemistry.html.

Apple. 2017. "Environmental Responsibility Report. 2017 Progress Report, Covering Fiscal Year 2016." Accessed on October 20, 2017. https://images.apple.com/environment/pdf/Apple_Environmental_Responsibility_Report_2017.pdf.

AT&T. 2015. "Maersk Teams with AT&T to Track and Monitor Cold Shipping Containers." Posted on September 9, 2015. http://about.att.com/story/maersk_teams_with_att_to_track_cold_shipping_containers.html.

Autogrid. n.d. "The Energy Internet Starts Here." Accessed on September 29, 2017. www.auto-grid.com/about.

Bolton, Dough. 2016. "Apple Recovered One Tonne of Gold by Recycling IPhones Last Year." *The Indipendent*. Posted on April 17, 2016. www.independent.co.uk/life-style/gadgets-and-tech/news/apple-iphone-products-devices-gold-recycling-environmental-report-a6987841.html.

Bressanelli, Gianmarco, Federico Adrodegari, Marco Perona, and Nicola Saccani. 2018. "Exploring How Usage-Focused Business Models Enable Circular Economy through Digital." *Sustainability 2018* 10 (639). doi:10.3390/su10030639.

Carbon Clean Solution Limited. n.d. "Innovation." Accessed on September 25, 2017. www.carboncleansolutions.com/technology/innovation.

Chandler, David L. 2017. "Researchers Design One of the Strongest, Lightest Materials Known." *MIT News*. Posted on January 6, 2017. https://news.mit.edu/2017/3-d-graphene-strongest-lightest-materials-0106.

Dubey, Rameshwar, Angappa Gunasekaran, Stephen J. Childe, Samuel Fosso Wamba, and Thanos Papadopoulos. 2016. "The Impact of Big Data on

World-Class Sustainable Manufacturing." *The International Journal of Advanced Manufacturing Technology* 84 (1): 631–45.

Ellen MacArthur Foundation. 2016. "Intelligent Assets: Unlocking the Circular Economy Potential." Accessed on September 5, 2017. www.ellenmacarthur foundation.org/assets/downloads/publications/EllenMacArthurFoundation_Intelligent_Assets_080216.pdf.

IBM. n.d. "What Is Cloud Computing?" Accessed on October 1, 2017. www.ibm.com/cloud-computing/what-is-cloud-computing.

IKEA. 2018. "IKEA Saves One Million Meals Through Food Waste Initiative." Posted on March 13, 2018. https://newsroom.inter.ikea.com/News/ikea-saves-one-million-meals-through-food-waste-initiative/s/96d248e2-98cd-436a-846e-ceda216da74d.

International Communication Union (ITU). n.d. "ICT Facts and Figures 2017." Accessed on June 20, 2017. www.itu.int/en/ITU-D/Statistics/Pages/facts/default.aspx.

Liang, Lu-Hai, and Laura Paddison. 2016. "Could 3D Printing Help Tackle Poverty and Plastic Waste?" *The Guardian*. Posted on November 6, 2016 www.theguardian.com/sustainable-business/2016/nov/06/3d-printing-plastic-waste-poverty-development-protoprint-reflow-techfortrade.

Lieder, Michael, Farazee M. A. Asif, and Amir Rashid. 2017. "Towards Circular Economy Implementation: An Agent-Based Simulation Approach for Business Model Changes." *Autonomous Agents and Multi-Agent Systems* 31 (6): 1377–402. doi:10.1007/s10458-017-9365-9.

McGill University. 2017. "A More Sustainable Way to Refine Metals." Published on June 7, 2017. www.mcgill.ca/newsroom/channels/news/more-sustainable-way-refine-metals-268517.

McKinsey&Company. 2015. "Unlocking the Potential of the Internet of Things." Posted on June 1015. www.mckinsey.com/business-functions/digital-mckinsey/our-insights/the-internet-of-things-the-value-of-digitizing-the-physical-world.

Mell, Peter, and Timothy Grance. 2011. "The NIST Definition of Cloud Computing." *National Institute of Standards and Technology* (NIST). Accessed on May 5, 2018. https://nvlpubs.nist.gov/nistpubs/Legacy/SP/nistspecial publication800-145.pdf.

Morrison, Alan, and Subhankar Sinha. 2016. "A Primer on Blockchain: Infographic." PWC. Posted on December 6, 2016. http://usblogs.pwc.com/emerging-technology/a-primer-on-blockchain-infographic/.

Muirhead, Sam. 2016. "How Open Source Can Accelerate The Circular Economy Shift." *Circulate News*. Posted on April 13, 2016. http://circulatenews.org/2016/04/how-open-source-can-accelerate-the-circular-economy-shift/.

Newlight Technologies. n.d. "Newlight Signs 10 Billion Pound Production License with IKEA." Accessed on September 27, 2017. www.newlight.com/newlight-signs-10-billion-pound-production-license-with-ikea-2/.

Norton, Steven. 2015. "Internet of Things Market to Reach $1.7 Trillion by 2020: IDC." *The Wall Street Journal*. Posted on June 2, 2015. https://blogs.wsj.com/cio/2015/06/02/internet-of-things-market-to-reach-1-7-trillion-by-2020-idc/.

Philips. n.d. "CityTouch Light Management System." Accessed on February 4, 2017. www.lighting.philips.com/main/systems/lighting-systems/citytouch#.

Rainforest Alliance. 2017. "Scaling up Sustainable Agriculture Through Technology: The Rainforest Alliance Launches Farmer Training App." Posted on April 4, 2017. www.rainforest-alliance.org/press-releases/farmer-training-app-launch.

Rujanavech, Charissa, Joe Lessard, Sarah Chandler, Sean Shannon, Jeffrey Dahmus, and Rob Guzzo. 2016. "Liam - An Innovation Story." *Apple*. Accessed on July 20, 2017. www.apple.com/environment/pdf/Liam_white_paper_Sept2016.pdf.

Schwab, Klaus. 2016. "The Fourth Industrial Revolution: What It Means, How to Respond." *WEForum*. Posted on January 14, 2016. www.weforum.org/agenda/2016/01/the-fourth-industrial-revolution-what-it-means-and-how-to-respond/.

Siemens. n.d. "Creating the Most from Wind." Accessed on October 1, 2017 www.industry.siemens.com/verticals/global/en/wind-turbine/Documents/E20001-A110-P550-X-7600.pdf.

Trucost. n.d. "Making the Business & Economic Case for Safer Chemistry." Accessed on September 12, 2017. www.trucost.com/publication/making-business-economic-case-safer-chemistry/.

Unruh, Gregory. 2015. "The Killer App for 3D Printing? The Circular Economy." *MIT Sloan Management Review*. Posted on December 8, 2015. http://sloanreview.mit.edu/article/the-killer-app-for-3d-printing-the-circular-economy/.

UPS. 2016. "UPS and Optoro Form Strategic Alliance to Enhance Retail Reverse Logistics Services." Posted on December 12, 2016. https://pressroom.ups.com/pressroom/ContentDetailsViewer.page?ConceptType=PressReleases&id=1482265436045-955.

Vodafone. 2016. "Vodafone and Philips Join Forces for Connected Lighting and Smart City Services." Posted on March 14, 2016. www.vodafone.com/content/index/media/vodafone-group-releases/2016/philips-connected-lighting.html.

Wang, Gang, Angappa Gunasekaran, and Eric W.T. Ngai. 2016. "Distribution Network Design with Big Data: Model and Analysis." Annals of Operations Research 1–13. https://doi.org/10.1007/s10479-016-2263-8.

Yin, Yadong. 2017. "Reprintable Paper Becomes a Reality." University of California. Posted on March 1, 2017. www.universityofcalifornia.edu/news/reprintable-paper-becomes-reality.

5 Business Models for a CE

5.1 Introduction

A business model is generally referred to as the way a company organizes itself to generate value for customers and thus revenues from its operations. Traditional business models, where the company purely focuses on increasing sales and loses track of its products after the point of sale, are no longer fit for the 21st century. As the Circular Economy (CE) progressively moved from theory to practice, new ways of conducting business took shape leading to solid economic models that address the environmental concerns outlined in the previous chapters. What is more, recent research (Kavadias et al. 2016) attests that circular business models are most likely to be successful and widely adopted to the point of transforming entire industries, thanks to a range of positive characteristics that foster organizations to be agile and adaptive in a more collaborative ecosystem. To be successful however, CE business models need to be carefully tailored to the specific set of capabilities and resources of each company; operationalized through modern technological advancements; and directed to the opportunities in the market in which the firm operates. Building on a number of studies attempting to frame CE business models and to define their key characteristics (Bakker et al. 2014; Bocken et al. 2014; Lacy and Rutqvist 2015; Lüdeke-Freund et al. 2018), we have defined four macro-categories:

- **Net-Zero Innovation** involves the operation of environmentally friendly production processes, with inputs and final products carrying a negligible or no ecological footprint, if a net positive impact on the environment is not achievable.
- **Servitization** is an innovative business model where the ownership of the equipment is not transferred to the customer. Instead of selling a product, the company charges the user for the service delivered by the asset itself.
- **Product Life Extension** focuses on creating products that last longer and remain economically useful; hence, its emphasis is on designing products for easy re-use/repair/refurbishment/re-manufacturing and on establishing reverse cycles for their treatment.

- **Product Residual Value Recovery** is about exploiting the residual value of a product, through its further treatment (recycling), when this cannot be re-marketed or has reached the end of its life cycle.

5.2 Net-Zero Innovation

The first CE business model is concerned with reducing the environmental impacts of production processes and products, to a point of not producing any environmental externality. In some instances, it is even possible to seek a positive impact on the environment (primarily by transforming the used product into nourishment for the geosphere). While R&D and manufacturing activities for net-zero processes and products have significantly developed in recent years (e.g. technologies for renewable energy in electric cars and biochemicals as input materials for biodegradable bags), it is the concept of producing goods that can have a positive contribution on the environment to have gained most attention lately (McDonough and Braungart 2002a). However, apart from a few exceptions like carpet tiles from Interface and mattresses from Naturepedic (products hitting the news in 2017 because they are developed through carbon-negative recyclable materials[1]), net-positive manufacturing requires a tremendous effort by companies, and at the moment the vast majority is simply not ready for the transition. Companies wishing to embark on such a journey must in fact re-invent their production processes altogether, phasing out all toxic materials and replacing them with ecologically friendly alternatives. Assuming that production processes continue to evolve towards circularity and that green material science keeps maturing, one can envision a progressive overtake by environmentally positive products. External forces are expected to concurrently enable the transition: a progressive scarcity and price volatility of environmentally harmful raw materials, and the enforcement of tougher environmental legislative frameworks (e.g. climate change regulations). Companies pursuing a business model based on net-zero innovation fall under one or more of the following categories:

- Firms producing environmentally friendly materials and products that are sold in the B2B marketplace. In recent years, the fashion and clothing industry has witnessed a growing interest for sustainable material innovation driven by push (increased environmental awareness of consumers and tighter regulations) and pull (new markets to conquer and the need to secure long-term viability of operations) forces. Fashion brands are increasingly looking for bio-based materials to use in their manufacturing processes, and new companies are emerging accordingly to supply the demand. Headquartered in Catania (Italy), Orange Fiber turns citrus juice by-products into a sustainable silk-like fabric that can be coloured and printed like standard textiles. The company has already supplied the luxury brand Salvatore Ferragamo for the development of its 2017 Capsule Collection. In the U.K., a company named Ananas Anam patented a process to convert a pineapple by-product into a unique material – Pinatex – used as an alternative to leather, plastic, and technical textiles in a variety of products across fashion (bags and shoes), automotive, aeronautic, and furnishings.[2] In Switzerland, Rohner makes an ecologically harmless synthetic fabric – Climatex – that shows high qualities of temperature balance, moisture reduction, and energy saving, making it highly suitable against climate obstacles in interiors, healthcare, automotive, transportation, clothing, and accessories (e.g. shoes). Apart from the production of fabrics, net-zero innovation is also finding other applications. Favini, for example, is an Italian producer of natural fibre-based paper solutions supplying fashion, luxury, design, IT, and technical sportswear. Also in Italy is GF Biochemicals, which developed a proprietary technology to produce levulinic acid, a bio-based chemical produced at commercial scale directly from biomass that replaces oil-based products in fabric care, skin care, foams, cleansers, colour cosmetics, and formulation aids.

- Businesses specialized in developing innovative net-zero products for the public. The Society for Research and Initiatives for Sustainable Technologies and Institutions (SRISTI) is an Indian grassroots organization that develops natural organic agro-products, like fertilizers and pest control herbal compositions, to diminish the impact of nitrogen-based fertilizers on the environment. In 2013, SRISTI partnered up with USAID to start transferring low-cost agricultural innovations and technologies in African countries as well. Another organization trying to resolve a critical environmental issue in the country is Bakey's, which sells one-time-use edible cutlery to reduce plastic waste. But multinational corporations are also active. In 2017, Nike announced the development of a chemical-free recyclable packaging solution for its sportswear, designed in tandem with Taiwanese firm Miniwiz. The durable, modular, and highly versatile solution (usable also as a backpack) is manufactured using post-consumer materials like milk and orange juice containers. The new packaging was first tested in China, before being adopted globally by the brand.[3]

- Companies producing green inputs and energy for their own operations. Some companies like Facebook, Google, and Ikea have already installed massive renewable energy plants for their own offices or stores. In Nevada (U.S.A.), electric car manufacturer Tesla is building a 10-million-square-foot factory designed to operate at net-zero energy consumption and has carbon-neutral production processes; all operations will be powered through solar, wind, and geothermal energy sources embedded within the factory itself. North American theme park Walt Disney World teamed up with Harvest Power – a specialized firm in anaerobic digestion processes – to meet its huge energy demand by processing food waste. Food scraps, used cooking oil, and grease are collected from the restaurants and hotels in the complex and then treated in a nearby massive system of tanks to produce electricity.

- Companies fostering the adoption of net-zero practices along their supply chains. Generally, this approach concerns primarily air emissions and water management. In the garment sector, a recent alliance between the International Finance Corporation (IFC) and Hennes & Mauritz (H&M) aims at boosting the adoption of renewable energy across the company's tier-1 and tier-2 suppliers[4] in China, India, and Bangladesh.[5] In a similar fashion, U.S. retailer Walmart revealed in its 2017 Global Sustainability Report plans to team up with WWF and other NGOs to create a dedicated platform featuring an emission reduction toolkit anticipated to help its suppliers worldwide take practical actions in reducing their carbon footprint. The project is part of a broader strategy aiming for the retailer to achieve a saving of one billion tonnes in emissions from its supply chain by 2030. A decarbonization of the supply chain is a growing concern among many brands, some of them committing to "science-based" carbon reduction targets[6] and seeking support from the Science Based Target Initiative, an organization set up by the WWF, UN Global Compact, the World Resource Institute, and the Carbon Disclosure Project (CDP) to drive climate action among international brands. Currently, 300+ companies, including super-brands like Coca-Cola, P&G, Dell, and Sony, have already embarked on the programme.

5.2.1 Profit Sources

Environmentally friendly products sold in the B2C sector can count – especially in developed countries – on an increasing base of environmentally conscious customers willing to pay a premium price. Cost-effectiveness is the other reason for producing green solutions through net-zero processes, either for self-use or to be sold. Indeed, by placing net-zero considerations right at the beginning of the design phase, companies can take decisions that reduce costs (e.g. no environmental liabilities and reduced H&S expenditures because of no chemicals being used) and concurrently enhance product value (McDonough and Braungart 2002b).

5.2.2 Most Suitable Products/Markets/Industries

Theoretically, all industries and markets are suitable for this business model and in fact the production of green alternative inputs/products has developed across all sectors in recent times. Certainly, highly pollut-ing industries facing tougher environmental regulations and mounting public pressure (oil and gas, chemicals, and automotive) would see more benefits in a timely adoption of this model.

5.2.3 Key Areas of Intervention for Implementation Strategy

Strong R&D efforts are required to come up with ecologically harmless alternatives and such determination can result primarily in innovative product design or discoveries in material science (enabling technology). The Cradle2Cradle approach (McDonough and Braungart 2002a) can serve as an effective roadmap for any business wishing to re-invent its production process and a growing number of companies, including super brands, are considering it. In May 2017, the French cosmetics multinational L'Oreal announced the C2C Certification for two of its products based on a positive assessment of their material health and material reutilization, as well as a positive valuation of renewable en-ergy, carbon management, water stewardship, and social fairness in the production processes (Lemmon 2017). Besides developing in-house ex-pertise and technology to make the transition happen, firms can also count on supporting organizations (external collaboration) as useful allies at any stage of the process, and most notably to lay the founda-tions of the new design process (e.g. information gathering regarding materials currently used and their toxicity, possible alternatives, etc.). In this respect, specialized consultancies (e.g. the Environmental Protection Encouragement Agency – EPEA) and peer-to-peer initiatives, like the Bio-based Industries Consortium in Europe, can play a significant role. The latter is a Brussels-based non-profit international association estab-lished in 2012 and counting 200+ members, all committed to invest in collaborative research, development, and exhibition of bio-based tech-nologies to "accelerate the innovation and market uptake of bio-based products and to position Europe as a world-leading, competitive bio-based economy where the basic building blocks for chemicals, materials and advanced biofuels are derived from renewable biological resources" (BioBased Consortium website[7]). The project currently counts on several renowned science-based and engineering companies (like Dupont Indus-trial Biosciences, Novozymes, Cargill, and BASF) which were signed as full members and cover agriculture, agro-food, technology providers, forestry/pulp and paper, chemicals, and the energy sector.

5.3 Servitization

The servitization business model implies a shift away from the typical transaction-based system of product sales and ownership, towards a more fluid approach whereby customers are provided with alternative service-based solutions (or Product-Service Systems – PSSs). Despite the conceptualization of this business model going back 30 years (Vandermerwe and Rada 1988), it is only in the past decade that a significant number of western firms have started to seriously consider it as an option, perhaps due to two primary factors: the development of technological innovations (e.g. smartphone applications, sensors, and IoT) that make servitization easier and cheaper to implement, and the mounting need to escape the price war affecting many businesses struggling to increase sales in already saturated markets. From a customer perspective, in fact, opting for service-based solutions can mean substantial savings – largely in terms of eliminating cost of ownership and maintenance expenses – an incentive that appeals to many, especially in periods of financial crises. Researchers have identified three main categories of PSSs (Tukker 2015):

- **Product-oriented services** consist of basically ancillary services (e.g. insurance contracts or consultancy) still largely centred on the selling of a product. From a CE standpoint, this category means very little and will therefore be left out from further discussion.
- **Use-oriented services**. Despite the focus here is still on the product being provided to the customer, the firm retains its ownership, selling instead the right to use the asset for either a certain amount of time or the full life of the product. Three subcategories of this model are easily identifiable. First is product leasing, whereby the service is guaranteed to a single user and a fixed rate is paid in return to the provider. By doing so, the firm can retain and monitor its assets, while facilitating the tracking, upgrading, or upcycling of material components. US-based carpet tile manufacturer Interface has been a pioneer of servitization through its "Evergreen Lease" programme. The company produces, installs, cleans, maintains, and replaces carpets, while customers lease the service of keeping a space carpeted, rather than buying carpet. In the energy sector, SunPower is an American corporation that leases out electricity-generating solar PV power systems. The company provides the design, permitting, financing, installation, operations, and maintenance of a solar energy system on a customer's property, while always maintaining full ownership of the assets. Next is product renting or sharing. Contrary to leasing, this subcategory does not envision exclusive rights over a product, therefore allocating sequential use to different users. Floow2, for example, is a business-to-business digital sharing marketplace where companies can rent, from other businesses experiencing overcapacity, anything ranging from office spaces to heavy machinery. Recently, Floow2 has expanded in the healthcare market by setting up a dedicated platform for the rental of specialized medical equipment and facilities. Usually, product renting or

sharing entails pay-per-use solutions, where the owner sells access to high value products on a per-use basis. Car sharing companies charge customers for the minutes they spend on each ride. Finally, there is product pooling, where multiple users share the product simultaneously. Carpooling operator BlaBlaCar is an example of this business model.

- **Result-oriented services.** These focus on the result needed by the client (e.g. going from "A" to "B", lighting a building, etc.) rather than the means used to achieve it (e.g. travelling by train rather than airplane, installing LED instead of typical light bulbs, etc.). Hence, via this kind of service agreements, one party commits to guaranteeing a certain service performance, regardless of the specific products used. Philips Lighting, for example, charges a fixed rate to provide and maintain lighting services to airports (e.g. Amsterdam Shipol) and cities (e.g. Washington D.C., Los Angeles, Amsterdam, etc.).

5.3.1 Profit Sources

The servitization model generates smaller, but continuous revenue flows as opposed to the selling of a product, generally based on one upfront payment by customers. Also, this model ensures greater customer loyalty and retention, as the company finds itself better aligned with customer expectations – product reliability and durability. Companies adopting servitization will hence be less subject to changes in customer preferences.

5.3.2 Most Suitable Products/Markets/Industries

The business model is best suited for expensive products, characterized by high production costs and short or infrequent usage; the ideal situation is when these products also require frequent maintenance operations and do not follow quick changes in style and fashion (Tukker 2015). That said, servitization has been successfully implemented in many industries: from complex and elaborated assets like cars, elevators, copiers, home appliances (Egerton-Read 2017a), and air conditioners (Egerton-Read 2017b), down to carpet tiles and tyres. As part of a differentiation strategy, the model appears to be very valuable in industries marked by fierce competition and aggressive pricing, like automotive. Also, there are important differences between servitization for B2B and B2C. In B2B transactions, the client is usually less interested in fashionable designs and add-ons, but more focused on product characteristics like reliability and high-quality performance. In terms of receptivity, acceptance and familiarity are higher among younger generations of customers, which generally have limited access to funds and for which the responsibility of ownership is less appealing.

5.3.3 Key Areas of Intervention for Implementation Strategy

Enabling technologies play a major role in mainstreaming servitization. Researchers at the Cambridge Service Alliance, a global partnership between businesses and universities, have selected the top technologies that are helping businesses transitioning towards a servitization of their products, among which stand out (Dinges et al. 2017): advanced predictive analytics to foresee product failures; communication technologies to remotely adjust machines and products; mobile platforms to access data for enterprise resource planning purposes and to interact with customers; consumption monitoring technologies capable of collecting and assessing large amounts of information to create customer-specific service offerings; and geospatial technologies to track machines, products (components), and users.

Especially thanks to predictive analytics, sensors, and machine-to-machine communication, companies today are able to get instant information about the physical status of a product and quickly decide to repair or replace it, as needed. The monitoring of large volumes of shared, rented, and leased products is now possible at low costs for the business, meaning more affordable pricing for interested customers. In addition to harnessing the latest technology, firms choosing to transform their products into services also need expertise with the most recent circular product design principles. By keeping ownership of the products, businesses can in fact maximize their value throughout the entire life cycle. Design concepts like durability, easy maintenance, and modularity become highly valuable during activities of disassembly, upgrading, recovery, and recycling.

5.4 Product Life Extension

As the name suggests, product life extension is about designing products built to last and to remain economically useful for as long as possible. This approach, sometimes referred to as "Classic Long-Life Model" (Bakker et al. 2014), is specific to those brands that place the product's characteristics of robustness, quality, and endurance at the heart of their marketing strategies. Examples are Patagonia (clothing), Miele (home appliances), and Rolls Royce (automotive). Specific to this business model are also all those reverse cycle activities aimed at prolonging the life cycle of a product or its functioning parts (re-use, repair, refurbishment, and re-manufacturing). Implementing such CE activities carries serious implications for companies as they redefine consumption patterns by slowing down disposal and replacement rates, and by meeting the real needs of their customer rather than promoting "wants". Therefore, this innovative approach to business, where firms place environmental stewardship and sustainable consumption at the heart of their strategy while concurrently remaining profitable through novel promotional activities and deeper customer engagement, has also been defined "sufficiency-driven business model innovation" (Bocken and Short 2016). A recent study on the adoption of CE among Standard & Poor's (S&P) 500 listed large cap firms in the period 2005–2014 shows that businesses operationalize this model primarily through maintenance and – to a lesser extent – refurbishment activities, while still undervaluing other valuable product life extension strategies like re-manufacturing (Bocken et al. 2017; Vogtlander et al. 2017).

5.4.1 Profit Sources

Companies exploiting this model need to secure revenues by charging a premium price for their durable and high-quality products (Bocken and Short 2016), as well as by providing customers with add-ons and upgrades, plus quality repairing and refurbishing services (Lacy and Rutqvist 2015). As a matter of fact, the lower number of units sold must be compensated by revenues generated via a range of complementary services. Businesses choosing this model also profit from enhanced loyalty by customers, who in fact manifest an increased trust in companies that phase out planned product obsolescence and align their interests with those of customers. Finally, businesses will gain unique insights into customer preferences, needs, and wants as the degree of contact between the parties will increase through the ongoing services provided. This information will help in the definition of better targeted future offerings.

5.4.2 Most Suitable Products/Markets/Industries

Product life extension strategies, like refurbishing and re-manufacturing, have proved effective for more complex assets in B2B niche markets like heavy machinery, photocopiers, and car components (Vogtlander et al. 2017). In particular, some product characteristics are the key to facilitate re-manufacturing activities, namely: the product's core being suitable for integration into restored versions; the components of the product asked to be returned having a high market value that does not depreciate much overtime; the original product being all made in a single factory and not assembled in various successive steps; and both process and product technology not changing too rapidly (Sundin et al. 2009). One of the most successful business examples of product re-manufacturing is CatReman, a subsidiary of Caterpillar. Since 1973, CatReman has been gradually expanding its re-manufacturing activities, now employing more than 3,500 people and producing restored parts for Cat machines and engines, as well as components for customers spanning several industries such as Perkins and Alcoa (industrial), Ford (automotive), and Honeywell (aerospace and defence). Designing for long life might prove rather challenging for those products that are subject to rapid techno-logical change, like consumer electronics. However, to overcome such obstacles, modular design is often an effective solution.

5.4.3 Key Areas of Intervention for Implementation Strategy

Companies which decide to tackle this circular business model need to focus on three different, but intertwined areas of intervention. First, there is a necessity to implement circular design principles to allow for easier disassembly and further processing of returned items. In doing so, designers will need to adopt strategies aimed at addressing the multiple challenges linked to the enhanced complexity of today's products and materials – e.g. the increased number of materials used and the presence of more combinations of different components and connections (Peiró et al. 2017). Next, it is vital to set up efficient reverse cycle channels, beginning with the collection of used products (an activity generally re-ferred to as take-back programmes), through the creation of dedicated return points, pickup services, and send-back programmes. Finally, if collection of used items can at times be accomplished by leveraging in-house expertise and facilities, sorting, re-processing, and re-marketing are often more complex activities that require partnering up with se-lected business partners (external collaboration).

But external collaborations can be essential also to devise a successful take-back programme. As a matter of fact, in some circumstances, it can be a rather complicated task, mostly because the linear economic para-digm incited firms to structure themselves in a way that they lost sight of products after point of sale. Additionally, return flows need to be pre-dictable, reliable, and match the working capacity of the infrastructure set up to collect and re-process the items (e.g. return points, refurbishing facilities, etc.). To tackle these issues, businesses have forged partner-ships with logistic operators like UPS, or specialized organizations like ecoATM, that facilitate the process of collecting used products from cus-tomers. In North America, Nespresso, a worldwide leader in single-serve coffee, leveraged UPS nationwide presence to assist its customers in re-turning used capsules. The partnership operates in 48 American states, where Nespresso customers can bring their bags of empty capsules to one of 88,000 UPS points spread across the territory. The logistics com-pany is then responsible for delivering the items to Nespresso's business partner AgChoice, which separates the aluminium from coffee grounds, hence commencing the recycling process.[8] North America is also home to another fruitful collaboration at the collection level. Numerous retailers have in fact teamed up with ecoATM, an organization that equips stores and malls with smart recycling kiosks for technological devices. When fed like a smartphone or an MP3 player, the kiosk instantly assesses the conditions of the product, determining its appropriate market value and compensating the user with cash. The process only takes a few minutes.

Apart from the issues to be addressed at the take-back scheme level, a company wanting to establish a complete set of reverse cycle operations must strategically think about the best options for the sorting and further re-processing of the collected goods. In the most basic scenario, things will be sorted according to whether they can be re-entered in the market. More advanced circular companies will establish complex sorting processes, where no item is discarded and multiple life extension options (re-using, repairing, refurbishing, and re-manufacturing) are in place. In the automotive industry, French carmaker Renault runs a state-of-the-art re-manufacturing plant in Choisy-le-Roy where not a single component of car carcasses that enter its premises get wasted – 40% are re-used to produce re-manufactured car parts like gearboxes, injectors, and turbocompressors; 50% are recycled; and the remaining 10% get valorized in treatment centres.[9] In the fast-fashion industry, efficient sorting of items returned is a crucial part of a business model based on material life extension, as each item would be treated differently according to its conditions. Items in an acceptable shape can be repaired or re-sold in low-income regions, while those in poor conditions used as inputs for the manufacturing of new collections or, if textiles are no longer suitable for wear, would be cascaded into other products like cleaning cloths or insulating materials for the auto industry.

Out of all CE business models, those based on product life extension are arguably the most disruptive for companies. To be successful, firms must ensure strong internal alignment, with closer and more frequent interactions among designers, operation managers, and marketing heads to guarantee all tasks being integrated towards shared circular goals. Indeed, as design policies (modularity, disassembly, re-use, etc.) will be established within the company, they will need to be communicated down to operations and marketing. An example of strong internal alignment is what allowed Dutch furniture company Desko to benefit from a circular business model rooted in a three-tier buy-back scheme. According to this model, Desko designers conceive furniture that lasts longer and is easy to disassemble and refurbish, so that the company can buy back the assets twice during their lifetime and return them to good working conditions: the first owner is paid 10% of the original purchase price when the item reaches end-of-use, the second is given 5%. Desko's sales force is then trained to market the refurbished furniture at 50% and 75% discounts, respectively.[10]

As the variety of cases presented illustrates, every situation is different, and a company needs to carefully select the most appropriate approach to bring its products back to life. Each process requires the establishment of very different operations, and thus careful strategic thinking. To reduce the likelihood of mistakes, companies can take advantage of specialized supporting tools, such as the Reverse Logistics Maturity Model (RLMM)[11] developed by the Ellen MacArthur Foundation in collaboration with Cranfield University and the Deutsche Post DHL Group.

RLMM is a comprehensive framework that provides key insights into how to set up and run effective return management processes in accordance with three different demand-driven archetypes: low value extended producer responsibility (mass production items distributed via retail networks, e.g. consumer electronics, shipping pallets, etc.); service parts logistics (like machinery and automotive parts); and advanced industrial products (complex items like medical equipment).

5.5 Product Residual Value Recovery

Product Residual Value Recovery can be implemented when the life extension of products is not feasible through re-use, repair, re-manufacturing, or refurbishing. In fact, under a CE scenario, recycling is considered the least efficient way of re-entering products into the value chain. Researchers have identified four broad types of recycling practices, divided according to their potential of recovering the residual value of a product (Bocken et al. 2016). While the first category does not belong to our definition of "recycling", given that applies to "re-using" a product for its original purpose and without modifications (e.g. donating a PC to a friend who will continue using it without altering any of its parts), the other three include: transforming used products (e.g. discarded tyres) into items of lower quality, without altering the chemical structure of the recycled material; converting discarded products (e.g. plastic bottles) through chemical or heat processes that break down the structure into core components (molecules) and then re-process them to create a completely new material or item; and finally generating energy from recycled materials.

In recent times, practices to transform discarded/used products have received increasing attention from the business sector. This tendency is arguably a consequence of recognizing landfills as mines,[12] often cheaper and easier to access than virgin natural deposits. Since 2012, Interface and its business partner Aquafil (an Italian multinational producer of carpet and textile yarn) have been working with coastal communities in the Philippines and Cameroon to collect and re-process discarded fishing nets from the bottom of the seas. When the local community retrieves a sufficient amount of nets, these are collected by Aquafil and transformed – through the Econyl Regeneration System – into nylon yarn to make Interface's carpet tiles. So far, the Net-Works project has helped reclaim 140+ metric tons of fishing nets from the oceans, with Interface now aiming to scale up the model in more geographical areas by 2020.[13] Probably also due to the success of this initiative, recycling fishing nets has become a conventional business activity in various parts of the world: Danish cleantech company Plastix has set up a certification for recycled fishing nets, while "Circular Oceans" is a three-year European-funded project launched during 2015 to inspire communities in the Northern fringe of Europe and in the Arctic region to realize the hidden economic opportunities of discarded fishing nets and ropes.[14]

Of course, it is also possible to have outputs generated from the processing of one's own used products/materials, hence creating a sort of closed loop within the same supply chain. Dell and Hewlett-Packard (HP) have established robust reverse cycling operations whereby plastic from discarded computers (Dell) and toner cartridges (HP) get recovered and turned into input material for new products. Today, recycled plastic is present in more than 90 different Dell products[15] and the percentage of HP ink cartridges manufactured with closed-loop recycled plastic exceeds 80%.[16] In the automotive sector, Fuji Heavy Industry – the parent company of Subaru – runs a manufacturing plant in Indiana (U.S.A.) where all manufacturing waste is re-processed through one of the methods previously described (material transformation or energy generation).

Industrial symbiosis arguably represents the most advanced concept to recover the residual value of products. It is basically an association between two or more industrial facilities or companies, in which the wastes or by-products of one become the raw materials for another. Kalundborg Symbiosis set up in Denmark since the 1980s is certainly the most prominent example of industrial symbiosis ecosystem in the world. It is designed to ensure a continuous flow of water, energy, and materials among several public and private enterprises, which include the world's largest producer of insulin, the world's leading enzyme producer, the largest sewage treatment plant in Northern Europe, the largest power plant in Denmark, and the largest oil refinery in the Baltic Region. More recently, China (that counts more than 1,500 industrial parks) has also taken decisive steps towards industrial symbiosis systems, as part of an ambitious nationwide CE plan[17] (McDowall et al. 2017). Since the turn of the century, Eco-Industrial Parks (EIPs) have appeared extensively across the country, under the supervision of the Ministry of Environmental Protection and the National Development and Reform Commission (Zhang et al. 2010). These institutions, together with the central government, have promoted a number of measures to support the establishment of EIPs, like: introducing stricter environmental and resource utilization standards or the provision of financial support and planning guidance (Yu et al. 2015). In 2005, Suzhou New District (SND) was selected to become one of new EIPs in the country and since then, it has grown to an astonishing size: more than 15,000 enterprises are involved, with many operating in IT, electronics, biotech, and medical equipment (Mathews and Tan 2016). Through participation in industrial symbiosis ecosystems, firms operating in Chinese EIPs have been found to be better placed to improve their competitive position, principally by lowering overall production costs and by reducing environmental externalities (Yuan and Shi 2009). The recycling of solid waste and industrial water at SND, for example, has reached 90+% with most companies relying on locally sourced and cost-efficient supplies of raw materials.[18]

5.5.1 Profit Sources

Product Residual Value Recovery has given birth to several companies that are fully dedicated to the provision of recycled components for production. One good example is Aquafil, based in Trento (Italy) and leader in nylon research and production. The company has developed a process to chemically recycle nylon that achieves the same fibre quality as virgin production. When the model is established in closed-loop operations (within the same company or supply chain), this usually leads to reduced production costs and avoidance of landfill taxes.

5.5.2 Most Suitable Products/Markets/Industries

Developing products using industrial waste, instead of post-consumer waste, can be advantageous, notably because the former generally has a more predictable composition, and its waste stream is more reliable (Singh and Ordonez 2016). But the real long-term competitive advantage linked to recycling activities is primarily attainable in industries where manufacturing heavily relies on rare-Earth elements.[19] Since 2012, Honda Motor has been using a dedicated recycling facility to extract metals from used car components – primarily the nickel-metal hybrid batteries of Honda vehicles. The process, enabled by a collaboration with Japan Metals & Chemicals, allows for the mass production of high-quality recycled rare metals then used in the manufacturing of new cars.[20]

Rare-Earth elements aside, products made of glass, paper, and plastic – for which recycling processes are now relatively mature – and with low cost and intense usage (e.g. water bottles) are generally well suited to re-enter production systems through recycling. Food is also a suitable candidate, thanks to the evolution in anaerobic digestion technology, which makes it possible to break down organic matter (such as animal or food waste) to produce biogas and bio-fertilizers. Construction and electronics are further industries to have displayed an enormous potential with this business model, particularly when considering urban mining. The construction sector has been the target of a number of important measures developed for the collection of specific end-of-life materials, such as the San Francisco "Demolition Debris Recovery Ordinance" in 2006 or the 2000 "Construction Materials Act" in Japan (Silva et al. 2017). For its part, the electronic industry produces tons of e-waste every year. In Europe and the U.S., much of these discarded products are shipped – legally or illegally – to third world countries,[21] where they get disposed of in open-sky landfills. Agbogbloshie, a former wetland and suburb of Accra, Ghana, is the largest e-waste site in the world. Poisons such as lead, mercury, arsenic, dioxins, furans,

and brominated flame retardants are known to be running into the sur-
rounding soil and water with obvious devastating consequences for the
environment and human health. Tests run by Greenpeace labs on water
and soil from Agbogbloshie revealed concentrations of toxins at levels a hundred times higher than tolerated.[22] Now, pioneering circular
companies are investigating ways to turn this global ecological problem
into an economic opportunity. For example, California-based BlueOak
Resources is currently building the first American urban mining refinery, a facility fully dedicated to recovering valuable metals like gold and
copper from e-waste.

5.5.3 Key Areas of Intervention for Implementation Strategy

As for the life extension business model, firms taking steps to execute
residual value recovery need to set up adequate reverse cycle channels for
the collection of by-products/waste. Similarly, implementing the right
enabling technology and infrastructure will be crucial. Major strategic
decisions will need to be taken as to whether develop in-house expertise and set up internal facilities or, rather, outsource these activities.
The former approach is what, for example, Apple is pursuing by leveraging its state-of-the-art recycling robot "Liam". Apple's move follows
its commitment to shift towards a 100% closed-loop supply chain that
would supply enough recycled material to manufacture the whole suite
of Apple products (Egerton-Read 2017c). One of the major reasons that
led Apple to invest internally on the development of new recycling capabilities was the intrinsic complexity of efficiently taking a smartphone
apart (Wiens 2016). In sectors where the collection and treatment of
used items are simpler, these activities can be outsourced to reverse logistic experts and specialized recycling organizations, like I:CO or Veolia.
Operating in the clothing industry, I:CO is a service provider specialized
in apparel reverse logistics, which manages the transport of used clothes
to its own plants, where items are then sorted for either re-use, recycling,
or energy generation. The company, with facilities across Europe, India,
and the U.S.A., has already attracted the interest of major brands like
H&M, Levi's, Intimissimi, Adler, and Reno. At the cross-industry level,
Veolia is a global provider of environmental management services, specialized in devising cutting-edge solutions for recycling by-products and
waste. The French-based company exhibits clients with various needs,
spanning: energy recovery from the by-products of whisky production,
turning biomass ash into a phosphate-rich fertilizer, or recycling used
plastic bags into refuse sacks.[23]

Table 5.1 Business Models for a CE

	Business Models			
	Net-Zero Innovation	Servitization	Product Life Extension	Product Residual Value Recovery
a Profit sources	Premium-price for conscious customers; Cost-effectiveness.	Smaller but ongoing revenues; Customer loyalty and retention.	Premium price for durable and high-quality products; Continuous revenue flows through add-ons and complementary services; Customer loyalty and retention.	Reduced production costs and avoidance of landfill taxes; Some companies are dedicated to the provision of recycled components to third parties.
b Most suitable products/markets/industries	Applicable in all industries; Highly polluting industries (oil & gas, chemicals, automotive) expected to benefit the most.	Expensive products with high production costs, sporadic usage, recurrent maintenance; Industries with high competition (e.g. automotive) and/or elaborated goods (e.g. elevators, aircon); Younger generations in B2C markets.	Complex assets (e.g. heavy machinery, photocopiers); Contained speed of change in process and product technology.	Products of low cost and intense usage, made of glass, paper or plastic (e.g. water bottles); Industries where rare-Earth elements play a key role (e.g. cars), but also food, construction and electronics; Urban mining (e-waste).
c Key areas of intervention for implementation strategy	R&D dept. (product design and material science); External partnerships for collaborative research.	Enabling technologies; Product design.	Product design; Reverse cycles (starting from take-back programmes), often requiring solid collaborations with external partners.	Reverse cycle channels for by-products and waste.

Table 5.1 offers a quick comparison of the four categories of CE business models, according to their sources of profit, industry suitability, and considerations for implementation.

5.6 Conclusions

This chapter presented four general approaches to business that companies can pursue to implement principles of circularity: net-zero innovation, servitization, product life extension, and product residual value recovery. While the environmental implications of the four CE business models are huge, businesses are increasingly considering them for their economic benefits as well (Linder and Williander 2017). When compared to existing linear systems of production, these models in fact reveal: new revenue streams and higher margins; greater differentiation in the market through a Sustained Competitive Advantage (SCA); stronger customers relationships and deeper understanding of their needs; reduced manufacturing costs; and increased brand value.

Being the CE still in its infancy, most companies are currently exploring one single business model – generally considered to be the best fit for the core activities of the firm. This is particularly true for established companies that have been operating in the linear economy for decades and for which the transition to more circular practices will inevitably require greater efforts than a start-up. However, the four CE business models can be leveraged in combination and this seems to be the preferred approach by new business ventures. Two examples of young companies leveraging multiple circular business models simultaneously are Mud Jeans and Share'ngo.

Mud Jeans is a young Dutch denim company built with a distinct circular profile in mind as it takes advantage of all four CE business models. The firm, with business partner Yousstex, has developed an innovative laser technique which dramatically reduces the impact of jeans manufacturing on the environment (net-zero innovation). Mud Jeans leases pair of jeans at €5 per month, giving the customer the option to buy the product after one year, or change model and extend the rental, or return the jeans and end the relationship. Free repairs are also included in the offering. For those clients who decide to keep the jeans, the company encourages recovery by offering financial incentives to return the item to the company when the life of the product eventually comes to an end (servitization). Returned jeans are then sorted so that materials continue to flow through one of three loops: cleaned and re-used; upcycled and sold as unique vintage pairs; or recycled (product life extension). Worn out jeans that go into recycling are shredded, cut into pieces, and blended with virgin cotton to create a new denim yarn (residual value recovery). Share'ngo is an Italian car sharing operator currently running fleets in several major cities. The company combines two circular business models together. First, registered users are charged on a pay-per-use basis (servitization). Second, each vehicle, equipped with a battery that can last for more than 100 km, is completely electrical (net-zero innovation).

Notes

1 Floordaily. 2017. "Interface Unveils Carbon Negative Carpet Tile". Posted on June 8, 2017. www.floordaily.net/flooring-news/interface-unveils-carbon-negative-carpet-tile and Sustainable Brands. 2017. "Braskem, Sealed Air, Naturepedic Unveil Renewable, Carbon-Negative Polyethylene Foam". Posted on June 20, 2017. www.sustainablebrands.com/news_and_views/chemistry_materials_packaging/sustainable_brands/braskem_sealed_air_naturepedic_unvei

2 Sportswear giant Puma already prototyped a model of shoes made of Pinatex.

3 Jessica Lyons Hardcastle. 2017. "Nike, Circular Economy Firm Miniwiz Develop Sustainable Packaging from Trash". *Environmental Leader.* Posted on March 27, 2017. www.environmentalleader.com/2017/03/nike-circular-economy-firm-miniwiz-develop-sustainable-packaging-trash/

4 Tier 2 companies supply Tier 1 with the materials and products needed, and then Tier 1 deals directly with H&M.

5 Textile World. 2017. "IFC and H&M Partner to Boost the use of Renewable Energy in the Garment Sector". Posted on April 4, 2017. www.textileworld.com/textile-world/knitting-apparel/2017/04/ifc-and-hm-partner-to-boost-the-use-of-renewable-energy-in-the-garment-sector/

6 They acknowledge the warming level of 2 degrees Celsius compared to pre-industrial temperatures, as described in the Fifth Assessment Report of the Intergovernmental Panel on Climate Change

7 http://biconsortium.eu/about/our-vision-strategy

8 Nespresso. n.d. "Nespresso Expands Recycling Partnership with UPS from 20 States to the Entire Continental U.S." Accessed on October 15, 2017. www.nestle-nespresso.com/newsandfeatures/nespresso-expands-recycling-partnership-with-ups-in-the-us

9 The manufacturing site at Choisy-le-Roy is also environmentally sound, using 80% less energy, 90% less chemicals, and water than regular manufacturing sites. Because the plant produces no waste, it is considered the most profitable among all Renault's sites.

10 www.circle-economy.com/case/desko/#.Wd7ynVt-rIU

11 www.ellenmacarthurfoundation.org/assets/downloads/ce100/Reverse-Logistics.pdf

12 It is essentially the process of reclaiming compounds and elements from large quantities of discarded products. In general, the conversation is about urban mines – landfills closed to densely populated urban areas – but other sites exposed to waste accumulation (like seas) can also be considered.

13 Net-Works. n.d. "Taking Net-Works Global". Accessed October 20, 2017. http://net-works.com/about-net-works/scaling-up/

14 www.circularocean.eu/

15 Dell. n.d. "Design for Environment. Closed-Loop Recycled Content." Accessed on October 25, 2017. www.dell.com/learn/us/en/uscorp1/corp-comm/closed-loop-recycled-content

16 HP. n.d. "HP Planet Partners. Product return & recycling." Accessed on August 19, 2018. http://www8.hp.com/us/en/hp-information/environment/product-recycling.html

17 The 2013 Circular Economy Development Strategies and Action Plan http://chinawaterrisk.org/research-reports/circular-economy-development-strategies-and-action-plan/ and the following Circular Economy Promotion Plan for 2015 http://chinawaterrisk.org/research-reports/circular-economy-promotion-plan-for-2015/

18 In 2010, the utilization rate of industrial solid waste and the recycling rate of industrial water reached 96% and 91%, respectively. Source: Mathews, John

A. and Hao Tan. 2016. "Lessons from China". *Nature* 44 (531): 440–42. Accessed on October 20, 2017.

19 Rare-Earth Elements (REES) are 17 chemical elements sharing comparable properties and therefore located in the same geological deposits. Their applications are manifolds, particularly in the high-tech sector, from computer hard drives to cameras and telescope lenses, from the catalytic converter of cars and aircraft engines to televisions and computer screens. They are: cerium (Ce), dysprosium (Dy), erbium (Er), europium (Eu), gadolinium (Gd), holmium (Ho), lanthanum (La), lutetium (Lu), neodymium (Nd), praseodymium (Pr), promethium (Pm), samarium (Sm), scandium (Sc), terbium (Tb), thulium (Tm), ytterbium (Yb), and yttrium (Y).

20 Honda. 2012. "Honda to Reuse Rare Earth Metals Contained in Used Parts." Posted on April 17, 2012. http://world.honda.com/news/2012/c120417eng.html

21 www.theguardian.com/global-development/2013/dec/14/toxic-ewaste-illegal-dumping-developing-countries

22 Greenpeace. 2008. "Chemical Contamination at e-Waste Recycling and Disposal Sites in Accra and Korforidua, Ghana". Accessed on July 5, 2017. www.greenpeace.org/archive-international/Global/international/planet-2/report/2008/9/chemical-contamination-at-e-wa.pdf

23 Veolia. n.d. "Leading the Circular Economy Sustainable Solutions for a Sustainable World". Accessed on October 31, 2017. www.veolia.co.uk/sites/g/files/dvc636/f/assets/documents/2017/07/Veolia_UK_Circular_Economy_brochure.pdf

Bibliography

Bakker, Conny, Marcel den Hollander, Ed van Hinte, and Yvo Zijlstra. 2014. *Products That Last: Product Design for Circular Business Models*. Delft, South Holland: TU Delft Library.

Bocken, Nancy, Ingrid de Pauw, Conny Bakker, and Bram van der Grinten. 2016. "Product Design and Business Model Strategies for a Circular Economy." *Journal of Industrial and Production Engineering* 33 (5): 308–20. doi: 10.1080/21681015.2016.1172124

Bocken, Nancy, Paavo Ritala, Pontus Huotari. 2017. "The Circular Economy. Exploring the Introduction of the Concept among S&P 500 Firms." *Journal of Industrial Ecology* 21 (39): 487–90. https://doi.org/10.1111/jiec.12605

Bocken, Nancy, and Samuel Short. 2016. "Towards a Sufficiency-Driven Business Model: Experiences and Opportunities." *Environmental Innovation and Societal Transitions* 18: 41–61. http://dx.doi.org/10.1016/j.eist.2015.07.010

Bocken, Nancy, Samuel Short, Padmakshi Rana, Steve Evans. 2014. "A Literature and Practice Review to Develop Sustainable Business Model Archetypes." *Journal of Cleaner Production* 65: 42–56. https://doi.org/10.1016/j.jclepro.2013.11.039.

Circle Economy. n.d. "Desko: Transforming the Furniture Industry with Buy Back Strategies." Accessed on November 16, 2017. www.circle-economy.com/case/desko/#.Wd7ynVt-rIU

Dell. n.d. "Design for Environment. Closed-Loop Recycled Content." Accessed on October 25, 2017. www.dell.com/learn/us/en/uscorp1/corp-comm/closed-loop-recycled-content

Dinges, Veit Florian Urmetzer, Veronica Martinez, Mohamed Zaki, and Andy Neely. 2017. "The Future of Servitization: Technologies That Will Make a

Difference." *The Cambridge Service Alliance.* https://www.researchgate.net/profile/Florian_Urmetzer/publication/280489377_The_Future_of_Servitization_Technologies_that_will_make_a_difference/links/55b6150408ae092e9655b478/The-Future-of-Servitization-Technologies-that-will-make-a-difference.pdf

Egerton-Read, Seb. 2017a. "How Otto Group Is Testing Out the Transition from Selling to Renting at Scale." *Circulatenews.* Posted on January 16, 2017. http://circulatenews.org/2017/01/otto-group-testing-transition-selling-renting-scale/

Egerton-Read, Seb. 2017b. "Why Air Conditioning as a Service Could Have a Huge Impact on Energy Usage." *Circulatenews.* Posted on February 15, 2017. http://circulatenews.org/2017/02/air-conditioning-service/

Egerton-Read, Seb. 2017c. "What Would It Mean If Apple Stopped Mining for IPhone Materials?." *Circulatenews.* Posted on April 21, 2017. http://circulatenews.org/2017/04/mean-company-like-apple-stopped-mining-iphone-materials/

Ellen MacArthur Foundation. 2016. "Waste Not, Want Not. Capturing the Value of the Circular Economy through Reverse Logistics." Accessed on October 17, 2017. www.ellenmacarthurfoundation.org/assets/downloads/ce100/Reverse-Logistics.pdf

Floordaily, 2017. "Interface Unveils Carbon Negative Carpet Tile." Posted on June 8, 2017. www.floordaily.net/flooring-news/interface-unveils-carbon-negative-carpet-tile

Hardcastle, Jessica Lyons. 2017. "Nike, Circular Economy Firm Miniwiz Develop Sustainable Packaging from Trash." *Environmental Leader.* Posted on March 27, 2017. www.environmentalleader.com/2017/03/nike-circular-economy-firm-miniwiz-develop-sustainable-packaging-trash/

Honda. 2012. "Honda to Reuse Rare Earth Metals Contained in Used Parts." Posted on April 17, 2012. http://world.honda.com/news/2012/c120417eng.html

HP. n.d. "HP Planet Partners. Product return & recycling." Accessed on October 25August 19th, 20187. http://www8.hp.com/us/en/hp-information/environment/product-recycling.htmKavadias, Stelios, Kostas Ladas, and Christoph Loch. 2016. "The Transformative Business Model." *Harvard Business Review.* October 2016. Accessed on October 3, 2017. https://hbr.org/2016/10/the-transformative-business-model

Lacy, Peter, and Jakob Rutqvist. 2015. *Waste to Wealth. The Circular Economy Advantage.* Basingstoke: Palgrave Macmillan.

Lemmon, Rory. 2017. "Two L'Oreal Products Achieve Cradle to Cradle Certification." *Circulatenews.* Posted on May 26, 2017. http://circulatenews.org/2017/05/two-loreal-products-achieve-cradle-to-cradle-certification/

Linder, Marcus, and Mats Williander. 2017. "Circular Business Model Innovation: Inherent Uncertainties." *Business Strategy and the Environment* 26 (2): 182–96. doi:10.1002/bse.1906

Lüdeke-Freund, Florian, Stefan Gold, and N. M. Bocken. 2018. "A Review and Typology of Circular Economy Business Model Patterns." *Journal of Industrial Ecology* In press. doi:10.1111/jiec.12763

Mathews, John A., and Hao Tan. 2016. "Lessons from China." *Nature* 44 (531): 440–42. Accessed on October 20, 2017. www.nature.com/polopoly_fs/1.19593!/menu/main/topColumns/topLeftColumn/pdf/531440a.pdf

McDonough, William, and Michael Braungart. 2002a. *Cradle to Cradle: Remaking the Way We Make Things.* New York: North Point Press.

McDonough, William, and Michael Braungart. 2002b. "Design for the Triple Top Line: New Tools for Sustainable Commerce." *Corporate Environmental Strategy* 9 (3): 251–58. https://doi.org/10.1016/S1066-7938(02)00069-6

McDowall, Will, Yong Geng, Beijia Huang, Eva Barteková, Raimund Bleischwitz, Serdar Türkeli, René Kemp, and Teresa Doménech. 2017. "Circular Economy Policies in China and Europe." *Journal of Industrial Ecology* 21 (3): 651–61.

Nespresso. n.d. "Nespresso Expands Recycling Partnership with UPS from 20 States to the Entire Continental U.S." Accessed on October 15, 2017. www.nestle-nespresso.com/newsandfeatures/nespresso-expands-recycling-partnership-with-ups-in-the-us

Net-Works. n.d. "Taking Net-Works Global." Accessed October 20, 2017. http://net-works.com/about-net-works/scaling-up/

Peiró, Laura, Fulvio Ardente, and Fabrice Mathieux. 2017. "Design for Disassembly Criteria in EU Product Policies for a More Circular Economy." *Journal of Industrial Ecology* 21 (3): 731–41. https://doi.org/10.1111/jiec.12608

Silva, Angie, Michele Rosano, Laura Stocker, and Leen Gorissen. 2017. "From Waste to Sustainable Materials Management: Three Case Studies of the Transition Journey." *Waste Management* 61: 547–57.

Singh, Jagdeep, Isabel Ordonez. 2016. "Resource Recovery from Post-Consumer Waste: Important Lessons for the Upcoming Circular Economy." *Journal of Cleaner Production* 134: 342–53. https://doi.org/10.1016/j.jclepro.2015.12.020

Sundin, Erik, Lindahl Mattias, and Ijomah Winifred. 2009. "Product Design for Product/Service Systems: Design Experiences from Swedish Industry." *Journal of Manufacturing Technology Management* 20 (5): 723–53. doi:https://doi.org/10.1108/17410380910961073

Sustainable Brands. 2017. "Braskem, Sealed Air, Naturepedic Unveil Renewable, Carbon-Negative Polyethylene Foam." Posted on June 20, 2017. www.sustainablebrands.com/news_and_views/ chemistry_materials_packaging/sustainable_brands/braskem_sealed_air_naturepedic_unvei

Textile World. 2017. "IFC and H&M Partner to Boost the Use of Renewable Energy in the Garment Sector." Posted on April 4, 2017. www.textileworld.com/textile-world/knitting-apparel/2017/04/ifc-and-hm-partner-to-boost-the-use-of-renewable-energy-in-the-garment-sector/

Tukker, Arnold. 2015. "Product Services for a Resource-Efficient and Circular Economy -A Review." *Journal of Cleaner Production* 97: 76–91. doi:https://doi.org/10.1016/j.jclepro.2013.11.049

Vandermerwe, Sandra, and Juan Rada. 1988. "Servitization of Business: Adding Value by Adding Services." *European Management Journal* 6 (4). doi:10.1016/0263-2373(88)90033-3

Veolia. n.d. "Leading the Circular Economy Sustainable Solutions for a Sustainable World." Accessed on October 31, 2017. www.veolia.co.uk/sites/g/files/dvc636/f/assets/documents/2017/07/Veolia_UK_Circular_Economy_brochure.pdf

Vidal, John. 2013. "Toxic 'e-waste' Dumped in Poor Nations, Says United Nations." *The Guardian.* Posted on December 14, 2013. www.theguardian.

com/global-development/2013/dec/14/toxic-ewaste-illegal-dumping-developing-countries

Vogtlander, Joost G., Arno E. Scheepens, Nancy M. P. Bocken, and David Peck. 2017. "Combined Analyses of Costs, Market Value and Eco-Costs in Circular Business Models: Eco-Efficient Value Creation in Remanufacturing." *Journal of Remanufacturing* 7 (1): 1–17.

Wiens, Kyle. 2016. "Apple's Recycling Robot Needs Your Help to Save the World." Posted on March 24, 2016. www.wired.com/2016/03/apple-liam-robot/

Yu, Fei, Feng Han, and Zhaojie Cui. 2015. "Evolution of Industrial Symbiosis in an Eco-Industrial Park in China." *Journal of Cleaner Production* 87: 339–47. https://doi.org/10.1016/j.jclepro.2014.10.058

Yuan, Zengwei, and Lei Shi. 2009. "Improving Enterprise Competitive Advantage with Industrial Symbiosis: Case Study of a Smeltery in China." *Journal of Cleaner Production* 17: 1295–302. 10.1016/j.jclepro.2009.03.016

Zhang, Ling, Zengwei Yuan, Jun Bi, Bing Zhang, and Beibei Liu. 2010. "Eco-Industrial Parks: National Pilot Practices in China." *Journal of Cleaner Production* 18: 504–9. https://doi.org/10.1016/j.jclepro.2009.11.018

Part III
CE Strategic Management

Part III is the core of this book for it brings the CE considerations formulated in Parts I and II down to a more practical level. It links the elements of the "CE Framework for Circularity in Business Strategy", CE-enabling technologies, and circular business models with traditional tools for strategic analysis, thus freely letting emerge customized business opportunities and action strategies. The rationale for this new lens to strategic management is to be found in the recognition that the changing socio-environmental and economic landscape of the 21st century presents a radically new set of threats and opportunities which cannot be effectively dealt with by companies pursuing business-as-usual approaches. To continue thrive, a new array of core competencies is required, one based on resources and capabilities created with circularity in mind.

A series of inter related analyses (like VRIE, 5-Forces industry model, PEST, and SWOT) are presented, discussed under a CE perspective, and supported by practical instruments specifically designed for circular thinking to help practitioners perform their assessments. The proposed CE Strategic Management process places at its core the dynamic tension between the existing strategy of the firm and its desired CE alternative. With this in mind, five sequential macro-activities are defined: Identify current strategy > Data collection and analysis > Definition of a preferred CE position > Gap analysis > CE strategy formulation > CE strategic planning.

6 Introducing the CE Strategic Process

6.1 Introduction

The CE does not aim at changing the profit-maximization paradigm of businesses. Rather, it suggests an alternative way of thinking to attain a Sustained Competitive Advantage (SCA), while concurrently addressing the environmental and socio-economic concerns of the 21st century. Indeed, stepping away from linear forms of production can lead to the development of new core competencies along the value chain (De los Rios and Charnley 2017) and ultimately superior performance that cuts costs, improves efficiency, and meets advanced government regulations or the expectations of sophisticated customers.

While the framework for circularity defined in Chapter 3 can serve as a basis for thinking strategically about CE implementation, the execution of a plan lies at the end of a lengthy and complex analytical process, one whereby firms seek to identify the best opportunities available to improve competitiveness in the marketplace. The aim of this chapter is to introduce the CE strategic process, a step-by-step guide to CE strategy definition that is supported by frameworks and concepts popular in management consulting, and forms the basis of Part III of this book. The first tool presented is the idea tree, a powerful concept to identify hotspots for CE implementation within the existing structure and operations of the firm.

6.2 Organizational Culture

Before introducing the CE strategic process and commencing the journey to discover how to attain an SCA, it is important to recognize that organizational culture is generally what determines the success or failure of a company approaching principles of circularity. Indeed, strategic decisions are naturally affected by the kind of culture developed within an organization, as this causes certain strategic issues to receive most attention, while others get overlooked.

Multinational consumer goods company Unilever provides a good example of how a company culture can be influenced top-down. Paul Polman, the group CEO, replaced his predecessor in 2009 and since then has radically altered the company's culture. Mr. Polman is driven by the vision of fully decoupling Unilever's growth from its environmental footprint and increase its positive social impact. Since Mr. Polman took office, Unilever's culture has focused on principles of sustainability and sustainable development, involving both employees and customers in a variety of green programmes and initiatives, like the Unilever Sustainable Living Plan.[1] Unilever's sustainability commitments have been crystallized in the corporate code of conduct, hence disclosing to the public the orientation of the company.[2] The document also includes the behavioural norms and ethical standards of the company, to which every Unilever's employee must adhere.

Despite being a difficult and time-consuming task, changing organizational culture is often regarded a key aspect to ensure strategic change takes place successfully and effectively. Strategists must therefore ask themselves whether the strategic change they have envisioned can occur within the existing cultural setting of the firm or this needs to change as well. Because culture is a source of stability for a company's employees and customers, it should generally be avoided to enforce changes too rapidly or in response to negative events (e.g. an environmental disaster caused by the company operations), favouring instead a cultural shift implemented in small steps and described as something positive and beneficial for all. If the positive aspect can arguably always be advocated when proposing circular solutions, pace of change is not always guaranteed. The matrix below (Table 6.1) lists four types of strategic change that can occur depending on differences in implementation speed and extent (Balogun and Hope Hailey 1999). Cultural adjustments, when required, would need to occur in a similar fashion.

- **Adaptation:** Changes with small extent and at low speed. This move does not require a change in strategy nor has a large impact on the company structure. Today, in the face of tightened environmental legislations, heightened environmental awareness of consumers,

Table 6.1 Sizing Up Change[3]

	EXTENT OF CHANGE	
	Realignment	Transformation
SPEED OF CHANGE — Incremental	Adaptation	Evolution
SPEED OF CHANGE — Big Bang	Reconstruction	Revolution

and price fluctuations, many companies have partially transitioned from using harmful production inputs like chemicals and plastics, to more circular bio-based materials. For example, Dutch multinational AkzoNobel has recently joined efforts with cleantech leader Photanol to naturally produce bio-based chemicals for the company's products instead of typical raw materials obtained from fossil fuels.[4]

- **Reconstruction:** Changes with small scope and at high speed. Oftentimes, reconstruction can be accommodated within the present culture, even if the organization is largely affected by the change. CE reconstruction can occur, for example, when a company succeeds in switching to closed-loop operations with the support of key suppliers and environmentally friendly providers. Carlsberg, for example, is investing heavily in circular packaging solutions, and in doing so has selected a group of "green" suppliers to partner with. The initiative, Carlsberg Circular Community (CCC), aims to develop products that are optimized for recycling and re-use, without compromising on quality (Niero et al. 2014). Such transformation can occur without major changes in the company's core business, especially because re-manufacturing or recycling activities occur externally.

- **Evolution:** Changes with large scope and at incremental speed. Such changes involve extended processes and several steps that may require a long time to complete. For example, leading car manufacturers like Nissan and BMW are slowly transitioning to electric engine technology in an effort to anticipate future trends in the industry. Though the vast majority of vehicles are still fuel-powered, BMW i3 and Nissan LEAF models are clear evidence that these companies have plans to step up their efforts towards zero-emission automobiles (Fingas 2016).

- **Revolution:** Changes with transformation-like extent and at high speed. Italian energy and resource group ERG, for example, has gone through a radical – and rapid – transformation of its business by selling out all activities related to oil and gas and re-investing in wind energy power plants.

Incremental and transformational CE changes (Evolution) are the ones most widely pursued by companies at this time. Organizations are in fact just starting to embed circular operations and in doing so they proceed in small steps often through pilot projects. They often begin with minor modifications affecting only part of their overall operations and then scale up gradually. Newly implemented circular practices – and the corresponding business model – get tested with a selection of products and processes, fine-tuned, and then expanded to more product lines and larger parts of the organization. For example, it took Interface many years and several incremental steps to become the CE reference firm that it is today. Similarly, other large multinationals in different sectors (e.g. Unilever, Nespresso, and Carlsberg in food and beverage; Philips, Ricoh, and Dell in electronics; Michelin and Renault in automotive; and Puma in clothing) are gradually embracing the change required to become circular and are undergoing transformations at multiple levels – sourcing, innovation, end-of-life product management, etc. – experimenting small- to medium-scale circular practices to ultimately understand how circular principles fit with the overall set of capabilities, resources, and business activities of the company.

6.3 The CE Strategic Process

Given the strategic importance of circular practices over the near future, CE must be accounted for in strategic decision-making. Executives willing to accept that businesses operate in an ever-changing environment, where strategies need to be continually re-shaped according to the latest opportunities and threats in the industry, shall focus on monitoring the complex context in which their companies operate, at both business and societal levels. The image below illustrates a standardized, cross-industry process for the assessment and definition of a CE strategy (Figure 6.1).

The fundamental steps of the strategic process are the following:

- **Identifying Current Situation**: Although not frequent, the state of firms approaching a circular path might already comprise components of CE practices and goals. A thorough assessment of the current strategy is crucial for understanding where a business stands in its circular journey and what steps shall be prioritized when laying

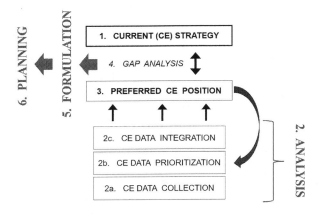

Figure 6.1 The CE Strategic Process.

down a preferred CE strategy. If, for example, a company has never embarked on a CE project before, a pilot involving only a tiny fraction of the business would be highly recommended to test the firm's readiness. Amongst the tools that can be used to investigate the current strategy of a company, the idea tree is a valid option to identify potential CE opportunities.

- **Data Analysis**: The analysis part of the strategic process involves data being collected, carefully examined, given priorities, and integrated with the chosen CE principles, business objectives, and areas of intervention. Business strategies will be built on the trends, strengths, weaknesses, opportunities, and threats inferred by the information collected at company, industry, and macro levels, with the assistance of frameworks like the value chain, VRIE, five forces, PEST, and SWOT. When seeking to define a new CE strategy, attention should be mainly given to often unexplored aspects of the business such as material management, sustainable design, opportunities for reverse cycles, attitude of suppliers and customers towards CE, etc. This sort of data will be leveraged to identify hotspots for CE implementation.

- **Determining Preferred CE Position**: The scenario resulting from having examined, prioritized, and integrated all the data will reveal the CE strategic options available. At this stage, the strategic quadrant can help a company choose its ideal positioning in the industry, hence determine its preferred CE attitude.

- **Gap Analysis**: The current and ideal positions of a company hardly concur, especially when circular principles are at stake. Hence, there will be a gap to be closed. In those cases when the gap is just too big given the actual CE readiness of the company, data will need to be rearranged (in terms of prioritization) so that an alternative "preferred CE reality" can be envisioned and assessed.

- **Strategy Formulation and Planning**: The final steps of the process involve deciding on a CE strategy, hence proceed to its formulation and planning.

6.4 Current Strategy Identification

Just a minority of companies have vision, mission, and strategic plans that truly reflect the strategies they implement. Thus, identifying and exploring the existing strategy is the first step of a company's journey towards a circular model. A deeper understanding of the current strategic plans and planning processes is, in fact, essential for envisioning a CE strategy for the firm. When looked through a CE lens, current business strategies can be categorized as: being already built around one or more CE principles (these businesses can be regarded as Circular

---

Case Study: Interface

Interface Inc., the US-based world's largest manufacturer of modular carpets, has a long-standing sustainability tradition. Founded in the early 1970s, in 1994 the company was set on a new course by its founder Ray C. Anderson, who moved the firm away from the traditional industrial system and towards a business model focused on sustainability. The company's growth strategy has since been based on circular principles and Interface's *Mission Zero* (a promise to eliminate any negative impact on the environment by 2020) is the overall framework that guides all aspects of the company's operations. This commitment is reflected in the vision of the company: "To be the first company that, by its deeds, shows the entire industrial world what sustainability is in all its dimensions: people, process, product, place and profits, and in doing so we will become restorative through the power of influence".[5]

Interface practices CE at multiple levels. Products are designed with sustainability principles in mind, such as closed loop and dematerialization. At the manufacturing stage, the firm has been the first carpet manufacturer in the world to employ a process for the separation of carpet fibre from backing, hence allowing for a maximum amount of end-use material to be recycled with negligible contamination. Finally, through its "Evergreen Lease" programme, Interface has been a pioneer in the servitization of carpets as they get produced, installed, cleaned, and replaced. As a result, customers lease the service of keeping a space carpeted, rather than buying a carpet. This programme allows Interface to retain ownership of the carpet, ensuring it is not disposed of in landfills, but rather properly recycled (Rogelio and Quinn 2003).

Economy pioneers, e.g. Interface, Philips, or Patagonia), embedding one or more CE projects but without a broad CE structure in place (e.g. companies that are using recycled products as inputs for their production lines but lack a formalized CE strategy), or entirely devised according to a linear production model (presently, most companies still fall under this category).

6.5 Idea Trees

According to Grant (2002), a strategy is the unifying theme that gives coherence and direction to the actions and decisions on an organization.

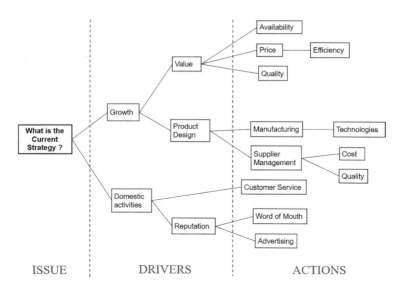

ISSUE   DRIVERS   ACTIONS

Figure 6.2 Idea Tree – What Is Your Current Strategy?

However, uncovering a business strategy by understanding the theme hidden behind the actions and decisions of a firm is difficult given the vast number of facts needed to be integrated. Idea trees can help in these efforts as they provide a simple way to cluster multiple factors together and create causal relationships between the various cells. Multiple attempts are generally required, with some trees having no use or being unfeasible, but all need to display the following two characteristics: be as comprehensive as possible and drill down until practical actions are unveiled, instead of having just high-level strategic themes. An example is reported above (Figure 6.2).

The next step would be to imagine how the current strategy could be affected if a CE cultural shift was to take place. As such, the drivers get identified and so are hotspots for CE implementation. The next diagram highlights two types of occurrences (Figure 6.3). First is the inclusion of new action cells that only a CE perspective would allow to recognize as potentially critical for the current strategy of the company (e.g. reverse cycle operations to improve the availability of inputs, perception by customer of the product's environmental friendliness, assess suppliers by their sustainability practices, enhance reputation through participation in sustainability forums, etc.). Next is the identification of cells, already present in the original tree, that would undergo a significant reevaluation and/or reinterpretation (e.g. the higher efficiency and cost savings that could derive from closed loops, the use of technologies such as 3D

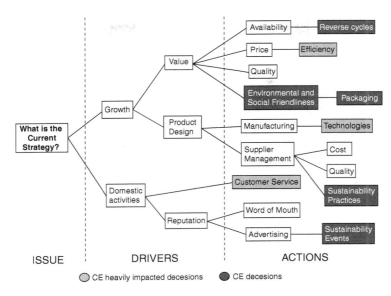

Figure 6.3 Critical Nodes under a CE Perspective.

printing, or the numerous CE practices that could make customer relationships tighter and more aligned). Regardless of the shape and structure of the tree that is deemed most appropriate to represent the current strategy of the firm, it must be describable and justifiable.

The power of idea trees can be further enhanced by weighting drivers, using rankings and expert judgement. In that situation, the idea tree continues to be a powerful tool up until strategy formulation, when actions get targeted and prioritized.

6.5.1 Supporting Methods for Idea Tree Analysis: Circular Brainstorming

Circular brainstorming is a valuable technique to detect any CE-oriented practice already in place and to facilitate thinking about possible developments. Also, it might be used to identify hotspots for CE implementation, even when "seeds of circularity" cannot be found across the organization. To conduct a successful circular brainstorming session, the following steps shall be followed:

a   Take the idea tree previously generated and focus on the CE actions identified as fitting for the current business strategy.

b   As a team, go through a careful examination of the six CE business objectives – regenerate, share, optimize, loop, virtualize, and

Table 6.2 Actions towards CE Business Objectives

REGENERATE	SHARE	OPTIMIZE
• By switching to renewable energy to power the company's operations or those of its suppliers. • By sourcing bio-based materials (composed, entirely or in significant part of biological products or renewable domestic agricultural materials). • By phasing out toxic production inputs. • By restoring ecosystems damaged by your operations.	• By switching to a Sensitization business model. • By finding new markets for unsold inventory stocks.	• By increasing the environmental performance of your operations. • By supporting suppliers diminish their environmental impacts. • By reducing the amount of waste produced in your value chain. • By finding a second life for the waste produced in your value chain.

LOOP	VIRTUALIZE	EXCHANGE
• By establishing reverse cycles for your products at their end of life. • By implementing re-manufacturing, refurbishing, and recycling processes. • By harnessing anaerobic digestion processes. • By finding circular solutions for your water demand.	• By reducing the material intensity of your products. • By switching to digital alternatives.	• By applying new technologies. • By choosing new products and services. • By replacing old materials with renewable solutions.

exchange – to inspire circular thinking (Ellen MacArthur Foundation 2015). The table above (Table 6.2) can be used as a guide to generate direct questions like: can we utilize waste as a resource? Can our production be more localized? Can we make it easier for users to self-repair our products? Can we design our product to be more modular?

c   Look for opportunities to become more circular, by mapping out:

• All "seeds of circularity" spread across the organization (CE-oriented practices): where in your current strategy are CE business objectives already being pursued? By what means, programme, initiative?

- Possible improvements of current CE-oriented practices: how can the existing procedure/system in place be scaled up across the organization, thus becoming a strategic CE objective?
- Hotspots for CE implementation in the absence of existing CE-oriented practices: what CE objectives could be incorporated into the existing strategy?

d Once the brainstorming session ends, collect all the ideas and place them on a board. Go through each of them and select those that most excite you.

The insights from idea trees, supported by exercises such as circular brainstorming, represent areas for further exploration. The next step in fact will be to investigate the different options according to the resources and capabilities of the firm, industry dynamics, external forces, and opportunities, hence distinguishing between those that are practically feasible from the ones that are not. With regard to the current strategy – now identified in its true form (i.e. actions rather than a crude mission statement) – it will be possible, at the end of the analytical process, to evaluate its ongoing consistency with the new objectives and genuine CE possibilities.

6.6 Conclusions

This chapter offered an overview of the CE strategic process, a step-by-step guide to strategy definition that will be further analysed in the following chapters of this section of the book (Part III). Central to this framework is the relationship between the current strategy of the firm and the preferred CE position that results from a thorough data analysis of the firm, its industry and wider context. The eventual gap between the two points represents the area around which to formulate and plan the implementation of a new strategy.

Organizational culture constitutes a key aspect to act upon before transitioning towards a CE strategy. Cultural adjustments need to anticipate the strategic change desired by the company and be appropriate to such plan in terms of extent and speed. At present, incremental and transformational CE changes (Evolution) are the ones most widely pursued by companies. The case of consumer goods giant Unilever was presented as a telling example of how a company culture can be shaped top-down with the aim of integrating sustainability principles at the very heart of a firm's strategy. Other examples of strategic change, induced by CE considerations, were given to suit all scenarios of Balogun and

Hope Hailey's typology (1999) – adaptation, evolution, reconstruction, and revolution.

The second half of the chapter addressed the first step of the CE strategic process: identifying the current strategy. While most firms are still centred around linear production processes, some have elements of circularity in them and a few are fully based on CE principles. The case of Interface was described as a classic example of the latter. The chapter ended with a focus on the idea tree, a tool useful for the identification of a business strategy and hotspots for CE implementation. It provides a useful guidance to navigate amidst the complexity of an organization, with the goal of unveiling practical CE actions meaningful for the business. To further support strategists in this initial assessment, circular brainstorming was also presented as a valuable method to map out all seeds of circularity already existing within the firm, as well as to spark new CE-related ideas.

Notes

1 www.unilever.com/sustainable-living/the-sustainable-living-plan/
2 www.unilever.com/about/who-we-are/purpose-and-principles/
3 Source: Adapted from J. Balogun and V. Hope Hailey, *Exploring Strategic Change*, 3rd edition, London: Prentice Hall, 1999.
4 Akzonobel. 2014. "AkzoNobel and Photanol Developing Chemical Compounds of the Future". Posted on September 17, 2014. www.akzonobel. com/for-media/media-releases-and-features/akzonobel-and-photanol-developing-chemical-compounds-future
5 www.interface.com/EU/en-GB/about/mission/Redesigning-Our-Company-en_GB

Bibliography

Akzonobel. 2014. "AkzoNobel and Photanol Developing Chemical Compounds of the Future." Posted on September 17, 2014. www.akzonobel.com/for-media/media-releases-and-features/akzonobel-and-photanol-developing-chemical-compounds-future
Balogun, Julia, and Veronica Hope Hailey. 1999. *Exploring Strategic Change.* London: Prentice Hall.
De los Rios, Irel Carolina, and Fiona J. S. Charnley. 2017. "Skills and Capabilities for a Sustainable and Circular Economy: The Changing Role of Design." *Journal of Cleaner Production* 160 (1): 109–22.
Ellen MacArthur Foundation. 2015. *Growth Within: A Circular Economy Vision for a Competitive Europe.* Accessed on September 5, 2017. www.ellenmacarthurfoundation.org/publications/growth-within-a-circular-economy-vision-for-a-competitive-europe.
Fingas, Jon. 2016. "BMW Reportedly Steps Up Its Electric Vehicle Plans." *Engadget.* Posted on December 9, 2016. www.engadget.com/2016/09/12/bmw-reportedly-steps-up-electric-car-plans/

Grant, Robert M. 2002. *Contemporary Strategy Analysis*. 4th edition. Hoboken, NJ: Blackwell Publishing.

Niero, Monia, S. H. Boas, Stig Irvin Olsen. 2014. "Carlsberg Circular Community: When a Company and Its Suppliers Join Forces to Implement Eco-Innovation." *Setac Europe 20th Lca Case Study Symposium*. www. forskningsdatabasen.dk/en/catalog/2261004393

Oliva, Rogelio, and James Quinn. 2003. "Interface's Evergreen Services Agreement." *Harvard Business School* Case 603-112, February 2003. www.hbs. edu/faculty/Pages/item.aspx?num=29680

7 CE Data Collection and Prioritization

Firm, Industry, and External Levels of Analysis

7.1 Introduction

The CE strategic process introduced the concept of Sustained Competitive Advantage (SCA), the real differentiating factor of a business in any industry setting. A firm obtains a competitive advantage after properly combining resources and capabilities – physical assets like machinery, patents, and even human resources, but also intangibles and non-easily transferable assets like knowledge, experience, stakeholder relationships, and culture – to develop a distinctive competence (Gluck et al. 1980; Porter 1980; Dierickx and Cool 1989; McGrath et al. 1996). Unfortunately, not all resources and capabilities are good enough to create a new core competence and so it becomes essential to properly assess them prior to investing in them. This is the purpose of data analysis, a process to collect, prioritize, and integrate information at company, industry, and external levels. The most established management tool used to evaluate resources and capabilities is the VRIE framework, introduced in 1991 by Barney, who is widely recognized as the main proponent of the Resource-Based View (RBV). To create an SCA, these resources and capabilities have to be valuable, rare, imperfectly imitable, and exploitable by how the firm is organized (Collis and Montgomery 1995), and the best place to look for the most appropriate candidates is the company's value chain (Barney 1991).

It is important to recognize that since the RBV model was first conceived, concepts in management theory central to corporate competitiveness have evolved, often leading to questioning the solidity of the RBV framework (Peteraf and Barney 2003). However, its central proposition of requiring valuable, rare, inimitable, and non-substitutable resources and capabilities to achieve an SCA remains valid and is today shared by more recent business concepts like "core competencies", defined as *"the collective learning in the organization, especially how to coordinate diverse production skills and integrate multiple streams of technologies"* (Prahalad and Hamel 1990, 84). This definition clearly highlights the enrichment from the original RBV explanation also revealing the strategic importance of a CE-enabling attitude for the progress of a company: it is not so much the value of individual resources that matters, but rather their synergistic combination (Laurie et al. 2006). In the short term, strategy is constrained by the resources and capabilities available, so it is shaped by what the firm has. But over the long run, strategy is about renewing and adding resources and capabilities to develop distinctive competences that can adapt quickly to changing environments (Zook 2007; Alexander and Martin 2013).

The strategic importance of being able to responsively and purposefully adapt an organization's resource base to changing environments led to define such capacity as "dynamic capabilities" (Teece et al. 1997), thus differentiating them from the standard operational capabilities of the company (Helfat et al. 2007). They are *"the firm's processes that use resources – specifically the processes to integrate, reconfigure, gain and release resources – to match and even create market change"* (Kraaijenbrink et al. 2010, 357). Once again, it is straightforward how strategic CE decisions seamlessly find their place in this second definition as well: a change from linearity to circularity is both evident and inevitable, but what is more is that pioneering companies are already producing that change in most industries. The advent of dynamic capabilities has been instrumental to step aside from the all-inclusive resources of the RBV and acknowledge the distinction between those resources that are inputs to the firm and the capabilities that enable the firm to select, deploy, and organize such inputs (Makadok 2001). Resources remain important for the life of the company, not per se, but because of the configuration conferred by dynamic capabilities (Ambrosini et al. 2009; Morgan et al. 2009).

But sources of value do not just exist inside of the organization. External linkages are also critical, especially for the development of key technological capabilities (Coombs 1996). By using collaborative arrangements oriented towards technology access, companies can multiply internal resources and display a broader array of core competencies (Teece et al. 1997) more rapidly and cost-effectively. Tools like the five forces model (Porter 1979) or the PEST framework (Aguilar 1967) allow to explore that external environment in detail and to create the knowledge base necessary for a later identification of the company's strengths, weaknesses, opportunities, and threats: the footing to fine-tune a preferred CE positioning.

7.2 The Value Chain

Through the RBV, firms are analysed in terms of what they can do when using their resources and capabilities. The connections between these different assets and processes are well illustrated with Porter's value chain (1985), a framework representing the various activities (primary and support) involved in the creation and sale of a product

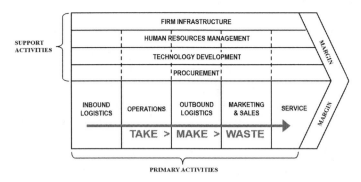

Figure 7.1 Porter's Value Chain Framework.[1]

or service. The activities are positioned in a sequential order inside an arrow-like diagram that evokes the typical linear approach still practised by most companies (Figure 7.1). As a company begins to look at its value chain through a CE lens, it will discover that all activities can undergo significant alterations. Indeed, to fully embrace the opportunities that the CE has to offer, organizations need to critically look at their set of resources and capabilities, while being committed to adjust their structure (potentially across all levels and departments) through core strategic decisions. In doing so, a new wealth of opportunities for creating SCA will unfold.

Primary activities are the backbone of product/service development. From inbound logistics to operations and sales, here is where the process of transforming raw materials into a marketable good takes place. Although all primary activities play an important role, especially in manufacturing contexts, operations and sales are arguably the epicentre of the value chain, where the greater effort is placed to make things work efficiently. The next diagram illustrates a standard value chain with the integration of some CE considerations concerning primary activities (Figure 7.2).

- **Inbound Logistics** is the umbrella term for the receiving, storage, and delivery of inputs, and includes relationships with suppliers. With the implementation of CE strategies, these activities will likely undergo significant changes, primarily as a result of the implementation of internal reverse cycle operations. In this regard, new flows of materials and products will require additional efforts in terms of warehouse space, as well as enhanced logistic planning and execution. For example, a company implementing a take-back programme to collect pre-owned products will need to extend its reach up to the drop-off/return points, where goods are collected. Drop-off points can be established either within

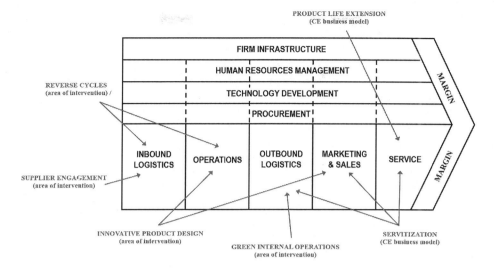

Figure 7.2 CE Impacts on Primary Activities.

the company shops and facilities, or outside the boundaries of the business, especially if the firm does not have a network of physical spaces available.

Inbound logistics can also be positively disrupted by closed-loop supply chain operations, with suppliers thoroughly interacting with the firm in the handling and processing of recycled production inputs. In this case, strong coordination with business partners will be vital to ensure constant and reliable flows of materials.

• **Operations** comprises all assets (e.g. machinery) and value-creating competencies (e.g. maintenance, assembly, testing, etc.) needed to transform inputs into the final product or service. Core CE activities like repairing, refurbishing, re-manufacturing, and recycling will give birth to a whole new set of operations within the company. As reverse cycles are established, and pre-owned products re-enter the company operations, infrastructure needs to be reinvented to accommodate these new streams of products, likely involving the purchase of new machinery or even entire facilities. Philips Healthcare, for example, has three refurbishment facilities in North America and Europe where pre-owned healthcare systems like X-ray generators and cardiovascular equipment are refurbished, upgraded, and quality tested. Quality testing and assurance is a particularly relevant feature in CE operations, for second-life products can still be perceived as low-quality assets by customers. Operations can also be affected by CE product design as production processes would need to be adjusted to efficiently manufacture products based on standardization, modularity, easy sorting, disassembly, and prolonged use. As an example, Renault's Choisy-le-Roi re-manufacturing plant processes car components that have been redesigned according to standardization principles to increase re-use ratio and to make sorting activities more fluid.

- **Outbound Logistics** is the suite of activities, like warehousing, order fulfilment, and transportation required to manage and distribute the outputs of operations. CE-inspired strategies have the potential to disrupt the traditional models of outbound logistics, particularly through the establishment of more localized value chains and as a result of placing operations closer to the company's main geographical markets. Take Riversimple[2], a UK-based small-scale carmaker. As part of its circular business model, the firm plans to build a distributed manufacturing network of factories to be more agile and minimize transportation costs across the supply chain. Each site will be located close to the market it serves and will produce around 5,000 cars annually. Such model is bound to be increasingly adopted by circular firms, and more conspicuously by those using 3D printing solutions in their manufacturing processes, for the technology allows for the easy establishment of small-scale production facilities. Also, by setting up factories and plants locally, companies can potentially enjoy a broader licence to operate and increased brand recognition.

  But outbound logistics is likely to undergo significant changes also for those companies pursuing a servitization business model, as goods need to be transported to locations where demand is the highest. Car-sharing operators, for example, have dedicated teams looking after their fleets 24/7, and their activities may be arranged to include moving cars around the city to meet demand patterns. A similar discourse applies to ensure quick movement of assets from and to maintenance points.

- **Marketing and Sales.** As discussed in Chapter 5, the CE training of Desko's sales force was instrumental to guarantee the success of its "three-tier buy back system". Customers need to be creatively and continually engaged through, for example, the offering of add-ons and upgrades as well as repair and refurbishing services, all activities facilitated by innovative product design. New approaches to marketing will be essential to companies pursuing servitization as the focus will shift from selling a product to the service it provides. One original solution has been tested successfully by Italian car-sharing operator Share'ngo. Any new user going through the registration process is presented with a series of personal questions to define a social profile of the individual, i.e. the degree to which he or she is actively involved in the community. On these grounds, a personalized pay-per-use fee is created: the greater the social activism of the individual (e.g. through volunteering), the lesser the per-minute rate that will be charged.

- **Service** refers to all the activities required to keep the product's value at the expected standards after being sold, and includes installation, customer support, repair, etc. Under a CE scenario, servicing activities are given a primary role in the company's value chain, particularly when the whole business model begins to lean towards product life extension or servitization. With the focus on post-sales activities, the CE competitive advantage of a company will likely be measured on its ability to effectively communicate its circular creed, integrate best practices along the entire value chain, and continually engage customers through a suite of ongoing services.

Secondary activities, although not directly involved in the physical creation of what is going to be sold by the company, are crucial for the smooth running of primary activities and in adding value to the final product or service. This second version of the value chain shows the integration of certain CE considerations concerning support activities, which have been grouped as either having a potentially major or minor impact (Figure 7.3).

- **Procurement** is about managing the acquisition of resources and services to meet the needs of the organization. With the release of the ISO 20400:2017, companies can now follow international guidelines for sustainable procurement. Notably, the standard places a strong focus on the inclusion of sustainability criteria into procurement policies and strategies and also makes explicit reference to the concepts of the CE. As a matter of fact, purchasing

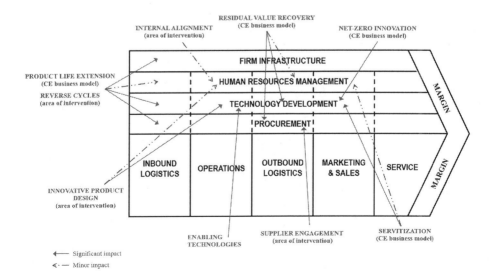

Figure 7.3 CE Impacts on Supporting Activities.

policies will progressively be adjusted to emphasize service-based solutions and second-life products over the acquisition of virgin resources, with procurement strategies being devised to strengthen procurer–supplier relationship around circular competences specific to the business model being pursued: net-zero innovation, servitization, product life extension, or residual value recovery (Witjesa and Lozano 2016).

Procurement activities will mostly be affected when the firm actively seeks supplier engagement in circular practices. It might indeed occur that a company decides to shortlist suppliers based on their willingness/capacity to participate in CE initiatives. At a subsequent stage, suppliers might also be ranked according to detailed CE criteria, such as the ability to deliver green raw materials/products, the capacity to work according to modularity principles, refurbishing skills, etc. In 2014, AkzoNobel took this path by teaming up with a supplier, Photanol, to develop a process capable of harnessing the power of the sun to produce green chemicals.[3]

- **Technology Development** has long been a crucial horizontal activity for linear firms and is going to be even more important for circular businesses (mainly those implementing servitization, residual value recovery, and net-zero innovation). Technological capabilities such as IoT and smart sensors will be essential to implement reverse cycle operations. CE product design is another facet of the business that will determine the technological know-how and polices of the company (e.g. modular technology and open source). Ultimately, all the CE-enabling technologies detailed in Chapter 4 carry a high potential for disruption in most industries, and as such can become a primary source of competitive advantage.

- **Human Resource Management** encompasses the key HR activities of recruiting, training, developing, compensating, and laying off personnel. For a CE strategy to be implemented effectively, strong internal alignment, both vertically and across departments, is a must. Most notably, firms will need their R&D, operations, and sales departments to work closely together to design products that can be easily refurbished or re-manufactured and sold without planned obsolesce in mind. Apart from development programmes for existing employees dedicated to familiarize with CE core concepts and best practices, new CE-specialized human resources are also likely to be needed such as senior executives with expertise in implementing CE business models, CE product designers, engineers specialized in green processes, skilled refurbishment professionals, experienced repair workers, etc.

Case Study: Philips

As part of its "Diamond Select" programme, in late 2014, Philips opened a facility in the Netherlands, where pre-owned healthcare machineries like magnetic resonance imaging (MRI), interventional X-ray (iXR), computed tomography (CT), and surgical imaging are refurbished and re-entered in the market as new and with full warranty, but at a lower price. Since then, the programme has expanded and the company now runs three similar facilities fully dedicated to CE-related operations for healthcare machinery. There, procurement activities and logistics are closely interrelated as the refurbishment process starts with the selection of pre-owned systems that mainly come back to Philips in the form of trade-in. Then, reverse cycle operations commence, with the deinstallation of systems by specialized workers, and their transportation to the refurbishing plants. To process these returned items, a new set of capabilities was needed: the way technology and operations fit into each other had to be optimized. Today, the collaboration is seamless, with the company's design and operation teams working together to ensure that newer refurbishment technologies are compatible with older system platforms.[4]

- **Firm Infrastructure** comprises all the various departments (like legal, finance, government relations, quality assurance, etc.) that perform behind-the-scene tasks and ultimately act as a glue in keeping the various parts of the organization together. These activities will be impacted to different extents by the implementation of CE operations, depending on the strategy being pursued. For example, transitioning to a product-as-a-service model will require the legal office to devise insurance contracts for the specific good being rented, whilst a product life extension business model will force the quality department to strengthen its quality assurance protocols.

7.2.1 Supporting Methods for Undertaking Value Chain Analysis: Interviewing Key Personnel

Below is a list of questions that can be asked to senior managers from different departments to establish how they perceive the degree of impact (significant or minor) that specific CE ideas would have on the company's value chain (Table 7.1).

Table 7.1 Value Chain CE Questionnaire

> OPERATIONS	> PROCUREMENT
• How might the planning and execution of our internal activities be disrupted by this idea? • How long could it take to ensure that The operations linked to the implementation of this idea will be as efficient as the existing ones'1 • How might the efficiency of our operations be affected by this idea?	• How does the efficiency of our sourcing activities might be affected by this idea? • How long might take to ensure that the sourcing activities linked to the implementation of this idea will be as efficient as the existing ones? • What suppliers might help us develop this idea? • What is the most environmentally conscious supplier out there?
> RESEARCH & DEVELOPMENT	> LOGISTICS
• How expensive would it be to develop this product? • How long would it take to design this product? • Is there any external partner that could help us in the process?	• Do we have the logistical capabilities to pursue this idea? • What would be the cost of acquiring new facilities to implement this idea?
> HUMAN RESOURCES	> SALES
• Winch employees might have the skills and capabilities required to implement this idea? • Are there current employees with a background in CE? • Do we have the internal expertise do pursue this CE idea?	• What sale techniques do we envision for marketing this CE product/service? • What portion of our clientele do we anticipate being willing to buy/ switch to this new CE product?

7.3 The VRIE Framework

An analysis of resources and capabilities aims to identify those activities, among the myriad characterizing the firm, that play a crucial role in delivering superior performance. Through the VRIE framework (Barney 1991), the contribution of a resource or capability to an organization is evaluated using four parameters: value, rareness, imitability, and potential for exploitation (Table 7.2).

7.3.1 Value

In a linear economy, the value of a resource or capability has traditionally been determined by how customers rate its contribution to the appeal of the final service or product (e.g. Ikea's unique design for easy assembly or the fast supply chain model of Zara). Because the CE prioritizes closed loops over linear ways of production, the value of a capability or resource

Table 7.2 VRIE Framework

	Valuable	Rare	Difficult to Imitate	Exploitable
Competitive Disadvantage	NO			
Competitive Equality	YES	NO		
Short-Term Competitive Advantage	YES	YES	NO	
Unused SCA	YES	YES	YES	NO
SCA	YES	YES	YES	YES

is no longer measured only in terms of customer satisfaction, but also by its contribution to the application of circular practices. As a simple example, the value of a machinery is not only determined by how good or fast it can make a product, but also for its ability to process used resources in place of virgin materials. Generally speaking, valuable capabilities and resources will be those that give the company an ability to retain or extract most value from a used product. Hence, the design capability of Ikea will have real CE value only to the extent to which the company will be able to maximize circular principles of modularity and disassembly. Zara's fast supply chain model could even be classified as a negative capability in CE terms as it generates large amounts of wasted products – which however get partly re-used or re-manufactured by both Zara and its suppliers through the establishment of appropriate take-back programmes.

7.3.2 Rareness

Rareness is the extent to which a certain resource or capability is shared among competitors. The more businesses have it, the lesser its uniqueness. As the CE is still in its infancy, circular pioneers have the opportunity to enjoy long-lasting competitive advantage by exploiting the many technological innovations mentioned in Chapter 4 and capabilities such as circular design, reverse cycles, and closed-loop supply chains. For example, Carlsberg's extensive work to apply circular principles along its supply chain is unique in the beer sector. Such exclusive capability to work closely with CE-oriented suppliers has benefited the company in many ways, namely a greater ability to manage costs (via reduced reliance on primary raw material) and securing compliance with ever-stricter regulations over waste and packaging.

7.3.3 Imitability

Imitability refers to how complex or costly (or both) is for competitors to imitate a certain resource or capability. When it comes to CE, the sooner a firm embarks on its circular journey, the harder it will be for competitors to catch up, especially in terms of brand image and support from the right business partners. Companies like Patagonia in the clothing industry are widely recognized as sustainability pioneers, making their brands both a major resource and primary source of competitive advantage. Because most of Patagonia's competitors are still largely anchored to linear business models, the company is enjoying superior brand image – especially among so-called green consumers.

7.3.4 Exploitation

Exploitation refers to how well a company is organized to exploit that source of SCA. In CE terms, it is about being able to capitalize on a resource or capability through one or more areas of intervention[5] as laid out in the "Framework for Circularity in Business Strategy" presented in Chapter 3. Vodafone's "New Every Year" service allows customers in the UK, Greece, the Netherlands, and Ireland to upgrade to the latest smartphone every 12 months, as long as their mobile phones are returned in acceptable conditions. By doing so, the company has focused on a business model based on access over ownership, in an effort to strengthen its relationship with customers. Through the establishment of return channels for pre-owned mobiles, Vodafone is exploiting its widespread network of shops that are now operating as collection sites as well.

7.4 Five Forces

The reasons leading to analyse an industry can be to compare various sectors or to better understand how profits may be maximized within a single industry. One of the most refined tools to conduct an industry analysis is the five forces model (Porter 1979). This is a framework that seeks to analyse the level of competition within an industry and develop a business strategy accordingly. Power of suppliers and buyers, threat of new entrants and substitutes, and degree of rivalry determine the competitive intensity and therefore attractiveness of an industry (Figure 7.4). Specific criteria are used to thoroughly analyse each of the five forces.

An industry analysis can also be of great interest for a business to understand the potential applications and benefits of circular practices. Indeed, some industries are more apt to circularity than others – due, for example, to the large amount of waste generated, high regulatory pressure, scarcity of raw materials, etc. Hence, using Porter's model to investigate how the five major forces can affect an industry under a CE perspective seems worthwhile. What follows is a presentation of all forces and their respective criteria, each one receiving two scores (high or low): the first one in relation to linear thinking and the second according to a circular interpretation.

A   **CE SUPPLIERS POWER:** It measures the power of those suppliers that have chosen to implement CE practices (Table 7.3). Their power is higher when:

- There is a low **concentration** of suitable suppliers that a CE-oriented company can choose from for a specific task.

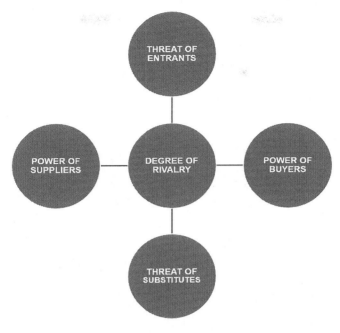

Figure 7.4 The Five Forces Model.[6]

Table 7.3 The Power of (CE) Suppliers

Their Power Is Highest When:	*Suppliers (Linear Perspective)*	*CE Suppliers (Circular Perspective)*
Concentration	LOW	LOW
Substitute CE Supplies	LOW	HIGH
Switching Costs	HIGH	LOW
Buyer CE Information	LOW	HIGH
Forward Integration	HIGH	HIGH

- There is a variety of environmentally friendly materials that can be used as **substitutes** to hazardous elements in the manufacturing of new products and customers manifest a good receptivity for such changes.
- There are low costs in **switching** from standard to CE suppliers in case former ones do not agree to CE standards or lack the required capabilities to do so competitively.
- **Buyer CE information** is high. Meaning that the buyer is knowledgeable about circular practices and can properly rank suppliers on their CE capabilities.
- **Forward integration** is high. It is often possible in a CE context for suppliers to decide moving into the firm's industry.

Table 7.4 The Power of (CE) Buyers

Their Power Is Highest When:	Buyers (Linear Perspective)	CE BUYERS (Circular Perspective)
Concentration	LOW	LOW
Price Sensitivity	HIGH	LOW (less relevant)
Switching Costs	LOW	HIGH
Backward Integration	HIGH	HIGH
Acceptable Substitutes	HIGH	HIGH

B   **CE BUYERS POWER:** Customer readiness for CE services/products reflects their power when making a purchasing decision (Table 7.4). Under a circular perspective, their power is greater when:

- There are few large customers to which CE products and services can be offered. Low **concentration** will make it harder for a company to penetrate a certain market if major buyers have no interest in its circular alternatives.
- **Price sensitivity** is low, meaning that consumers base their decisions on CE-related quality more than price. Small fluctuations do not influence the so-called green consumer, generally willing to pay a premium price for products that meet his/her sustainability expectations. Besides, efficiently produced circular goods and services are generally less expensive than their linear counterparts, making the issue relatively minor.
- **Switching costs** are high, implying that changes in purchasing behaviour (i.e. switching to another firm) result from reasoned decisions not just based on price, but on a long-term commitment to adopt circular alternatives.
- **Backward integration** is high. In a CE context, it is not unlikely to witness a buyer integrating backwards to take over the firm.
- They can buy **substitute products** that meet their minimum CE standards (high).

C   **THREAT OF CE SUBSTITUTES:** Assuming an industry context already geared towards circularity (Table 7.5), the importance of CE substitutes increases:

- If **Switching Costs** for buyers are low. However, transitioning to circular practices (i.e. changing to a CE substitute) generally goes beyond costs, implying lifestyle changes for consumers and the redesigning of business models for companies. Hence, the likelihood that low switching costs alone might lead customers to change their buying preferences is minor.
- When their **Price–Performance** ratio is high. However, there is little margin to play on this dimension as seeking an optimal

Table 7.5 The Threat of (CE) Substitutes

Their Threat Is Highest When:	Substitutes *(Linear Perspective)*	CE Substitutes *(Circular Perspective)*
Switching Costs	**LOW**	**LOW** (less relevant)
Price–Performance	**HIGH**	**HIGH** (less relevant)
Suitability of Alternatives	**HIGH**	**HIGH**

combination of price vs performance is already a fundamental tenet deeply embedded in the CE perspective. Maximizing the utilization rate of goods is paramount in CE business models to secure customers loyalty.

- If **Suitability of CE alternatives** is high. In the opposite situation, customers may prefer to continue using linear products or services. This is particularly true when circular products are offered through innovative business models (e.g. servitization) that customers are still not familiar with. As a result, it is advisable for CE companies to develop proper awareness-building and customer-engagement practices to make sure the economic and environmental advantages of adopting circular alternatives are fully grasped by the public.

D **THREAT OF NEW CE ENTRANTS** is high in industries where the barriers to entry for new CE-oriented start-ups are low, meaning that industries are open to be disrupted by innovative circular practices (Table 7.6). As a result, we really talk about *"barriers to disrupt"* rather than the usual *"barriers to entry"*. More specifically, the threat is high if:

- Existing firms have not already developed CE expertise applied to production processes and products' development. On the other hand, when established companies have successfully converted to CE practices, they are said to possess a **cost advantage** from the CE proprietary knowledge nurtured either internally or through industry-wide CE programmes. Currently, there are a few industries with large multinationals (e.g. Interface, Ricoh, Philips, Tesla, etc.) retaining CE cost advantage.
- **Economies of scale** have not been achieved, making it easier for new companies to establish themselves. However, even when economies of scale are present and consolidated, new CE entrants can be a threat as circular practices are predominantly about innovation and often have the potential to utterly disrupt production processes and products. Hence, from the perspective of a new entrant, the obstacles linked to economies of scale may

often be overcome by investing in innovative circular alternatives. The automotive industry, for example, has historically been an arena limited to established large players. Yet, electric carmaker Tesla has taken big steps revolutionizing the industry, with its mission to accelerate the world's transition to sustainable transportation by producing affordable electric vehicles for the masses. To achieve that goal, the company in 2014 began the construction of a 10-million-square-foot factory in Nevada, powered only by renewable energy through a combination of geothermal, wind, and solar sources.[7]

- **Brand value and reputation** of existing linear companies is low. However, even when confronted with high brand value firms, CE entrants may overcome this barrier by pursuing strategies that aim at educating customers on the advantages of CE alternatives. For example, Coca-Cola and Pepsi are such dominant brands that competitors with cheaper, nearly identical products have traditionally been unable to break in effectively. However, as the issue of water scarcity worsens worldwide, new CE companies that manage water efficiently through innovative production processes may decide to compete in the beverage industry by highlighting, via awareness-building campaigns, the unsustainable business practices of large multinational rivals. The same idea may apply to other industries and markets like clothing, where the cultivation of cotton and some specific manufacturing processes (like those involved in the production of jeans)[8] are very resource- and water-intensive. Patagonia, for example, differentiates itself from the mass market by offering made-to-last outdoor clothing, manufactured using the least environmentally impactful processes and materials.

- **Regulatory system** is relaxed (low) making new entries easy. Currently, in several geographies, market access for CE companies is still restricted by outdated regulatory barriers that limit the development of circular industrial processes, products, and business models. In 2016, a study by the European Commission found the EU still affected by regulatory obstacles specifically linked to the collection of waste streams, the uptake of secondary resources, and product design for re-use, repair, or recycling.[9] Notably, these regulatory hurdles often are not the result of a single policy, but rather caused by an intricate merger of inconsistent regulations linked to:[10]
  - Making waste generation preferable compared to CE practices like industrial symbiosis or closed internal loops.
  - Limiting the intake of appropriate waste streams through high-quality treatment facilities, causing instead improper disposal or incineration.

Table 7.6 The Threat of (CE) Entrants

Their Threat Is Highest When:	*New Entrants (Linear Perspective)*	*CE New Entrants (Circular Perspective)*
COST ADVANTAGE	LOW	LOW
SCALE ECONOMIES	LOW	LOW
BRAND VALUE AND REPUTATION	LOW	LOW
REGULATORY SYSTEM	LOW	LOW (very relevant)

o Encouraging the production of goods less suitable to be looped back into the economic system through re-use or recycling.

o Enforcing requirements (safety protocols, end-of-waste criteria, etc.) blocking the access to and/or development of markets for secondary raw materials.

o Waste requirements focusing of quantity rather than quality.

On the bright side, a few local, regional, and national institutions have recently started to adopt CE-friendly policies, laws, and regulations,[11] thereby making some industries more appealing to companies willing to invest in CE strategies.

E **CE RIVALRY** is the level of competition that CE businesses can bring to existing linear firms within an industry and is determined by how ease circular practices can be implemented while causing high impact (Table 7.7). CE implementation can basically occur at three levels: energy, material, and process. The energy aspect has to do with switching to renewable sources (solar, wind, biomass, etc.) for either production or use of a product (e.g. electric cars). In terms of material, the greater the number of components in a product that could be environmentally friendly, the higher its CE potential. Examples can be pesticide-free cotton and green polymers in the clothing industry or natural products for agribusinesses (such as the ones developed by the Indian-based grassroots organization SRISTI[12]). Finally, at a process level, the attention is towards availability of reverse cycle options and the costs associated with their implementation. Regardless of the circular aspect that is nourishing rivalry against conventional companies, this will be higher:

• If **Concentration** is low and existing firms are largely dissatisfied with their existing position in the market. Having many players wanting to change their situation is the perfect ground for CE businesses to enter solo or through a partnership with a non-CE existing business.

• When **Fixed Costs** are high. This is particularly true in industries that favour business models based on maximizing asset utilization rates. However, while reducing fixed costs can represent

Table 7.7 CE vs Not-CE Rivalry

The Degree of Rivalry Is Highest When:	Among Linear Firms	Between CE and NO-CE Firms
CONCENTRATION AND BALANCE	LOW	LOW
FIXED COSTS	HIGH	HIGH (less relevant)
DIFFERENTIATION	LOW	HIGH
CAPACITY	HIGH	LOW
GROWTH	LOW	HIGH

an important competitive edge for some firms, it is generally more relevant for CE businesses to look at variable costs, as their expenditures will remain constant, while the rising price of raw materials can have a devastating impact on non-circular companies.

- If **Differentiation** is high, meaning the distinction between CE and non-CE products is evident and forces customers to make a definite decision on what to buy.
- In a scenario of under-**capacity** (low), where it is reasonable to expect many CE businesses entering the market solo. In a crowded competitive market (overcapacity, i.e. high), it is instead more likely to assume CE start-ups partnering with existing companies, as these would search for ways to differentiate from direct competitors and target new customer niches.
- When market **Growth** accelerates (high). That is when CE companies have the opportunity to target "virgin" customers with powerful green messages. It is a fact that some CE products (theoretically ready) are only waiting for new generations of consumers. Asset sharing, for example – from cars to houses – is a market rapidly growing among the younger generations as they seem less attached to the idea of "owning", as their parents have been.

7.4.1 Supporting Methods for Undertaking CE Industry Analysis: Interviewing Key Personnel

A review of the five forces model has revealed that the CE power of each force (buyers, suppliers, entrants, substitutes, and rivalry) to influence its industry dynamics is determined by the sum of several criteria. Hence, properly assessing such criteria is key to get an accurate picture of reality. What follows is a list of questions – not meant to be exhaustive – specifically designed for that end.

A   **The Power of CE Suppliers**

- Concentration: How many suppliers have expertise in CE practices? How many suppliers have the capabilities to develop such expertise?
- Substitute CE supplies: Are there bio-based ingredients that could be used as substitutes in the manufacturing of our products? What can we expect customers receptivity to be over such changes?
- Switching costs: What are the costs of switching from standard to CE suppliers in case former ones do not agree to CE standards or lack the required capabilities to do so competitively (infrastructure, know-how, etc.)? Can switching costs be lowered by forging partnerships with CE suppliers?[13]
- Buyer CE information: What is the CE awareness amongst buyers? How likely is it for buyers to discern between suppliers on grounds of CE skills and expertise?
- Forward integration: What are the organizational characteristics of CE suppliers (size, financial resources)? Under what circumstances could CE suppliers capitalize on their expertise to expand along the value chain?

B   **The Power of CE Buyers**

- Concentration: If a few large customers dictate industry practices, how likely is it for them to accept a CE perceptive? Could CE alternatives alter the customer base of the industry?
- Price sensitivity: Based on the available industry data, is the typical customer a green/conscious consumer? Are customers willing to pay a premium price for CE products?
- Switching costs: Are customers aware and educated about the long-term savings that switching to a CE product typically generates? What initial investment are they willing to make?
- Backward integration: What are the characteristics of major CE buyers (size, financial resources)? Can CE buyers capitalize on their expertise to expand along the value chain?
- Acceptable substitutes: Are there products that barely meet future regulatory standards, but offer significant financial advantages?

C   **The Threat of CE Substitutes**

- Switching costs: What is or could be the difference in cost between CE and linear products?
- Price–Performance: What price–performance differences exist between CE and linear products?
- Suitability of alternatives: How attached are customers to existing products (explore attachment/detachment trends)? Is the

offering of CE product and services already present and radically transforming purchasing habits (e.g. servitization)?

D   The Threat of CE Entrants

- Cost advantage: Are there firms in the industry that have developed specific CE capabilities or proprietary knowledge leading to superior performance? Has the industry been suffering from technological lock-in in the last five years?
- Economies of scale: Is there potential for CE newcomers to overcome barriers imposed by scale economies? What is the real potential of CE innovation to attract investments?
- Brand value and reputation: How strong and solid is the brand image of leading linear companies? What is the potential for CE newcomers to differentiate themselves on grounds of sustainability and being green advocates, therefore nullifying the advantage of existing companies? How environmentally impactful is the industry overall?
- Regulatory system: Are there limitations in the industry for CE newcomers due to obsolete laws and regulations that did not envisage CE practices and processes? On the contrary, are there CE-oriented rulings – present or on the horizon – which would favour the market penetration of CE companies?

E   The Degree of CE Rivalry

- Concentration and balance: How are existing players performing within the industry? Are they satisfied with their current positioning or seek ways to innovate? Does the industry environment facilitate the creation of partnerships and alliances?
- Fixed costs: What are the fixed costs for operating in a linear fashion? Do fixed costs greatly outweigh variable costs? Will fixed costs be lowered by applying CE principles?
- Differentiation: What is the level of CE adoption across the industry? To what extent can CE players differentiate themselves from linear firms? How will differentiation be clear for customers?
- Capacity: Is over- (or under-) capacity in the industry seasonal or steady? How complex and lengthy would it be for existing businesses to start developing CE practices internally? Are there opportunities for CE firms to partner with existing linear companies by bringing in their know-how and capabilities?
- Market Growth: What customer segments (baby boomers, millennials, etc.) are feeding the market growth?

7.5 PEST Analysis

As Political, Economic, Social, and Technological (PEST) trends hold the potential to radically alter the dynamics of an entire industry, the PEST analysis was developed to investigate and assess the main external issues that can influence the environment in which a company operates (Aguilar 1967). When it comes to the CE, it is important to recognize the key external events that might promote – or sometimes impede – the development of circular practices in our industry. The entire CE itself is in fact an alternative industrial system that originated from the recognition of global major trends happening outside of the business environment, namely:

- The release of tougher environmental regulations in various countries (climate change laws, landfill protocols, etc.) has pushed businesses to re-invent their industrial processes [political change].
- Since 2000, the continued increase in price of raw materials has had a huge impact on the profitability and survival of many companies [economic change].
- The constant increase in human population and expansion of the middle class have dramatically altered the demand for goods and services. With standard production processes requiring levels of energy and resources that are simply not going to be available over the long run, the need for alternative business models is inevitable [social change].
- Technological developments, like sensor and trace-and-return systems, IoT, big data, and digital technology, made it easier for firms to implement alternative business practices aimed at recapturing value from pre-owned assets [technological change].
- Major advances in measurement systems have helped scientists comprehensively assess the status of the natural environment, leading to the recognition that the Earth is reaching system-wide global tipping points that might undermine the very existence of the human enterprise [technological change].

From these few generic examples, it transpires how the CE is a response to major global trends, and even more importantly, it is supported by them. This makes embracing the new economic paradigm a launch pad for business opportunities.

7.6 Supporting Methods for Undertaking PEST Analysis: Interviewing Key Personnel

To facilitate the identification of major CE trends occurring outside the company, a team of strategists with different expertise should address the following guiding questions:

POLITICAL
- Is there any global agreement (e.g. COP 21) likely to have an impact on the key processes of the industry?
- What environmental laws limiting or banning certain environmentally impactful activities are being adopted in the markets

and geographies served by the industry? For example, in April 2017 El Salvador's Legislative Assembly voted a total ban on mining activities concerning gold and other metals.[14]

- What regulations that would favour the adoption of CE practices across the industry are likely to be adopted and over what time frame? For example, in 2015 France introduced the Energy Transition Law with the objective, among others, to combat planned obsolescence of products.[15]
- What economic instruments that would favour the adoption of CE practices in the industry are being approved? For example, the tax breaks on repairs effective in Sweden from January 2017;[16] carbon tax; or incentives to green products/services, like car sharing and bio-based products.
- What existing laws and regulations, that limit the adoption of CE practices, are likely to be removed and over what time frame? For example, rating systems, standards, and codes of practice are currently being developed by several organizations to facilitate the approval process of government regulators over green building materials and speed up their widespread adoption.

ECONOMIC
- Which raw materials have their reserves projected to run out under a business-as-usual scenario?[17] What is the likely time frame for this to occur and how significant are these raw materials for the industry?
- Is there any raw material whose price has been significantly fluctuating or increased during the last five years? What is the expected trend for the future?
- What is the likely impact of economic instruments specifically developed by financial institutions and insurance companies to facilitate the adoption of CE practices by the private sector? For example, leasing arrangements for products with circular potential, valuation and risk models that suit the characteristics of circular businesses, new financing tools for supply chains that go beyond the currently available working capital solutions.[18]

SOCIAL
- Is the typical customer in the industry an environmentally conscious citizen, who is likely to prioritize green products and services?
- Is the industry experiencing a shift away from *ownership-need* typical customers? What markets/geographies are mostly affected by the change?
- Are the geographies served by the industry affected by overpopulation? What is the expected trend for the coming years?
- Are the geographies served by the industry experiencing an urbanization growth? Is this expected to continue during the coming years?

- What is the digital awareness of the average customer? How can further economic development in the area change purchase patterns and choices?

TECHNOLOGICAL

- What CE-oriented technologies are likely to be adopted on a large scale across the industry? How would such an adoption affect companies in the industry?
- What CE-oriented technologies can cause the market to expand?
- What CE-oriented technologies introduced by start-ups or existing companies are likely to disrupt production and delivery systems?

A PEST analysis does not need to be a one-off exercise, but rather its effectiveness is much higher when trends are monitored overtime. Also, government agencies, universities, consultants, think tanks, NGOs, suppliers, and customer groups should all be engaged by companies to accurately identify or verify the importance of shifts in the four domains. An ongoing and accurate assessment of trends will eventually allow a company to distinguish between changes that are likely to occur rapidly (one to two years), relatively soon (three to five years), or more gradually (longer than five years).

Once a PEST analysis is completed, a company should go back to the first step of the CE strategic process (i.e. the idea tree) to establish if the detection of future trends brought to light any additional ideas, not recognized in the first instance. Also, the outcome of a PEST analysis should be used to evaluate the impacts (positive or negative) that trends might have on each of the ideas already conceived. In the next chapter, PEST will be used in connection with the five forces model to evaluate impacts of macro trends on an industry dynamics.

7.7 Conclusions

In this chapter, we have looked at the process of data analysis, and particularly how to perform data assessments at firm, industry, and external levels using a CE lens. Traditional strategic tools infused with CE principles and ideas were leveraged to capture and prioritize useful information, highlighting the key dynamics that favour or hinder CE adoption.

The first tools to fall under our microscope were the value chain and VRIE framework. On this occasion, it was discussed through reasoning and examples (e.g. Philips) how some activities inside a firm – both primary and supportive – can be boosted to play a crucial role in delivering superior performance. The development of core CE competencies, distinctive and valuable, can lead to SCA. Next, it was Porter's five forces model. Not surprisingly, when the CE was used to interpret the various criteria, most of the traditional dynamics shaping competitive intensity, and thus industry attractiveness, no longer held. Almost like a mirror, risks were replaced by opportunities and vice versa. Finally, the focus shifted towards the external environment as data also need to be collected and analysed outside of the firm's boundaries and immediate context. The strategic tool chosen for this task was PEST. Here, discussion of the political, economic, social, and technological macro trends introduced in Chapter 1 deepened a bit further to explain the rapid adoption of CE practices worldwide.

Notes

1 Source: Adapted from Porter, Michael E. *Competitive Advantage.* 1985 (p. 37). New York: The Free Press.
2 Riversimple. n.d. "How the Business Works". Accessed on March 3, 2017, https://www.riversimple.com/how-the-business-works/
3 The sustainable technology mimics the ways plants use photosynthesis. AkzoNobel. 2017. "Akzonobel and Photanol Developing Chemical Compounds of the Future". *AkzoNobel.* Posted on September 17, 2014. www.akzonobel.com/news_center/news/news_and_press_releases/2014/akzono bel_and_photanol_developing_chemical_compounds_of_the_future.aspx
4 Philips Healthcare. 2014. "Refurbishing Solutions for MRI Systems". *Philips Healthcare.* Accessed on February 14, 2018. www.philips.com/c-dam/cor porate/about-philips/sustainability/sustainable-planet/circular-economy/ refurbished-medical-products/case-study-ce-philips-healthcare.pdf
5 They include: innovative product design, reverse cycles, green internal operations, supplier engagement, internal alignment, and external collaboration.
6 Source: adapted from Porter, Michael E. 1979(p. 141). "How Competitive Forces Shape Strategy". *Harvard Business Review.*
7 Tesla Motors. n.d. "Tesla Gigafactory". Accessed on April 23, 2018, www.tesla.com/gigafactory
8 The following video by WorlDynamics assesses the textile industry from a CE perspective, identifying and quantifying its major environmental impacts. https://youtube/65zR2nU0sBU
9 Technopolis Group. 2016. "Regulatory Barriers for the Circular Economy. Lessons from Ten Case Studies". Accessed on February 15, 2018. http://ec.europa.eu/DocsRoom/documents/19742
10 Technopolis Group. 2016. "Regulatory Obstacles to Circular Economy on Selected High Potential Markets". Accessed on February 15, 2018. http://ec.europa.eu/DocsRoom/documents/16041/attachments/3/translations/en/renditions/pdf.
11 For example, the French Consumption Law with its Article L111-3 requiring manufacturers to disclose information about the availability of a product's spare parts; the 2017 Swedish tax (VAT) break on repair activities; or the Circular Economy Policy developed by the City of Amsterdam (available at: www.amsterdam.nl/en/policy/policy-0/circular-economy/).
12 SRISTI (Society for Research and Initiatives for Sustainable Technologies and Institutions) produces a wide range of green agro-products extracted from natural herbs that include plant growth promoters and organic pesticides (the full list of products is available at: www.sristiinnovation.com/herbal-agro-products-helping-hands-for-farmers.html).

13 A fitting example of tight buyer–supplier relationship is offered by the closed-loop cooperation between Jaguar and Novelis. The client (Jaguar) sells end-of-life material – car carcasses made of aluminium – to the supplier (Novelis) that processes and re-sells recycled aluminium to the client, which then manufactures the main body of new vehicles for its customers. www. cisl.cam.ac.uk/publications/publication-pdfs/cisl-closed-loop-case-study-web.pdf

14 The New York Times. 2017. "El Salvador's Historic Mining Ban". Posted April 1, 2017. www.nytimes.com/2017/04/01/opinion/sunday/el-salvadors-historic-mining-ban.html

15 French Government. 2015. "Energy Transition". Accessed on June 7, 2018. www.gouvernement.fr/en/energy-transition

16 Jason, Margolis. 2017. "Sweden Tries to Curb Buy-and-Throw-Away Culture through Tax Breaks". *PRI*. Posted on January 2, 2017. www.pri.org/stories/2017-01-02/sweden-tries-curb-buy-and-throw-away-culture-through-tax-breaks

17 Key references to investigate projected scarcity of raw materials include: 'G. V. Mudd, "The Environmental Sustainability of Mining in Australia: Key Mega-Trends and Looming Constraints," *Resources Policy* 35, no. 2 (2010)' and 'Ellen MacArthur Foundation, "Towards the Circular Economy 3: Accelerating the Scale-Up across Global Supply Chains." (2014)'

18 ING Economic Department. 2015. "Rethinking Finance in a Circular Economy". Accessed on June 25, 2017. www.ing.nl/media/ING_EZB_Financing-the-Circular-Economy_tcm162-84762.pdf

Bibliography

Aguilar, Francis Joseph, 1967. *Scanning the Business Environment*. New York: Macmillan.

AkzoNobel. 2017. "Akzonobel and Photanol Developing Chemical Compounds of the Future." *AkzoNobel*. Posted on September 17, 2014. www.akzonobel.com/news_center/news/news_and_press_releases/2014/akzonobel_and_photanol_developing_chemical_compounds_of_the_future.aspx

Alexander, Allen T., and Dominique Philippe Martin. 2013. "Intermediaries for Open Innovation: A competence-Based Comparison of Knowledge Transfer Offices Practices." *Technological Forecasting and Social Change* 80 (1): 38–49.

Ambrosini, Véronique, Cliff Bowman, and Nardine Collier. 2009. "Dynamic Capabilities: An Exploration of How Firms Renew Their Resource Base." *British Journal of Management* 20 (S1): S9–24.

Barney, Jay. 1991. "Firm Resources and Sustained Competitive Advantage." *Journal of Management* 17 (1): 99–120.

Collis, David J., and Cynthia A. Montgomery. 1995. "Competing on Resources: Strategy in the 1990s." *Harvard Business Review* 73 (Jul–Aug): 118–28.

Coombs, Rod. 1996. "Core Competencies and the Strategic Management of R&D." *R&D Management* 26 (4): 345–55.

Dierickx, Ingemar, and Karel Cool. 1989. "Asset Stock Accumulation and Sustainability of Competitive Advantage." *Management Science* 35 (12): 1504–11.

Ellen MacArthur Foundation. 2014. "Towards the Circular Economy Vol.3: Accelerating the Scale-Up across Global Supply Chains." Accessed on September 5, 2017. www.ellenmacarthurfoundation.org/publications/towards-the-circular-economy-vol-3-accelerating-the-scale-up-across-global-supply-chains

French Government. 2015. "Energy Transition." Accessed on June 7, 2018. www.gouvernement.fr/en/energy-transition

Gluck, Frederick W., Stephen P. Kaufman, and A. Steven Walleck. 1980. "Strategic Management for Competitive Advantage." *Harvard Business Review* 58 (Jul): 154–61.

Helfat, Constance E., Sydney Finkelstein, Will Mitchell, Margaret Peteraf, Harbir Singh, David Teece, and Sidney G. Winter. 2007. *Dynamic Capabilities: Understanding Strategic Change in Organizations*. Oxford: Blackwell.

ING Economic Department. 2015. "Rethinking Finance in a Circular Economy". Accessed on June 25, 2017. www.ing.nl/media/ING_EZB_Financing-the-Circular-Economy_tcm162-84762.pdf

International Organization for Standardization (ISO). 2017. "ISO 20400:2017 Sustainable procurement — Guidance." Accessed on March 23, 2018. www.iso.org/obp/ui/#iso:std:iso:20400:ed-1:v1:en

Kraaijenbrink, Jeroen, J.-C. Spender, and Aard J. Groen. 2010. "The Resource-Based View: A Review and Assessment of Its Critiques." *Journal of Management* 36 (1): 349–72.

Laurie, Donald L., Yves L. Doz, and Claude P. Sheer. 2006. "Creating New Growth Platforms." *Harvard Business Review* 84 (5): 80–90.

Makadok, Richard. 2001. "Towards a Synthesis of Resource-Based and Dynamic Capability Views of Rent Creation." *Strategic Management Journal* 22: 387–402.

Margolis, Jason. 2017. "Sweden Tries to Curb Buy-and-Throw-Away Culture through Tax Breaks." *PRI*. Posted on January 2, 2017. www.pri.org/stories/2017-01-02/sweden-tries-curb-buy-and-throw-away-culture-through-tax-breaks

McGrath, Rita Gunther, Ming-Hone Tsai, Sankaran Venkataraman, and Ian C. MacMillan. 1996. "Innovation, Competitive Advantage and Rent: A Model and Test." *Management Science* 42 (3): 389–403.

Morgan, Neil A., Douglas W. Vorhies, and Charlotte H. Mason. 2009. "Market Orientation, Marketing Capabilities, and Firm Performance." *Strategic Management Journal* 30 (8): 909–20.

Mudd, G. V. 2010. "The Environmental Sustainability of Mining in Australia: Key Mega-Trends and Looming Constraints." *Resources Policy* 35 (2): 98–115.

Peteraf, Margaret A., and Jay B. Barney. 2003. "Unraveling the Resource-Based Tangle." *Managerial and Decision Economics* 24 (4): 309–23.

Philips Healthcare. 2014. "Refurbishing Solutions for MRI Systems." *Philips Healthcare*. Accessed on February 14, 2018. www.philips.com/c-dam/corporate/about-philips/sustainability/sustainable-planet/circular-economy/refurbished-medical-products/case-study-ce-philips-healthcare.pdf

Porter, Michael E. 1979. "How Competitive Forces Shape Strategy." *Harvard Business Review* 57 (2): 137–45.

Porter, Michael E. 1980. *Competitive Strategy: Techniques for Analyzing Industries and Competition*. New York: Free Press.

Porter, Michael E. 1985. *Competitive Advantage*. New York: The Free Press. Accessed on February 15, 2018. http://forleadership.org/wp-content/uploads/Competitive-Advantage.pdf

Prahalad, Coimbatore K., and Gary Hamel. 1990. "The Core Competence of the Corporation." *Harvard Business Review*, 68 (3): 79–91.

Riversimple. n.d. "How the Business Works." Accessed on March 3, 2017. www.riversimple.com/how-the-business-works/

Technopolis Group. 2016. "Regulatory Barriers for the Circular Economy. Lessons from Ten Case Studies." Accessed on February 15, 2018. http://ec.europa.eu/DocsRoom/documents/19742

Technopolis Group. 2016. "Regulatory Obstacles to Circular Economy on Selected High Potential Markets." Accessed on February 15, 2018. http://ec.europa.eu/DocsRoom/documents/16041/attachments/3/translations/en/renditions/pdf

Teece, David J., Gary Pisano, and Amy Shuen. 1997. "Dynamic Capabilities and Strategic Management." *Strategic Management Journal* 18: 509–33.

Tesla Motors. n.d. "Tesla Gigafactory." Accessed on April 23, 2018. www.tesla.com/gigafactory

The New York Times. 2017. "El Salvador's Historic Mining Ban." Posted April 1, 2017. www.nytimes.com/2017/04/01/opinion/sunday/el-salvadors-historic-mining-ban.html

Witjesa, Sjors, and Lozano Rodrigo. 2016. "Towards a More Circular Economy: Proposing a Framework Linking Sustainable Public Procurement and Sustainable Business Models." *Resources, Conservation and Recycling* 112: 37–44.

Zook, Chris. 2007. "Finding Your Next Core Business." *Harvard Business Review* 85 (4): 66–76.

8   CE Data Integration

8.1 Introduction

Given the general difficulty of being all things for all people, decisions must be made, and so a company must choose! For example, IKEA low-cost and simple assembly appeals to a specific target of consumers, and so does BMW engineering excellence. However, when considering environmental sustainability, the satisfied client base gets potentially broader as the topic surpasses traditional market segmentations; it equally touches young and old, male and female, rich and poor, and sophisticated and simple buyer. The result, in terms of target audience, compares what is generally expected when combining multiple distinctive competencies (e.g. quality and effectiveness), an effort traditionally not pursued by many companies in a linear economy given the time and investment required to obtain them. The significance of core competencies linked to environmental sustainability and the subsequent ability of a company to outperform competitors by doing things differently could prove decisive in years to come.

Yet, because of the intense pressure of competing over costs and quality in the short term, most companies do not spend sufficient time developing a corporate view of the future and this leaves them without the core competencies necessary to tap into new opportunities. As a result, they fail to achieve and/or sustain the sort of competitive advantage that would lead to higher than normal performance levels, often a necessary requirement to survive in today's marketplace. While the previous chapter dealt with the initial steps of data analysis (i.e. collection and prioritization), this section of the book is about integration. By combining macro (PEST) and industry (five forces) data, a company can reach a good understating of the environment – present and future – in which it intends to compete. Then by adding to the equation the specific reality of the firm, managers can soundly identify the strengths, weaknesses, opportunities, and threats (SWOT) unique to the company.

8.2 PEST vs Five Forces Matrix

Chapter 7 discussed the PEST analysis as a way to recognize changes in either the political, economic, social, or technological arenas and foresee CE trends. Here, we continue the conversation to see how that macro-level data can serve the interests of a company. One of the most effective ways to harness the results of a PEST analysis is to link them to an industry analysis, hence creating a PEST x five forces matrix. The first table below lists the chief CE-related global occurrences expected to have implications across industries (Table 8.1). Apart from identifying those changes that are most imminent, a distinction is also made on whether the anticipated events are expected to occur fast

Table 8.1 CE Outlook Using PEST Analysis

	SUPPLIERS	BUYERS	SUBSTITUTES	NEW ENTRANTS	RIVALRY
POLITICAL			New laws and regulations limiting the selling and use of polluting processes, products, and services will lead to a mass market for CE alternatives **(Suitability of CE Alternatives)**	Governments are expected to take action to overcome limitations and complexities of outdated legislatory systems that hinder market access for CE companies **(Regulatory System)** / Governments will promote CE legal frameworks that will include incentives for companies adopting circular practices **(Regulatory System)**	
ECONOMIC	As the economic benefits of the CE go mainstream, more and more suppliers will be willing to collaborate on CE practices, therefore reducing concentration **(Supplier Concentration)**		Scarcity of raw materials will prompt companies to adopt circular practices to secure sources of inputs from pre-owned assets **(Suitability of CE Alternatives)** / High prices of raw materials lead to adopt circular practices in order to secure inputs from pre-owned assets **(Suitability of CE Alternatives)**	Financial institutions will develop new credit and financial solutions specifically tailored for enabling the adoption of CE practices, thereby facilitating market access to new companies **(Regulatory System)**	New CE practices will lead to a reconceptualization of production costs and positioning **(Fixed Costs / Growth)**
SOCIAL		Greater awareness of global/local environmental issues will encourage people to choose CE products and services even if prices are higher **(Price Sensitivity)**	As environmental issues worsen, more people will opt for CE alternatives when facing a purchasing decision **(Switching Costs)** / Older generations that are not acquainted with digital technology will gradually leave space to tech savvy individuals who will drive the demand for innovative digital services **(Suitability of CE Alternatives)**	As the ecological impacts of man-made activities worsen, new entrepreneurs will recognize these as business opportunities and offer "green" alternatives. **(Brand Value & Reputation)** / As the global middle class grows, pressure on finite resources will increase and so will the demand for CE alternatives, hence opening the doors for new green companies **(Scale Economies)**	As more customers will accept CE solutions, their selection will shift more towards product type rather than brand **(Concentration / Differentiation)**
TECHNOLOGICAL	Developments in CE-related technologies (renewable energy, refurbishing, trace and return) are making it possible for companies to internalize production processes **(Substitutes / Switching Costs / Buyer CE information)**	Major breakthroughs in CE enabling technologies are driving down the cost of CE-related operations, making it possible for companies to offer CE products and services at convenient prices **(Switching Costs)**	Developments and widespread adoption of CE enabling technologies will improve the price-performance of CE products and services **(Price-Performance)**		

Rapid change	Slow change	Incoming change

or slow. Just as an example, by crossing the "buyers" force with the "technological" trend, the following consideration regarding switching costs transpires: "Major breakthroughs in CE enabling technologies are driving down the cost of CE-related operations, making it possible for companies to offer CE products and services at convenient prices.

To better comprehend how global trends can affect specific industries, the second table offers a CE analysis specific for the automotive sector (Table 8.2). In this case, the generic consideration previously made about switching costs, for example, takes shape becoming:

> major breakthroughs in CE enabling technologies (smartphone applications, digital platforms, sensor systems for instant communication of the car fuel levels, tires consumption, etc.) are driving down the cost of CE-related operations thereby making it possible for companies to offer car sharing at convenient prices.

Table 8.2 CE-PEST Analysis for the Automotive Industry

AUTOMOTIVE INDUSTRY				
SUPPLIERS	**BUYERS**	**SUBSTITUTES**	**NEW ENTRANTS**	**RIVALRY**
POLITICAL		Following COP21 commitments, the release of laws and regulations aiming at curbing Co2 emissions at country level (through incentives to buyers of electric cars and bans over the selling of fossil fuel engines) will gradually make the production and selling of electric vehicles more convenient for car manufacturers **(Suitability of CE Alternatives)**	Governments will promote: CE legal frameworks (e.g. to rate the durability and reparability of car components and standards to measure them); mandatory information about the lifetime of the vehicle and its parts; extension of minimum legal warranties; spare parts that must be widely available and affordable for a minimum number of years; lower taxes on repair service activities that will include incentives for companies adopting circular practices **(Regulatory System)**	
ECONOMIC As more and more firms start implementing CE practices (e.g. Renault, Caterpillar primarily through closing the loop of car components; Tesla by producing electric vehicles for the masses; Mercedes offering car sharing services) a larger number of suppliers will be involved, thereby increasing concentration **(Concentration)**		Reserves of lead expected to run out by 2030. This might prompt companies to adopt circular practices to secure volumes of production inputs from pre-owned assets **(Suitability of CE Alternatives)** High prices for metals will prompt car-makers to adopt circular practices to secure volumes of production inputs from pre-owned vehicles **(Suitability of CE Alternatives)**		Profit margins are moderate and opportunities for expansion limited. Reinterpreting fixed costs offers opportunities for market growth and a more relaxed competition **(Fixed Costs / Growth)**

SOCIAL		Greater awareness of environmental and health issues connected with Co2 emissions will encourage more people to choose electric cars and car sharing services, already booming in Europe and the United States (**Price Sensitivity**)	Greater awareness of environmental issues will prompt more people to opt for CE alternatives when facing a purchasing decision between a normal car and a CE alternative, such as subscribing to a car sharing service or buying an electric vehicle (**Switching Costs**) — Older generations that are not familiar with digital technology will be gradually replaced by tech savvy people who will drive the demand for car sharing (**Suitability of CE Alternatives**)	As the ecological impacts of man-made activities worsen in relation to Co2 and consequently climate change, new companies will be able to enter the automotive industry by providing alternative solutions (e.g. Uber, Tesla, Share'Ngo etc.) (**Brand Value & Reputation**)	Companies focused on CE solutions, such as electric vehicles or car sharing, are generally not the usual car manufacturers, as they target a different customer profile (**Differentiation / Concentration**)
TECHNOLOGICAL	Major breakthroughs in CE enabling technologies (smartphone applications, digital platforms, sensor systems for instant communication of the car fuel levels, tires consumption, etc.) are driving down the cost of CE-related operations thereby making it possible for companies to offer car sharing at convenient prices (**Switching Costs**)		Developments in CE enabling technologies (like trace-and-return system to manage flows of returned car components, and digital technology to access information about shared vehicles) is fostering the price-performance of CE services like car sharing (**Price-Performance**)		

Rapid change	Slow change	Incoming change

8.3 SWOT Analysis

Although there is no clear trace about the origins of the SWOT framework, after several decades, it continues to be regarded as a solid technique for strategic decision-making and pervades the academic literature (Helms and Nixon 2010). Arguably, its value lays in its simplicity and unstructured approach as it invites to consider all the important aspects in a firm's environment and organize ideas so that the company's strengths can be identified to grasp external opportunities, while its weaknesses recognized to avoid external threats. The analysis consists in identifying all possible strengths and weaknesses of the organization under scrutiny. These can vary significantly and be related to management, operations, finance, image, or other factors important for the company. Threats and opportunities are instead recognized by assessing the external environment.

Critics to this technique have argued against such simplicity and excessive degree of subjectivity (Hill and Westbrook 1997; Panagiotou 2003), but the SWOT, in its bare state, should be intended simply as a list:

It conveys no information in itself, but a way of helping us to think about the information we already have. And for a busy manager, confronted by endless everyday pressures and unused to standing back to think about long-term issues, it is a particularly useful list, as demonstrated by its continued popularity.

(Kay et al. 2006, 43)

Another important aspect when performing a SWOT analysis is to consider that it should not be envisioned as a never-to-be-repeated exercise, but rather be ongoing (Houben et al. 1999). The dynamic environment in which a company operates causes the relative importance of a strategic factor to change constantly; hence, a proactive management team should maintain an up-to-date perception of what new opportunities become on offer and what risks might the company be facing in the future.

Regarding its relevance, the SWOT has a universal applicability as testified by its varied use to analyse firms in all types of sectors (e.g. health, agriculture, tourism, manufacturing, electronics, construction, textile, oil and gas, financial, IT, etc.) and countries (Ghazinoory et al. 2011). At a territorial level, SWOT also found worthy applications in the environment area, to analyse, for example, the consequences of a City Council implementing an EMS (Lozano and Valles 2007) or to formulate a portfolio of actions towards enabling sustainable energy development (Markovska et al. 2009).

Of course, for a proper data integration process, the SWOT list can and should be further analysed. Indeed, there have been significant contributions to its methodological development over the last two decades (Ramos et al. 2000) often through the integration of other methods, like the balanced scorecard (Ip and Koo 2004), multiple-attribute decision-making (Kangas et al. 2003; Yüksel and Dagdeviren 2007), Resource-Based View (Marti 2004), and core-competence tree (Coman and Ronen 2009). For the purpose of this book (i.e. integrate CE considerations into the SWOT), two dynamic[1] approaches have been created: the Dynamic CE-SWOT[2] and the CE-TOWS Matrix[3] (Weihrich 1982).

The first approach is a four-step process that starts by considering the results of a PEST analysis from an environmental (CE-oriented) perspective. CE opportunities, threats, strengths, and weaknesses are then identified, before a list of actions is finally created. The second approach builds on the traditional SWOT analysis to generate an enhanced version of the matrix, called CE-TOWS. This tool matches together the various elements identified in each of the four categories (Strengths–Weaknesses–Opportunities–Threats) to define pragmatic actions for CE implementation. Although slightly different in how they unfold, the two approaches systematically map all collected information according to whether they are perceived as a company's strength or weakness, with the same objective of identifying concrete CE actions to exploit opportunities and prevent threats. Thanks to their capacity of integrating different information together and connecting issues from different levels of analysis, both methods are ideal to understand how to approach a circular strategy.

8.3.1 SWOT Adaptation #1: The Dynamic CE-SWOT

The Dynamic CE-SWOT has been specifically conceived to guide the analytical process of integrating CE consideration into a SWOT analysis. The assessment starts from an in-depth analysis of environmental macro-trends and CE enablers (a further investigation of data previously gathered with the PEST analysis) to then detect relevant risks and opportunities for the business and finishing off with a list of selected actionable solutions based on strengths and weaknesses. The tool thus creates logic connections between the global socio-economic and environmental trends and the specific profile of the company under scrutiny. Figure 8.1 summarizes the four steps for conducting a Dynamic CE-SWOT Analysis.

This enhanced focus on external megatrends concerning sustainability resonates well with one of the most alluring concepts for sustainable business development devised in recent years: Shared Value (Porter and Kramer 2011). The notion suggests sustainability as a means to increase the competitive advantage of a firm, while concurrently benefitting its many stakeholders (including the environment, i.e. the silent stakeholder). The creation of Shared Value revolves around the crucial activity of embedding environmental (and social) considerations at the very heart of a company business model. In doing so, businesses are prompted to innovate their practices to fully grasp the market opportunities linked to the countless unmet needs caused by the (un)sustainable developmental path of the 21st century. Food giant Nestlé is one of multinational corporations to have embraced the SV approach. By reinventing the business model for its coffee, the company has teamed up with its suppliers to concurrently tackle poverty, mitigate environmental degradation, and boost productivity (Porter and Kramer 2011).

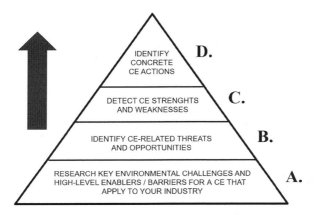

Figure 8.1 Performing a Dynamic CE-SWOT Analysis.[4]

A   **Research the Key Environmental Challenges and High-Level Enablers/ Barriers for a CE that apply to Your Industry.** Start with researching the key environmental challenges that have or will have an impact in the geographies you are serving. The analysis shall have a local/ regional/national or even international focus, depending on the company's reach. As a guide, the following macro-categories developed by the World Resource Institute (Metzger et al. 2012) can be used:

- Reduce greenhouse gases (GHGs); adapt to climate variability and extremes (sea level rising, floods, etc.).
- Develop alternatives for scarce natural resources (energy, materials, etc.).
- Produce food without disrupting natural systems (think about the impact of fertilizers).
- Ensure supply of freshwater (water quality, quantity, etc.).
- Preserve and restore ecosystem services (natural flood control, natural pest regulation, etc.).
- Eliminate chemical, air, and water pollution; mitigate health risks (waste management, toxics, etc.).

The collected data shall then be matched – into a matrix – against the PEST trends identified in the previous step of the CE Strategic Process. These will either promote or halter the development of circular practices in your industry, as it happened, for example, regarding: recent technological solutions that are making it easier for firms to implement alternative business practices aimed at recapturing value from pre-owned assets (technological change); major developments in measurement systems that have helped scientists comprehensively assess the status of the natural environment and realize the surpassing of natural tipping points that might undermine the very existence of the human enterprise on Earth (technological change); the massive growth in human population that is dramatically altering the demand for goods and services (social change); the continued increase in price of raw materials that has had a huge impact on the profitability and survival of many companies (economic change); and the announcement of tougher environmental regulations in various countries (climate change laws, landfill regulations, etc.) pushing businesses to re-invent their industrial processes (political change).

B   **Identify CE-related Threats and Opportunities.** Continue your analysis by conducting an in-depth investigation of the correlations found through step A Identify threats and opportunities specific to the organization. As the CE is essentially about innovation and collaboration, these two aspects will need to be prioritized when performing this assessment. Questions to be asked might include the following:

Threats

- Is there any fact or trend that could potentially negatively impact the organization? Where would the impact be felt (for example, increased costs, decline in revenues, damage to intangibles, loss of tangible assets, fiercer competition)?
- Is there any fact or trend that could potentially negatively impact my value chain (from raw materials extraction to production and distribution, consumption and disposal)? Is any key supplier already exposed to the risk(s)?
- Is any competitor already being negatively impacted by facts or trends identified in step A? How likely is it for the same occurring to my organization?

Opportunities

- What unmet needs related to the facts and trends identified in step A can be addressed through circular actions?
- Is any competitor already tapping into this opportunity?
- Is there any emerging CE-enabling technology that we can leverage to exploit this opportunity (i.e. satisfy this unmet need, tackle this environmental challenge)?
- What kind of collaborations (across departments, along the supply chain, with specialized CE organizations, or other institutions) could help us exploit this particular opportunity?

C   **Detect (CE) Strengths and Weaknesses.** Now that you have a clear picture of the broader dynamics unfolding around the company, narrow down your analysis at the firm level by concentrating on your core existing strengths and weaknesses. To begin with, the strategist shall make a comprehensive list of both categories. Most data are expected to already be available from the application of the various tools discussed in the previous chapters, but holding a brainstorming session at this stage will not hurt while on the contrary ensure that all possible solutions are brought to light.

Weaknesses:
Having previously worked on recognizing CE threats and trends, as you now go through the list of the firm's weaknesses, it will be easier to identify the ones more likely to reinforce those negative environmental externalities. To get ready for the next step (identification of concrete CE actions), try to write down a list of solutions that can help overcome the most relevant weaknesses. In doing so, keep in mind that the CE is fundamentally about (technological) innovation, novel partnerships, and previously unexplored solutions. Be creative!

Strengths:
As you create the list of company's strengths, do not be satisfied with clearly defined and highly celebrated core competencies.

The focus is on CE solutions and it may be that crucial capabilities have gone unnoticed if circularity has never been approached seriously by the firm before. It may in fact be that your company is unconsciously already exploiting one or more circular strengths to achieve or maintain competitive advantage. To help you with this task, you can use, as a reference, the comprehensive list of areas for circular action developed by Cristoni and Tonelli (2018) (Table 8.3). Go through each item and ask yourself whether your company is or could easily be well positioned in that area. Remember though that strengths can also be found elsewhere, for example, the company's culture or values or in the company's in-depth knowledge of a CE technology. Once you have completed your list, start asking yourself which strengths can be (further)

Table 8.3 Possibilities for Circular Action in the Value Chain

Design

1. Dematerialization
2. Optimise input materials
3. Increase longevity (design for durability)
4. Design for recycling

Sourcing

5. Engage suppliers on environmental programmes
6. Switch to circular feedstock

Production

7. Maximize overall environmental performance of operations
8. Switch to renewable energy to power operations
9. Explore circular applications for solid waste streams
10. Investigate circular water resources
11. Tackle packaging waste

Distribution Shipment

12. Optimize logistics (distribution strategies)
13. Address unsold inventory stock

Use

14. Maximize utilization rate (intensity of product use)

End Use

15. Focus on re-use/re-distribution of the product(s)
16. Focus on maintenance/repair
17. Focus on re-manufacturing refurbishment of product(s) or products parts

leveraged for implementing CE solutions in relation to the opportunities previously identified.

D **Identify Concrete CE Actions.** At this point, you shall be able to come up with a list of actions that are coherent with both the external changes occurring at the macro level and the characteristics of the firm. As the CE is a radically new approach to business, still surrounded by uncertainty and risks, it is recommended to start focusing on just a few actions. This will allow the firm to allocate the right amount of resources (personnel, time, investments, etc.) rather than dissipating them pursuing too many projects. Actions can vary greatly, depending on the results of the assessment. For example, a local manufacturer of wind turbines or solar panels might decide to investigate the possible applications of IoT technology to its products (business weakness) in light of the new opportunities offered by recent technological advancements (technological change) and shifting customer preferences that favour servitization (social change). Alternatively, a carmaker might decide to build on its expertise in car sharing (business strength) to export this service to a developing country, following the recognition of a rapid population growth in the area, further strengthened by rising middle class and urbanization trends (social change).

8.3.2 SWOT Adaptation #2: The CE-TOWS Matrix

This tool is presented as a simpler and more straightforward alternative than the previous one and it is arguably more suitable for start-ups or small firms. The CE-TOWS Matrix takes into deeper consideration the connections among the four categories Strengths–Weaknesses–Opportunities–Threats of the SWOT, allowing strategic action to become clearer. Differently from the Dynamic CE SWOT, this approach follows the traditional SWOT analysis and only adds a further step to it, where the manager is asked to identify the interrelations between elements of the SWOT list.

- **STEP 1**: As in the case of a normal SWOT, we commence by identifying all the strengths of the company, while keeping an eye out for those that might also prove useful for facilitating CE implementation, and which will become our focus in the later stage (populating the TOWS quadrants). There will of course also be weaknesses that can hinder the business from growing and concurrently prevent the establishment of CE solutions. To identify these, the first step is, once again, to start from a comprehensive list of all weaknesses.
- **STEP 2**: Maintaining a CE perspective, research the most relevant opportunities and threats that transpire from the PEST analysis. Remember that major trends promoting, preventing, or slowing down the development of circular practices are occurring in every industry.

- **STEP 3**: Thoroughly compare the identified CE-related threats and opportunities with the list of business strengths and weaknesses to identify the most suitable areas for CE actions.

The challenge in TOWS is producing integrated statements that make sense of the information that has been identified in prior analyses. To help visualize how a CE-TOWS Matrix should look like, we offer two very different examples from the clothing industry.

Case Study: Zara

Zara, the world's largest retailer, is a Spanish clothing and accessories brand based in Arteixo, Galicia. The company is the flagship brand of the Inditex group and owns close to 6,500 stores across roughly 90 countries around the world. Zara has conquered a market leader position in the fashion industry by exploiting the fast-fashion business model (Table 8.4). Thanks to its low-cost and quick value chain, Zara is able to continually provide its stores with the latest fashionable clothes at cheap prices. The brand has a global outreach and targets the mass market. As far as sustainability is concerned, Zara has implemented several noteworthy initiatives to help reduce its overall environmental impact. In 2012, the company signed the DETOX Commitment drafted by Greenpeace, whereby the brand committed to eliminate all discharge of hazardous chemicals from its supply chain and products by 2020.[5] More recently, the Spanish retailer joined the 2020 Circular Fashion System Commitment,[6] a not-for-profit initiative that aims at accelerating the transition towards an effective circular fashion system by implementing design strategies for cyclability; increasing the volumes of used garments collected and resold; and boosting the share of garments made from recycled post-consumer textile fibres.

As part of Inditex, the company also follows the sustainability principles embedded in the environmental policies of the Group. Besides a general environmental sustainability policy, Inditex has in place specific procedures for water management, energy management, biodiversity protection, and the stewardship of ancient and endangered forests.[7] More related to CE, Inditex has also focused efforts on strategies for closed-loop industrial practices. In November 2015, the Group started releasing clothes under its "Join Life" initiative, which featured the use of sustainable raw materials like Refibra Lyocell, a fibre created from recycled cotton and wood harvested from sustainably managed forests.

Table 8.4 CE-TOWS Matrix: Zara

S	• The company's complete control over its supply chain is an opportunity to implement CE practices quickly and efficiently and to strengthen the relationships with key suppliers and business partners. • The company's global outreach is an opportunity to take advantage of local/regional CE-oriented laws and regulations and implement customized CE solutions that fit with the different geographies in which it operates; • The massive number of strategically-located stores can be leveraged for effectively implementing take-back programmes and return schemes, repair services and other CE activities that will help the company further loyalize its customers; • Zara's success in online sales could potentially be leveraged to implement online marketplaces where people trade pre-owned products, and the company get a fee for every transaction completed.	• The extremely successful fast-fashion strategy pursued by Zara means massive amounts of goods are produced and quickly discarded. Hence the company might soon be facing multiple CE-related threats connected to: resources scarcity, increased price of raw materials, pressure from environmental groups, tougher environmental legislations, and reduced licences to operate; • The company's huge appeal on the younger generation of consumers might become a threat given they are more aware of the environmental problems connected with the current economic paradigm.
W	• Target segment which is not extremely consumer loyal and might go for cheaper and newer collections could be loyalized through servitization and other CE strategies that focus on extending/strengthening the relationship with customers.	• The pursued strategy of no/little advertisement can prevent the company from defending itself against environmentally-conscious customers or engage with them in case of new CE activities.
	O	T

Case Study: Patagonia

Patagonia Inc. is a privately held American clothing company which focuses mainly on high-end outdoor clothing. The high quality of its products allows the firm to charge a premium price to customers. The sales strategy of Patagonia focuses on selective distribution to retailers and a limited number of proprietary stores (Table 8.5). The company was founded by Yvon Chouinard in 1973, and has always been considered an environmentally

(Continued)

conscious business. Besides its many external environmental initiatives (for example, the company devotes 1% of annual sales to the preservation and restoration of the natural environment), Patagonia has been the first major retail firm to switch to all organic cotton and to use all non-toxic dyes and materials. One of the key pillars of the company's selling strategy is to manufacture, repair, and re-use products so that they "last a lifetime". For this reason, Patagonia is regarded as an anti-materialistic company, one that prompts its customers not to discard old items in favour of newer ones. In 2013, this stance has been formalized with the name of "Worn Wear initiative", which is built around the concept of the 4Rs: "Reduce, Repair, Re-use, and Recycle".[8] The programme allows customers to return their damaged Patagonia items, regardless of how old they are, to the company for repairing at no or little cost. Now, the initiative is bound to expand through the launch of a dedicated online platform whereby Patagonia will sell used clothing and outdoor equipment sourced from its customers. In Europe as well as in the U.S., Patagonia is registered as a Benefit-Corporation (B. Corp.), a new type of for-profit entity committed to pursue social as well as environmental objectives besides economic growth, hence freeing the company from the legal obligation to solely attain maximum returns for shareholders.

Table 8.5 CE-TOWS Matrix: Patagonia

S	• The long-standing environmentally friendly culture of the company can pave the way for rapid implementation and executives' buy-in of new CE strategies, that will further strengthen relationships with old customers, while appealing to new "green" generations. • Patagonia's customer loyalty incentives can be further enhanced through servitization and other CE strategies that focus on extending/strengthening the relationship with customers.	• Patagonia's in-depth knowledge of green materials and sustainable production processes may in the future be overtaken by business models based on net-zero innovation.
W	• The company charges a high premium price for its items, which could potentially be lowered by implementing cost-effective CE production strategies and CE enabling technologies.	• The low number of stores can become a barrier for the implementation of large-scale effective take-back programmes and return schemes, which could become necessary following tougher environmental legislations.
	O	**T**

8.4 Conclusions

Data integration is an important part of the CE strategic process, where the results of prior assessments on resources and capabilities of the firm, industry dynamics, and PEST are brought together to an actionable level. In the first instance, the PEST analysis conducted in Chapter 7 was combined here with the industry five forces to create a matrix that provided a comprehensive outlook of the impacts that CE macro-trends can have across industries. A focus on the automotive industry was then considered to understand the full potential of the method. The second half of this chapter dealt with the SWOT, and in particular two improved versions of the original framework, specifically devised for the CE: the Dynamic CE-SWOT and the CE-TOWS Matrix. Unlike the standard SWOT, these tools provide the manager with a list of thoughtful actions for CE implementation.

The Dynamic CE-SWOT is a four-step process that starts with a detailed investigation of the global socio-economic and environmental trends shaping the firm's industry. Inspired by the Shared Value concept of Porter and Kramer (2011) and the sustainability SWOT (Metzger et al. 2012), it is a tool mainly intended for larger organizations that experience poor communication among departments and work with multiple stakeholders. The CE-TOWS Matrix is instead simpler and targets start-ups and small companies. It basically takes the SWOT list of threats, opportunities, weaknesses, and strengths, and creates direct connections among the various categories, eventually deriving strategic actions. This second adaptation of the SWOT has been applied to two clothing firms: the notorious fast-fashion brand and world's largest retailer Zara, and Patagonia, a privately held American outdoor clothing company whose strategy focuses on conscious consumerism. The very different sets of actions resulting from these two examples reinforce the statement that CE strategies need to be carefully tailored to the specificities of each organization.

Notes

1 Assigning actions is what gives the analysis its dynamic nature.
2 The Dynamic CE-SWOT has been inspired by the Sustainability SWOT (sSWOT) engineered by the World Resource Institute. Eliot Metzger, Samantha Putt del Pino, Sally Prowitt, Jenna Goodward, and Alexander Perera. 2012. "sSWOT a Sustainability SWOT". The World Resource Institute. www.wri.org/publication/sswot.
3 In the TOWS matrix, the interdependence of S and W with O and T is central to the integration of issues identified in prior analyses (Weihrich, 1982). This attitude addresses one of the bigger concerns raised over the years about the SWOT: *"Very Interesting, but What Do We Do with It Now?"* (T. Richard. Dealtry, 1992, 1).

4 Image adapted from the work of Eliot Metzger, Samantha Putt del Pino, Sally Prowitt, Jenna Goodward, and Alexander, Perera. 2012. "sSWOT a Sustainability SWOT". The World Resource Institute.
5 Greenpeace International. 2012. "People! Zara Commits to Go Toxic-Free". Posted on November 29, 2012. www.greenpeace.org/international/story/7554/people-zara-commits-to-go-toxic-free/.
6 For more information about the project visit www.globalfashionagenda.com/commitment/.
7 Inditex. n.d. "Our Commitment to the Environment". Accessed February 25, 2018. www.inditex.com/en/our-commitment-to-the-environment.
8 Limei Hoang. 2017. "Patagonia's Circular Economy Strategy". *The Business of Fashion*. Posted on January 16, 2017. www.businessoffashion.com/articles/news-analysis/how-patagonia-transformed-the-circular-economy.

Bibliography

Coman, Alex, and Boaz Ronen. 2009. "Focused SWOT: Diagnosing Critical Strengths and Weaknesses." *International Journal of Production Research* 47 (20): 5677–89. doi:10.1080/00207540802146130.

Cristoni, Nicolò, and Marcello Tonelli. 2018. "Perceptions of Firms Participating in a Circular Economy." *European Journal of Sustainable Development* 7(4): 105–18. doi: 10.14207/ejsd.2018.v7n4p105.

Dealtry, T. Richard. 1992. *'Dynamic SWOT Analysis': Developer's Guide.* Birmingham: DSA Publications.

Ghazinoory, Sepehr, Mansoureh Abdi, and Mandana Azadegan-Mehr. 2011. "SWOT Methodology: A State-of-the-art Review for the Past, a Framework for the Future." *Journal of Business Economics and Management* 12 (1): 24–48.

Greenpeace International. 2012. "People! Zara Commits to Go Toxic-Free." Posted on November 29, 2012. www.greenpeace.org/international/story/7554/people-zara-commits-to-go-toxic-free/.

Helms, Marilyn M., and Judy Nixon. 2010. "Exploring SWOT Analysis–Where Are We Now? A Review of Academic Research from the Last Decade." *Journal of Strategy and Management* 3 (3): 215–51. doi:10.1108/17554251011064837.

Hill, Terry, and Roy Westbrook. 1997. "SWOT Analysis: It's Time for a Product Recall." *Long Range Planning* 30 (1): 46–52.

Hoang, Limei. 2017. "Patagonia's Circular Economy Strategy." *The Business of Fashion*. Posted on January 16, 2017. www.businessoffashion.com/articles/news-analysis/how-patagonia-transformed-the-circular-economy.

Houben, Ghislain, Kwan Lenie, and Koen Vanhoof. 1999. "A Knowledge-Based SWOT-Analysis System as an Instrument for Strategic Planning in Small and Medium Sized Enterprises." *Decision Support Systems* 26 (2): 125–35.

Inditex. n.d. "Our Commitment to the Environment." Accessed on February 25, 2018. www.inditex.com/en/our-commitment-to-the-environment.

Ip, Y. K., and L. C. Koo. 2004. "BSQ Strategic Formulation Framework a Hybrid of Balanced Scorecard, SWOT Analysis and Quality Function Deployment." *Managerial Auditing Journal* 19 (4): 533–43. doi:10.1108/02686900410530538.

Kangas, Jyrki, Mikko Kurttila, Miika Kajanus, and Annika Kangas. 2003. "Evaluating the Management Strategies of a Forestland Estate-the S-O-S

Approach." *Journal of Environmental Management* 69: 349–58. doi:10.1016/j.jenvman.2003.09.010.

Kay, John, Peter McKiernan, and David Faulkner. 2006. "The History of Strategy and Some Thoughts About the Future." In *The Oxford Handbook of Strategy*, edited by D. Faulkner, and A. Campbell, 21–46. Oxford: Oxford University Press.

Lozano, Macarena, and Jose J. Valles. 2007. "An Analysis of the Implementation of an Environmental Management System in a Local Public Administration." *Journal of Environmental Management* 82 (4): 495–511. doi:10.1016/j.jenvman.2006.01.013.

María Viedma Marti, José. 2004. "Strategic Knowledge Benchmarking System (SKBS): A Knowledge-Based Strategic Management Information System for Firms." *Journal of Knowledge Management* 8 (6): 31–49. doi:10.1108/13673270410567611.

Markovska, Natasa, Verica Taseska, and Jordan Pop-Jordanov. 2009. "SWOT Analyses of the National Energy Sector for Sustainable Energy Development." *Energy* 34 (6): 752–56.

Metzger, Eliot, Samantha Putt del Pino, Sally Prowitt, Jenna Goodward, and Alexander Perera. 2012. "sSWOT a sustainability SWOT". *The World Resource Institute*. Accessed on September 15, 2016. pdf.wri.org/sustainability_swot_user_guide.pdf.

Panagiotou, George. 2003. "Bringing SWOT into Focus." *Business Strategy Review* 14 (2): 8–10.

Porter, Michael E., and Mark R. Kramer. 2011. "The Big Idea: Creating Shared Value. How to Reinvent Capitalism—and Unleash a Wave of Innovation and Growth." *Harvard Business Review* 89 (Jan–Feb): 62–77.

Ramos, Paulo, Ana Salazar, and João Gomes. 2000. "Trends in Portuguese Tourism: A Content Analysis of Association and Trade Representative Perspectives." *International Journal of Contemporary Hospitality Management* 12 (7): 409–16. doi:10.1108/09596110010347266.

Weihrich, Heinz. 1982. "The TOWS Matrix—A Tool for Situational Analysis." *Long Range Planning* 15 (2): 54–66.

Yüksel, İhsan, and Metin Dagdeviren. 2007. "Using the Analytic Network Process (ANP) in a SWOT Analysis – A Case Study for a Textile Firm." *Information Sciences* 177 (16): 3364–82. doi:10.1016/j.ins.2007.01.001.

9 Determining Your Preferred CE Position

9.1 Introduction

With Chapter 9, we exit from the analysis of the CE strategic process to address the following phase: determining a preferred CE position. This target state, together with the previously identified "current situation" (see Chapter 6) will, in turn, serve to determine the gap that needs to be filled by the new CE strategy.

Identifying the most attractive strategic position within an industry is an essential step in any strategy development process; hence, there are already tools which are well tested and consolidated for the task. One of these, which seems the most appropriate for a calibration based on the new circular dynamics that are disrupting the business environment, is the strategic quadrant with its seven positions (Faulkner and Bowman 1992). This chapter then continues with an assessment of the internationalization approaches that a business is faced with when considering overseas markets. Building on the existing typical internationalization strategies (Bartlett and Ghoshal 1989) and by assessing cases of circularity already visible across industries, we imagine how internationalization decisions might look like in the context of a true CE.

9.2 Strategic Quadrant

The strategic quadrant, or strategy clock (Faulkner and Bowman 1992), developed from the current in disagreement with Porter's (1985) four generic strategies, according to which a business could maximize performance either by striving for low-cost production or by differentiating its products offering. According to Bowman and Faulkner (1996), it is instead the customer's perspective of value that needs to be analysed and used to compare all available products in terms of price (rather than cost) vs quality. The perceived quality of a product or service is determined by subjective and objective components – size, materials, and lifespan – and so is price (Parnell 2006). In the strategic quadrant, value is represented by the perceived quality–price ratio, which can be delivered in multiple combinations along the continuum that exists between providing great quality only to a particular group of wealthy customers (i.e. high specialization) and offering cheap products for a level of quality just above base line. While the "low price, hence low quality" statement – or vice versa – is true most of the times, in some instances, firms can offer a comparative low price thanks to technological innovations or economies of scale (White 1986; Hill 1988), delivering the ideal value proposition of high quality at low price. As illustrated later, the strategic quadrant helps to plot the different market positions according to where a company intends to stand relative to its competitors (Figure 9.1).

Regardless of the opportunities in the industry, the positioning – present or desired – of a firm needs to be based on real facts. The firm's internal competencies previously identified will determine where a company stands and how far it can move inside the quadrant. A stronger stance on aspects like good cost control systems, economies of scale, experience curve benefits, superior technology, and low-cost inputs will favour a positioning towards the low end of the price axis; superior performance in innovation, R&D, know-how, patents, location, and brand recognition will instead support a high degree of perceived quality.

With environmental considerations progressively becoming a priority at par with the economic performance for both policymakers and business executives (WEF 2017), the criteria to determine the seven positions in the quadrant are arguably to be re-assessed critically with the aim of granting CE matters some weight in the determination of quality perception and ultimately provide a more comprehensive evaluation of the

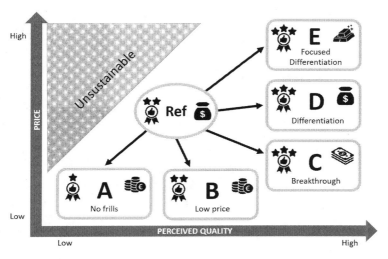

Figure 9.1 The Strategic Quadrant.

company positioning in the marketplace. What follows is an explanation of each competitive position, looked first from a traditional linear economic perspective and then through a more environmentally friendly lens.

Centre: Industry Reference

The industry reference has traditionally been defined according to customer expectations about the standards for an average product or service. It is normally where leading brands are located as they possess the power to offer such level of quality and still compete on price. Industry reference firms tend to share, in fact, common attributes: target the mass market with the aim of conquering the largest possible share; being large enough to influence both industry's dynamics and expectations from customers.

Under a CE scenario, industry reference businesses can be defined according to their capacity to deliver price-competitive alternatives to conventional linear products, while concurrently achieving advanced circular practices and negligent environmental impact. Companies of this kind have placed sustainability and the very heart of their businesses and invested significant resources in implementing environmentally sound production systems. They have thoroughly investigated the main ecological impacts of their products and industrial processes from a life cycle perspective and embraced innovative circular solutions to reduce them. Notwithstanding the efforts made on the environmental side, these companies remain able to provide customers with cost-effective solutions as they have managed to find and exploit economic opportunities lying behind existing inefficiencies. In doing so, they have attained multiple benefits such as superior alignment with customer expectations and increased customer loyalty, enhanced brand image, efficiency increases in both production and supply chain processes, and cost savings related to environmental taxes and price of raw materials. A CE-oriented company in this position represents an example of sustainability for all competitors (e.g. Interface in the carpet tile sector or Renault's Choisy-le-Roy plant in the automotive industry).

Position A: No Frills

"No frills" are those companies that, with respect to reference firms, offer products and services of lesser overall quality and with fewer features, but for a better price.

In the CE, the concept of "no frills" business can be applied to firms that, although pursuing some random circular activity, decide not to place circularity at the heart of their strategies. The quality or magnitude of circular practices in these firms is low and therefore cannot be of great value to informed customers. Numerous companies in all industries are today positioned here, ranging from those that use only a small amount of recycled materials in their production processes, to those able to collect and re-process (through re-manufacturing or refurbishing) only a negligible fraction of the items sold. Companies – especially smaller ones –

are sometimes forced in this position by the lack of resources and capabilities essential for wider implementation of CE practices.

Position B: Low Price

The low-price position is occupied by those firms that intend to compete on price, either on a permanent basis or to conquer new market share by driving competitors out of business. They have the capabilities to offer products or services of an equivalent value to those offered by the reference, but at a lower price. Usually, this position is achieved by businesses that, through a limited portfolio of products, have achieved extremely low production costs.

At this point of CE evolution, there are still no companies operating in this position of the quadrant. It can be reasonably anticipated that over time, more efficient production by CE companies will allow them to price their products lower than those coming out from linear processes. The anticipated price increase in raw materials will be a propelling force in this sense.

Position C: Breakthrough

Breakthrough firms are in the best position as they deliver products/services that are concurrently of greater value and less pricey than those of the industry reference. This unbeatable position is clearly highly attractive and evidently rather difficult to achieve. It leads to higher market share, but because of the low profit margins, the company must manage its costs effectively for growth to be sustained.

Circular firms in this position employ business practices that are superior to those of the reference. Despite being both fully circular, breakthrough firms are taking advantage of some unique technology or internal know-how to offer advanced circular performance. True examples of this kind of firms are possibly yet non-existent at this stage, but as more and more organizations adopt Cradle-2-Cradle in their production (McDonough and Braungart 2002), we can expect some being able to implement net-positive processes earlier than others, that might also have phased out negative externalities but not yet devised environmentally friendly outputs.

Position D: Differentiation

Differentiators are those companies that provide a better product (generally meaning additional or more attractive features) at an average price.

Under a CE scenario, companies pursuing this position focus on new green solutions to create a replicable business model that targets the mass market. In the automotive sector, for example, Renault can be viewed as being a CE reference thanks to the closed-loop approach deployed at its Choisy-le-Roy plant. However, when it comes to product offering, the French company is still heavily reliant on a sales model centred around ownership. Firms offering car sharing are a perfect example of CE differentiators, as they engage customers in a way that is radically different from the traditional approach utilized by the reference firm. The fee paid by a car sharing user is typically low enough for virtually anyone to access the service.

Position E: Focused Differentiation

Focused differentiation is about high-quality offering and relates to the original definition of differentiation strategy suggested by Porter (1985). Companies in this position can charge a premium price for their products and have customers still buying them. For example, they might be offering new technological features that no other firm can provide, like a more powerful engine for cars.

Similarly, under a circular perspective, position "E" is occupied by firms that focus on offering high-quality CE products and services in niche markets. This position might, for example, be suitable for established luxury brands that transition towards circularity or newcomers that target the luxury market through a unique and superior CE performance or features. Following on with the automobile example, US-based electric car manufacturer Tesla produced the Roadster, the first fully electric luxury sports vehicle, with a zero-emission engine that does not compromise speed or power.

Unsustainable

Unsustainable companies are those which offer a product or service whose price/benefit ratio is not competitive. New companies starting in this position do not achieve the necessary market share to survive and established firms falling into this position need to exit it as quickly as possible by either reducing prices or increasing product quality.

Firms, which today do not embrace circularity because it is still cheaper for them to continue exploiting the natural environment by means of linear business processes, will in the future become unsustainable. The impacts of soaring resource prices, environmental regulations banning the use of resource-intensive production systems, and customer preferences shifting towards net-zero impact products are just now beginning to be felt but will eventually become strong enough to relocate linear companies in the quadrant.

9.2.1 Supporting Methods for Market Positioning: Interviewing Key Personnel

The first step in this analysis is to thoroughly map out all circular companies currently operating in the industry and consider those that can be perceived as a "CE reference" – that means firms that have established CE principles at the heart of their business processes, hence achieving low environmental impacts, while being price-competitive. Examples of CE leaders in various industries are: Patagonia (clothing), Renault (automotive), Philips (lighting), Interface (flooring), and Desso (furniture). This exercise allows the manager to recognize the core competencies required to be a CE leader and grasp if/when/where/how these would fit with the strategic plans and capabilities of the firm.

Once the CE industry reference has been identified, the next step is in fact to compare that reality against your company's plans and core competencies. This activity, supported by questions like the ones listed below, allows one to rationally recognize the strategic CE positioning most appropriate for the company to pursue:

- **CE Industry Reference**: Do we possess the set of circular capabilities deployed by the CE industry reference? If not, what would be the effort (time, investments, human resources) required to develop such expertise? Will we be able to implement circular principles widely across the company whilst keeping the cost of our products competitive in the market?
- **No frills**: Are we totally lacking the resource or capability needed to make a firm transition to CE? Are there high costs associated with a large-scale implementation of CE principles? Is there any specific CE practice that we could implement at low cost and from which benefit greatly?
- **Breakthrough**: Do we possess any unique CE capability/technology/ expertise that would help us to achieve greater circular performance at lower costs compared to the CE industry reference? Would that competitive advantage be difficult for other companies to replicate?
- **Differentiation**: Can customer needs be satisfied in a way that is different from the offering of CE reference firms (e.g. service instead of product, sharing, high standard re-used products)? Would our business model lead to an expansion of the existing market?
- **Focused Differentiation**: Will the cost of implementing high-quality CE alternatives be so high that any surplus would need to be passed onto customers (i.e. premium price)? Are there customers willing to pay such a premium?

9.3 Approaches to Internationalization

Although little gets written about international strategies (Ariño et al. 2004), internationalization has marked the history of many companies around the world, especially over the last few decades. Four generic approaches to international growth have been identified by the academic literature, depending on degrees of global integration and local responsiveness: export, multidomestic, global, and transnational (Bartlett and Ghoshal 1989) (Figure 9.2). The advent of circular thinking is now bringing a new wealth of opportunities for businesses operating in an international context, but it is important to identify the most appropriate approach before moving forward. Next, we present these internationalization schemes and consider how the CE has an impact on them.

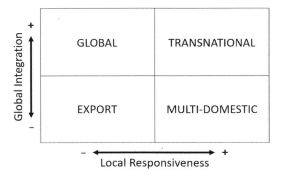

Figure 9.2 International Strategies.[1]

- **Export.** Through this strategy, the firm aims at expanding in foreign markets by relying on the same core competencies developed at home. As the export strategy does little to adapt the firm's products to the needs and wants of the targeted foreign customers, this approach works best in globalized markets, where customer's expectations are similar across geographical boundaries.

  In a CE context, this strategy has been successfully pursued with the use of technological breakthroughs such as digital platforms and smartphone applications. Firms like AirBnB, Car2Go, and Uber have all built on the success in their domestic markets to expand internationally by enabling more and more users to join their digital space and enjoy their services. The business model is replicated abroad in the same format and without adaptation to local markets. Pursuing an export strategy in the CE might also mean exporting domestic circular capabilities. For example, Renault has been operating its Choisy-le-Roi re-manufacturing plant since 1949. With the projected shortages and high price of some key resources (e.g. lead, metals, etc.), the company could decide to export its circular know-how and technical capabilities to establish similar plants in other parts of the world.

- **Multidomestic.** Adaptation to local needs is the key success factor of this strategy. Businesses that operate in industries characterized by high differentiation in local customer preferences tend to follow an international strategy based on decentralization at the country level, where local operations are managed almost autonomously. As a result, the company's products and services are tailored to meet the expectations of each regional market.

  As in the case of exporting, applying a multidomestic strategy within a CE context implies making use of the technological advancements that support circularity. For example, as 3D printers are starting to be deployed locally to craft products according to individual preferences, for the future we can envision local manufacturing hubs where products are made with local available resources – primarily waste materials – with minimal environmental impact. In such a context, multidomestic companies would use 3D printing technology to provide highly differentiated – or even customized – products, without the need of transporting materials and components from one part of the globe to another. Companies like Shapeways and 3D Hubs are already tapping into this largely unexplored market, offering customers the opportunity to create customized designer products. In January 2015, Chinese firm Shanghai WinSun Decoration Design Engineering Co. hit the headlines[2] thanks to its pioneering construction project featuring five-storey homes entirely created with 3D printing technology. The material used for the walls was a mixture of recycled construction waste, glass, steel, and cement.

- **Global.** Global strategies are about taking advantage of cheap labour and other location-related benefits, like low-cost natural resources. Outsourcing and offshoring are the essentials of a global strategy, which has traditionally been implemented in highly competitive industries where cost-effectiveness is the key to success. Setting up a global strategy translates in establishing long value chains with each step of the production process executed in a different country or region of the world, carefully chosen based on its economic advantages.

  In a true CE context, global strategies shall not survive as they would gradually be replaced by shorter and less complex value chains. For example, industries with high repair, refurbishing, and re-manufacturing potential will tend to set up re-collection and re-processing facilities closer to their final customers. This trend is already visible as the large majority of today's plants for reverse cycle activities are being set up right at the heart of the company's market, from Philips' refurbishing facilities in the USA[3] and The Netherlands to Caterpillar's re-manufacturing centre in Singapore.[4]

- **Transnational.** This strategy combines the cost-effectiveness of the global strategy with the local focus of the multidomestic approach. To achieve it, local operations are managed with a sort of hybrid approach in mind: each local subsidiary works to adapt itself to the specificities of its market whilst taking advantage of local resources and capabilities to contribute to the overall operation of the company.

  As the implementation of circular operations gradually gains more and more momentum within companies, we can picture a future where closed-loop activities will be integrated into existing trans-national plans. A car manufacturer, for example, might centrally decide which CE business strategy to implement globally (e.g. collection of pre-owned vehicles for components repairing vs servitization and design for durability), but local subsidiaries will determine which business partners to engage with and how to set up dedicated facilities for circular activities.

These four, of course, are not the only possible approaches to internationalization. There are other routes available – and sometimes necessary – especially when the company is based in small or emerging economies (Dawar and Frost 1999). Companies facing intense competition at home from multinationals, based in large developed countries, can decide to internationalize by re-defining their business model: focus on steps of the value chain, hence becoming suppliers to others and provide, for example, distribution and after-sale services (dodger strategy). Under a CE perspective, this is a route that can represent significant opportunities for companies who are struggling to compete in normal circumstances. As a matter of fact, supplier engagement and empowerment are fundamental circular activities, as revealed by examples like the Jaguar–Novelis relationship (see Chapter 3).

Under specific conditions, the reverse process might also be possible: witnessing firms in emerging economies becoming worldwide competitors by working their way up the value chain. In these cases, we would see an exploitation of the competitive advantage developed over the years by progressively integrating higher-value activities and international capabilities.

There is also the social entrepreneurship scenario concerning the expansion of firms that originate in developing countries with a mission of solving a specific environmental (and often social) problem and then pursue internationalization by replicating the same products, services, and operations in other regions of the world, including developed nations. The common success factor of these firms is essentially their ability to devise solutions that are at the same time innovative, sustainable, and deployed to target an evident socio-environmental concern. Such start-ups embrace circular principles at their core and therefore sit in a prime position for growth in a CE setting. In this respect, India is a case in point, with a vast portion of its population living off small-scale farming, an activity that is both causing serious environmental damages and trapping people in poverty and poor working conditions. Hence, the need to radically disrupt outdated farming practices in the country is strongly felt. SRISTI, for example, is a grassroots-based organization that equips farmers with a range of environmentally friendly and reasonably priced products to boost crop yields. Amongst its offering is a widely adopted nitrogen-free fertilizer which can play a pivotal role in reversing the damages inflicted to soils and water sources by nitrogen-based products. In October 2013, the United States Agency for International Development (USAID) announced a partnership with SRISTI[5] to share its low-cost agricultural innovations and technologies with African countries – initially Kenya as a pilot study – as a way of promoting local sustainable development. The Israel-based CropX is another telling example of how small organizations with environmentally oriented solutions deployed in emerging economies can rapidly achieve international recognition. The firm has devised an effective, yet simple system of sensors to optimize crops irrigation and design out waste of water resources. Originated to help Israeli farmers make the best of scarce water reserves in the region, the firm has recently entered the US market and now provides its irrigation systems to some of the largest farms in the country.

9.3.1 Supporting Methods for Internationalization Decision-Making: International Strategic Alternatives Checklist

To identify the most suitable route to internationalization, managers should consider all possible approaches previously presented. We propose the following checklist to help with the task. The alternatives with most dots circled shall later be prioritized for a more detailed assessment. In fact, recognizing what needs to be done to enhance competitiveness in the global market is just the first step. The real challenge is how to develop an international organization around a newly identified CE strategy (Ghemawat 2008) and that takes us back to the CE strategic process and in particular what will be covered in the next chapter: gap analysis, strategy formulation, and planning.

Export Strategy. Suitable when the following requirements are met by the firm:

- Core circular capability can be exported as is to different geographies.
- CE-enabling technology (e.g. digital sharing platforms, smartphone applications, etc.) can be leveraged with minimal effort (time, money, human resources, etc.) to penetrate different markets.
- Costs for exporting circular capability as is are low.
- Running costs for managing circular services are low and similar in all geographies.
- Expectation from customers is similar despite geographical and cultural differences.
- Customers' acceptance of circular products/services is similar across geographies.

Multidomestic Strategy. Suitable if the following requirements are met by the firm:

- Customer needs and preferences vary across geographies.
- To be managed efficiently circular practices require an in-depth knowledge of local contexts.
- Core circular capability cannot be exported as is to different geographies; barriers (e.g. regulatory) exist for replication across different markets.
- The collection of used products and further processing like repair, refurbishing, and re-manufacturing are among the core circular capabilities needed.
- CE-enabling technology (e.g. 3D printing) can be leveraged to suit different local preferences.
- Costs of exporting essential circular capabilities are high.
- Local subsidiaries possess the adequate CE expertise to conduct circular operations autonomously.

Global Strategy. Suitable under the following conditions:

- The number and location of existing suppliers in the value chain do not prevent the company from adopting circular principles.
- Regardless of their location, suppliers have the willingness and expertise to be involved in circular programmes/projects (this might entail narrowing down the overall number of suppliers used and prioritize those more apt at supporting the development of circular actions).
- The environmental performance of suppliers can be monitored through existing responsible sourcing programmes and technology (e.g. audits, blockchain, etc.).
- Outsourcing and offshoring can be further strengthened by allocating certain circular processes to external business partners, which possess the unique capabilities to do a better job.

Transnational Strategy. Suitable if the following requirements are met by the firm:

- Local subsidiaries possess the adequate expertise to implement CE circular operations autonomously.
- Customer needs and preferences vary across geographies.
- The selected geographies can positively contribute to the overall operation of the company by providing valuable local resources and capabilities.
- Historically, there has been strong control by the HQ so that subsidiaries have never been fully autonomous in their decisions.

- Local suppliers and other stakeholders can be easily trained to adopt the circular practices centrally decided by HQ.

Additional aspects to consider when the company is based in small or emerging economies include:

- The firm's mission is concerned with solving a specific environmental (or social) issue.
- The firm has devised an innovative solution that can be replicated in other regions of the world affected by the same problem.
- The firm possesses a set of capabilities or technologies that are unique in the market.
- The firms' products/services are cost-effective and can compete globally with existing non-CE alternatives.

9.4 Conclusions

Having completed CE data analysis (Chapter 7 and 8), the manager is able to properly assess the firm's position in its industry and determine future repositioning efforts based on the resources and capabilities of the company so that new opportunities can be tackled, and future risks mitigated. A tool to easily visualize where a company sits compared to its competitors is the strategic clock (Faulkner and Bowman 1992), which uses perceived price and quality as its two dimensions. Although today most companies that consider circularity are still in their initial stages (Position A: "no frills") – not yet having placed CE principles at the heart of their strategies ("reference" position) – it seems reasonable to predict that at some point in the future, CE production will become more efficient and attract a firmer commitment by managers and entrepreneurs, allowing prices of CE products to drop below the outputs of traditional production systems (Position B: "low price"). The anticipated price increase in raw materials compared to the savings in using second-hand inputs will accelerate the transformation, but until then, CE firms will likely find most success by focusing on a differentiation of their offering (Positions D: "differentiation" and E: "focused differentiation") and targeting specific niches of green customers.

To determine the preferred CE position of a company, we advise for the identification of the industry reference as a starting point, followed by a comparison against the firm's own plans and core competencies. A series of guiding questions were provided in the chapter to help with this process. The remaining of the chapter dealt with internationalization, a process that sometimes is a choice and otherwise a necessity, but that many companies have undertaken over the past few decades. After introducing the four generic approaches identified by the academic literature – export, multidomestic, global, and transnational (Bartlett and Ghoshal 1989) – a discussion of how these might look like under a CE perspective followed. While some current examples were provided, much of the analysis was based on considerations of what the future might bring, and for the majority of industries the high local responsiveness typical of transnational and multidomestic approaches appeared to offer the most promising returns. Given that the typical classification of international strategies is based on large firms in mature industries and developed countries, this chapter also discussed alternative routes for companies based in small or developing economies: the "dodger" strategy of becoming a supplier by focusing on steps of the value chain, the long-term ambitious strategy of forward integration, and the internationalization of local circular firms that originate with the mission of solving a specific environmental (and often social) problem. To support management in an internationalization assessment, a checklist was finally provided to identify the specific strengths of the organization under each scenario.

Notes

1 Source: adapted from Bartlett, A. Christopher, and Sumantra Ghoshal 1989. *Managing across Borders: The Transnational Solution.* Cambridge: Harvard Business Press.
2 Ollie Gillman. 2015. "The Villas Created Using 3D Printers: £100,000 Five-Storey Homes Made Using Construction Waste in China". *Daily Mail.* Posted on January 19, 2015. www.dailymail.co.uk/news/article-2917025/ The-villas-created-using-3D-printers-100-000-five-storey-homes-using-construction-waste-China.html.
3 www.usa.philips.com/healthcare/solutions/refurbished-systems.
4 www.americanmachinist.com/beyond-cutting-zone/caterpillar-opens-remanufacturing-center-singapore.
5 https://2012-2017.usaid.gov/india/news-information/press-releases/united-states-and-india-help-improve-farming-africa.

Bibliography

Ariño, Africa, Pankaj Ghemawat, and Joan E. Ricard, eds. 2004. *Creating Value through International Strategy.* London: Palgrave Macmillan.
Bartlett, Christopher A., and Sumantra Ghoshal 1989. *Managing across Borders: The Transnational Solution.* Cambridge: Harvard Business Press.
Bowman, Cliff, and David Oakley Faulkner. (1996). *Competitive and Corporate Strategy.* London: Irwin.
Dawar, Niraj, and Tony Frost. 1999. "Competing with Giants: Survival Strategies for Local Companies in Emerging Markets." *Harvard Business Review* 77 (Mar–Apr): 119–132.
Ellen MacArthur Foundation. n.d. "e-Choupal. Improving Income Levels of Indian Farmers through Better Access to Information". Accessed on March 15, 2018. www.ellenmacarthurfoundation.org/case-studies/improving-income-levels-of-indian-farmers-through-better-access-to-information.

Faulkner, David, and Cliff Bowman. 1992. "Generic Strategies and Congruent Organisational Structures: Some Suggestions." *European Management Journal* 10 (4): 494–500.

Ghemawat, Pankaj. 2008. "Reconceptualizing International Strategy and Organization." *Strategic Organization* 6 (2): 195–206.

Gillman, Ollie. 2015. "The Villas Created Using 3D Printers: £100,000 Five-Storey Homes Made Using Construction Waste in China". *Daily Mail*. Posted on January 19, 2015. www.dailymail.co.uk/news/article-2917025/The-villas-created-using-3D-printers-100-000-five-storey-homes-using-construction-waste-China.html.

Hill, Charles WL. 1988. "Differentiation Versus Low Cost or Differentiation and Low Cost: A Contingency Framework." *Academy of Management Review* 13 (3): 401–12.

McDonough, William, and Michael Braungart. 2002. *Cradle to Cradle: Remaking the Way We Make Things*. New York: North Point Press.

Parnell, John A. 2006. "Generic Strategies after Two Decades: A Reconceptualization of Competitive Strategy." *Management Decision* 44 (8): 1139–54.

Porter, Michael E. 1985. *Competitive Advantage: Creating and Sustaining Superior Performance*. New York: Free Press.

USAID. 2013. "United States and India Help Improve Farming in Africa". Posted on October 30, 2013. https://2012-2017.usaid.gov/india/news-information/press-releases/united-states-and-india-help-improve-farming-africa.

World Economic Forum. 2017. "The Global Risks Report 2017 12th Edition". www3.weforum.org/docs/GRR17_Report_web.pdf.

White, Roderick E. 1986. "Generic Business Strategies, Organizational Context and Performance: An Empirical Investigation." *Strategic Management Journal* 7 (3): 217–31.

Wright, Peter. 1987. "A Refinement of Porter's Strategies." *Strategic Management Journal* 8 (1): 93–101.

10 Gap Analysis, CE Strategy Formulation, and Planning

10.1 Introduction

Having performed the recommended analyses (value chain, five forces, PEST, and SWOT) and taken broad strategic decisions over where the company would like to be in the future (strategic clock and internationalization assessment), the next step before formulating and planning a detailed CE strategy is for the business to undergo a gap assessment. Under a CE perspective, such analysis would ideally include information covering the firm's material and waste flows, and its environmental impacts.

Once the gap is known, management can commence the four-step approach to formulate a CE strategy. This will mean taking key decisions regarding the CE business model(s) to adopt and the roll-out approach. Finally, senior management will need to decide whether the strategy will be implemented top-down, bottom-up, or rather by involving employees only to a limited extent.

10.2 Gap Analysis

The aggregated results from previous analyses serve to establish where a business stands relative to its desired market position. The concept of strategic gap (Ansoff 1965) reflects the discrepancy between an organization (i.e. its inherent capabilities) and the external environment. The gap can be positive or negative (Harrison 1996), depending on whether the organization has or does not have the management, technologies, policies, and resources to grasp the opportunities and cope with the threats, requirements, and responsibilities imposed by the external environment (Hofer 1978). As illustrated (Figure 10.1), under CE considerations the organization–environment gap tends to expand if the former does not renew itself, given that circular thinking creates new opportunities, but also exposes the company to new risks, while forcing upon it additional requirements and responsibilities.

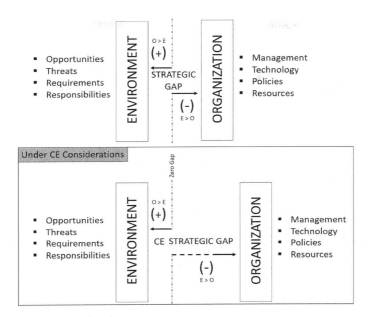

Figure 10.1 CE Strategic Gap.

Since the CE is fundamentally about gradually reducing the environmental damage associated with the manufacturing and use of products, a gap analysis for CE strategy formulation shall include environmental studies aimed at understanding material and waste flows, and direct environmental impacts.

Material Flows. An in-depth understanding of the flows of all substances and materials entering the company is crucial to fully assess the consequences of implementing circular material management in business operations. For example, there might be resources whose global reserves are predicted to be depleted soon and thus need to be preserved through closed-loop operations. Or, the company might realize that there are a high number of toxic substances used in production and therefore the best strategy would be to focus on identifying suitable bio-based alternatives.

Waste Flows. Apart from the typical waste generated at the site level (resource waste), a comprehensive waste flow analysis can be intended to look at the broader picture and include at least two additional categories (Lacy and Rutqvist 2015): wasted lifecycle and capacity waste. The former occurs when the lifecycle of a product is not maximized to its full potential through, for example, design for durability or product life extension interventions. Capacity waste arises if the physical utilization rate of a product is not 100%, which occurs, for example, when a car carries only one passenger or if it remains parked for long periods of time.

Environmental Impacts. The environmental impacts of a company's products and processes are many and can be assessed thoroughly through a Life Cycle Assessment (LCA), or by using more simple methods like dedicated matrixes and tables. Such a study can reinforce the company's understanding of its main deficiencies relative to CE principles and prove a valuable source of information in the definition of suitable strategies moving forward.

Only by deepening these types of environmental assessments a company will be able to properly estimate the gap between current and desired CE positions. Swedish clothing company Filippa K is a telling example of how an environment-based gap analysis can help a business achieve a desired circular strategy. Prior to establishing its CE plans, Filippa K spent more than two years conducting in-depth LCA assessments of its products' range, with every phase of the garments' lifecycle examined and later fine-tuned, for a minimum ecological impact. The result has been a line of high-quality circular products, called "Front Runners" that are built to last and get collected by Filippa K at the end of their life via a dedicated take-back scheme. The company has now plans to make its entire collections sustainable by 2030.

10.2.1 Supporting Methods for CE Gap Analysis: Environmental Impacts Table

Conducting an environmental impact analysis is an excellent way to understand the fundamental gaps that an organization needs to bridge through its CE strategy. When this analysis cannot be performed through LCA – due, for example, to a lack of economic resources or commitment from top management – the table below can be used as a simple alternative to quickly detect the main environmental impacts associated with the company operations (Table 10.1).

The table offers a short, yet comprehensive list of the major damages caused by businesses on the four key biological dimensions of air,[1] water,[2] soil,[3] and living organisms (flora and fauna). To simplify the assessment process, only two grading options shall be used: low or high intensity of impact. Because nowadays environmental awareness is widespread across the business sector, it is reasonable to believe that conducting this sort of assessments should be rather straightforward, especially if the HSE (Health, Safety, and Environment) department provides support.

Table 10.1 Environmental Impacts Table

Environmental Impact	Description
GHGs Emissions	Release of carbon dioxide, methane, nitrous oxide, hydrofluorocarbons (HFCs), and perfluorocarbons (PFCs) in the air.
Air pollution	Release of volatile organic compounds (VOC), particulate matter, carbon monoxide, lead, sulphur dioxide, and nitrogen dioxide in the air.
Nitrogen release	Major sources of nutrient pollution include surface runoff from farm fields and pastures and discharges from septic tanks and feedlots.
Phosphorus release	Major sources of nutrient pollution include surface runoff from farm fields and pastures and discharges from septic tanks and feedlots.
Land use change	Green fields converted to cropland/ industrial sites.
Water pollution	Major causes of water pollution are: sewage waste, release of soil nutrients like nitrogen and phosphorus, waste water used for industrial purposes, chemical waste, and thermal pollution from factories and power plants.
Chemical pollution	Release of toxic substances, plastics, endocrine disrupters, heavy metals, and radioactive contamination into the environment.
Biodiversity loss	Important direct drivers affecting biodiversity are habitat change, climate change, introduction of invasive species, overexploitation of natural resources, and pollution of water, air, and soil.

10.2.2 Supporting Methods for CE Gap Analysis: Circular Readiness Assessment

To perform a comprehensive CE gap analysis, the environmental impacts identified earlier should guide a more sophisticated evaluation of the current degree of circularity in place at the company. Managers can, for example, conduct a "Circular Readiness Assessment" (Cristoni and Tonelli 2018), an exercise which considers 17 different areas for circular action scattered along the value chain (design>sourcing>production>distribution/ shipment>use>end use). Figure 10.2 illustrates the conceptual map of the online tool,[4] which is also useful to size up the utmost CE potential acquirable by the industry and use such information as a benchmark.

By self-evaluating against each of the 17 areas, firms are able to acknowledge and discuss their specific relevance in the industry, as well as how mature the company is compared to what the external environment would demand in terms of opportunities, threats, requirements, and responsibilities. The final output of the assessment is a snapshot of the organization, visually illustrating the company's CE position compared

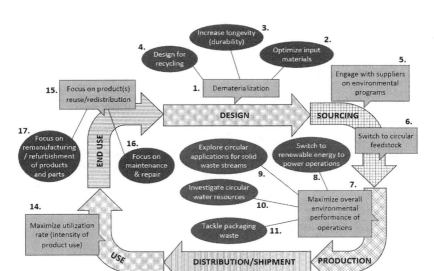

Figure 10.2 The Key Areas of Circular Action.

with the industry average, hence highlighting the areas most neglected or of greater strategic interest.

10.3 Formulating a CE Strategy

Now that the gap has been determined, a CE strategy can be formulated. This means tackling the identified flaws by devising a set of operational decisions that can bridge the gap between actual and preferred positions.[5] The firm has already identified the market position it wants to occupy (strategic quadrant) and is aware, through previous internal analyses, of what resources and capabilities are needed; hence, minimal efforts are required at this stage to ensure that the chosen strategy remains tangible in terms of budget constraints. A four-step process can be used to guide managers in this task.

Step 1. Identify where is the value being lost. Environmental assessments and gap analysis show the company where the circular value being lost is in terms of, for example, low product's utilization rate, modest closed-loop recycling, and so on. Next is to assess the potential for value creation by exploring what prevents such value from being realized and giving priorities to actions. Broad categories of barriers to be investigated are: technical (e.g. lack of technology or expertise), infrastructural (e.g. lack of facilities to establish CE processes, lack of external infrastructure that would support the adoption of CE products like electric cars, etc.), commercial (e.g. customers not ready for the CE alternative offering), and regulatory (e.g. specific laws and regulations limiting the intended CE practices).

Step 2. Determine how should the value be captured. Having identified the circular value to be potentially extracted, the company needs to determine the ways in which it intends to capture it. Major decisions will involve the type of business model to be implemented and the enabling technologies to be used, so that the transition can be as smooth and cost-effective as possible. The company will then need to consider all operational decisions and implications for the organization: e.g. R&D (process vs product innovation), product range (narrow or broad), marketing (product or brand), reward systems (employees and suppliers, or customers), and organizational structure (functional or project-based).

Step 3. Decide on the appropriate roll-out approach and set quantitative targets. As most companies have never embarked on a circular journey, the roll-out of their first circular efforts needs to be pondered carefully. Depending on the specific features of both the firm and the external environment, the approach can vary from small-scale time-bound pilot projects to a step-by-step CE implementation stirring the whole organization. When customers play an important part in the devised CE strategy and the company needs to confirm their full support before committing for long-term alterations, time-bound pilots seem most appropriate. For example, in May 2017, Nespresso, the world leader in coffee machines, capsules, and accessories, launched a six-month trial aimed at collecting used capsules from households in the Royal Borough of Kensington and Chelsea, London. Nespresso clients were given recycling bags dedicated for capsules that would then be collected by Suez, a waste management company. These bags would then be processed at a Nespresso waste-recycling site.[6] Approaching circularity by means of pilot projects is also the preferred option when a new technology needs testing prior to large-scale implementation. In 2017, Unilever announced a groundbreaking technological process, called CreaSolv®, to recycle sachet waste and use it to create new sachets for Unilever products. To test the viability of the technology, the company opened a dedicated pilot plant in Indonesia.[7]

Step 4. Envision a CE continuous improvement process. Upon launching the first CE programmes, operations should aim for a state of continuous improvement in value creation and cost reduction. This means seeking improvements in scale, logistics, and processes which will be facilitated by a deeper understanding of how the value is lost and waste streams are created. The quality in collecting, storing, and analysing data will determine the basis on which the company can further its development.

In choosing the most appropriate course of actions for the realization of new CE organizational objectives, it is important to remember that organizational know-how and technical capabilities do not always need to be fully developed internally. Firms may also want to look outside in search for valuable CE business partners. In the clothing industry, for example, many retailers and apparel brands today rely on specialized service providers for reverse cycle capabilities. I:CO through its innovative take-back system and global infrastructure helps firms like Calzedonia, H&M, Levi's, Puma, and M&S keep clothing and shoes in a closed production loop.

10.3.1 Supporting Methods for CE Strategy Formulation: Decision Priority Matrix

The decision priority matrix is an easy-to-use tool to map and prioritize CE actions according to effort (time, complexity, money, and other resources) and value (Figure 10.3). To help with the plotting process, it might be useful to ask the following questions:

- Would performing this action require things to be done differently than what the current processes allow for?
- Does the potential for value creation justify the disruption?
- Could the required know-how and technical capabilities be acquired through partnerships?
- What barriers could prevent an easy implementation of the idea?

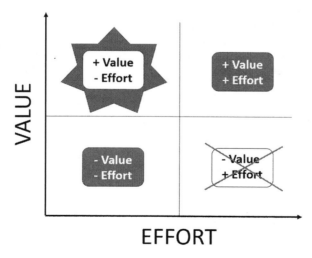

Figure 10.3 Decision Priority Matrix.

Clearly, the CE actions that should be addressed first are those with a high impact and requiring little effort (top-left). If this quadrant is empty or the company has additional resources to deploy, management could then consider either immediate low-impact actions or further investments for long-term high-impact activities.

10.3.2 Supporting Methods for CE Strategy Formulation: The Three-Step Process for Piloting CE Ideas

To conduct a pilot, managers shall follow at least the following three steps:

i.   Develop a trial plan. First, a decision must be made over what CE product or service to test. Next, it needs to be determined when, how, and with whom to do the testing. Feedback forms are also essential to engage customers through open exploratory questions aimed at discovering what worked and what did not, how the offering could be improved, and how people perceive it compared to existing linear products/services.
ii. Create a prototype or a simulation (in case of CE services). The prototype will need to have all the essential traits of the final offering so that trial users will have the same experience as the final customer.
iii. Collect feedback and, if necessary, modify the prototype accordingly.

10.4 CE Strategic Planning

After the strategy has been formulated, it is usually formalized in a document called Strategic Plan, where the course of actions gets crystallized to guide implementation. There is some level of debate over the usefulness of having such a written document. While it serves to formalize the strategic direction of the firm, facilitate communication over its desired future, and detail the action plans to feed into budget, it can also restrict flexibility and not allow for new opportunities to be properly recognized (Dutton and Duncan 1987). As demonstrated by cases of successful strategies that have not been planned and vice versa, there should not be a fixed rule for planning, but it is probably safe to argue that under a CE scenario – where uncertainty and inexperience are generally common at first – most firms would benefit from such a tool that conveys formalization, communication (to employees, shareholders, suppliers, customers, regulatory bodies, etc.), and control. A plan can help coordination, thus avoiding the risk of discrepancies between intentions and actions during implementation (Mintzberg and Waters 1985).

Strategic planning varies significantly depending on the specific attitudes and skills of the management team. There are many options around who to involve, responsibilities, and processes, but in general, three main approaches define how a strategic plan (and its implementation) can look like: top-down, bottom-up, and hybrid.

Top-down: It is the traditional and still most widely accepted approach. A top-down perspective recognizes the organizational hierarchy of the company and restricts the planning process to the top management, plus possibly external consultants or functional managers. Once approved, the plan gets handed down for its implementation (Skinner 1969; Wheel Wright 1984). The drawbacks of top-down planning are connected to the risk of being too vague, impractical, and difficult to be communicated across the organization (Kim et al. 2014). In fact, the distance between top management and employees implies a gap between managerial intentions and organizational actions that if not controlled can lead to a discrepancy between "intended" and "realized" strategies (Mintzberg 1978). So far, most CE strategies have been executed top-down, owing to the commitment of visionary CEOs, like Ray Anderson (founder of Interface), Paul Polman (CEO of Unilever), or the Garrone family (owner of ERG).

Bottom-up: It is a lengthy planning process that lacks structure and promotes acceptance through wide employee participation (Bartlett and Ghoshal 1994). The whole organization gets involved in strategic activities, with functional managers making unit-level plans later aggregated for validation by top management (Witcher and Butterworth 2001). One problem with this type of processes is that employees usually do not have a company-wide perspective and therefore propose ideas that do not match the overall strategy of the company. Although this process has the potential to trigger more innovation than the top-down alternative, oftentimes it is also difficult to integrate the different perspectives into one single action plan. The involvement of employees in decision-making can of course be the outcome of a structured approach, but also arise spontaneously, as in the case of Audi back in March 2017, when the union representing +40,000 workers at the plant in Ingolstadt (Germany) asked management to start considering the production of electric cars, to keep pace with other Audi's sites like the one in Neckarsulm.[8] Since the CE is a rather multifaceted and innovative concept, bottom-up processes do not seem to be the best approach for strategic planning, particularly if the company operations are complex, requiring in-depth expertise to understand CE implications and opportunities.

Hybrid: To reduce the limitations of the previous two approaches, some organizations opt for hybrid solutions, where ideas gathering occurs bottom-up, but the final implementation plan is devised by the top management only (Kim et al. 2014). In the case of young and small companies, for example, founders can provide guidance, while the planning process should instead be driven by a multidisciplinary team of representatives from all functions; the workforce should be engaged at the very early stages to establish communication policies and brainstorm ideas for future products, which will then be filtered by the steering committee before final approval by the founders. Even though evidence is lacking as to whether employees have been involved in the early stages of a shift towards circularity in pioneering CE companies, there is no doubt that staff represent a valuable source of information and insight.

10.4.1 Supporting Methods for Strategic Planning: Alternative Approaches Checklist

To help identify the most suitable strategic planning approach, managers can use the following checklist. The alternative with most dots circled shall then be studied in more details.

A **top-down** planning process is worth pursuing if:

- Most individuals in the top management possess significant CE knowledge/expertise.
- Most of the executives and top managers have served the company for 10+ years.
- The firm's processes are few and relatively simple.
- The organization's workforce is not too large.
- Implementation of the CE plan is not expected to be too pervasive and disruptive for the company's operations.
- Top management intends to roll out the CE programme in the short term.
- Operational jobs within the company are relatively easy and do not require relevant technical skills or capabilities.
- Company's culture has historically neglected environmental awareness and stewardship (implying being "green" is not a reason why employees choose to work for the company).

A **bottom-up** process is worth pursuing if:

- The firm's top management does not have significant CE expertise.
- The firm's processes are multiple and complex.
- Implementation of the CE plan will have a major impact on a large number of processes and operations (i.e. most employees/workers will be affected).
- Top management intends to roll out the CE programme over the long term.
- The company has a track record of successfully engaging employees on key decisions and programmes.
- Operational jobs within the company are relatively complex and do require relevant skills or capabilities.
- Company's culture has historically embraced environmental awareness and stewardship (employees tend to choose this company because of its environmental efforts).

A **hybrid** process is worth pursuing if:

- Some individuals in the top management possess significant CE expertise.
- Top management intends to roll out the CE programme over the medium term.
- The company has already successfully engaged employees on some key decisions and programmes.
- Operational jobs within the company are relatively complex and do require relevant skills or capabilities.
- Company's culture has embraced environmental awareness, though this is not a primary focus (some employees might have chosen to work for the company because of its environmental efforts).

10.5 Conclusions

A strategic CE gap is the inevitable divergence between where a business stands relative to its desired market position. Given the novelty of circular principles in many industries, the gap identified at the end of a strategic analysis (and supported by a detailed assessment of the company's material and waste flows and environmental impacts) can be quite substantial, as the external environment constantly evolves always becoming more complex, presenting new opportunities, threats, requirements, and responsibilities, while the average company still lacks the necessary managerial skills, technologies, policies, and resources to promptly react. The experience of Swedish clothing brand Filippa K showed how environmentally oriented gap analyses can be used as a valuable decision support tool for CE strategy development. Tools like the circular readiness assessment help identify the fundamental gaps an organization needs to bridge through a CE strategy.

Having clearly marked the direction in which a company wants to move, the next step is for a strategy to be formulated and planned. In the formulation stage, a company needs to quantify the potential pay-off of recovering the value being lost, determine how should that value be captured (i.e. what CE business model to adopt and CE-enabling technologies to leverage), define a roll-out approach, and envision a CE continuous improvement process. Finally, top management will need to decide whether strategic planning will occur top-down, bottom-up, or through a hybrid approach. The process of strategic planning acts as a type of agenda builder – creating and prioritizing a limited array of strategic issues (Dutton and Duncan 1987). To avoid missing opportunities, managers should critically consider the role of the planning process and restrain from using a rigid plan of actions. The top-down perspective is efficient and coherent, but may end up being impractical if rejected by operational managers. A bottom-up approach has greater employee ownership and is in touch with the real capabilities of the firm, but likely to be slow and fail to see the big picture. Finally, a hybrid approach is a middle ground solution where founders can have an initial input by flashing out their vision for the future, but an interdisciplinary team of executives from all functions is tasked with managing the process, and employees' contribution is limited to brainstorming ideas for new products.

Given the intrinsic complexity of CE (particularly when looked from the standpoint of an organization that has relied on linear systems of production since its inception), businesses are recommended to think tactically prior to involving the whole organization in strategic planning activities. Rather, a soft approach is suggested, whereby the final strategic decisions remain in the hands of top management and staff is only engaged in the early stages to gather insights through questionnaires or surveys.

Notes

1 For a more thorough description of this environmental impact at global level: www.youtube.com/watch?v=jnchKNoRjeM&t=145s.
2 For a more thorough description of this environmental impact at global level: www.youtube.com/watch?v=Ukwhn4Blac8&t=3s.
3 For a more thorough description of this environmental impact at global level: www.youtube.com/watch?v=h5nSAfYKwxo&t=24s.
4 The tool is freely available at www.worldynamics.com/circular_economy/web/assessment/main.
5 It is of interest to note that a zero gap is not achievable due to factors that go beyond human control, like imperfect information and time delays (Harrison 1996). A company shall look to achieve a level of positive gap judged to be a good strategic fit.
6 George Ogleby. 2017. "Nespresso Launches Coffee Capsule Recycling Service in London". *Edie*. Posted on May 13, 2017. www.edie.net/news/5/Nespresso-launches-coffee-capsule-recycling-service-in-London-borough/.
7 World Business Council for Sustainable Development. n.d. UNILEVER CreaSolv® process. Accessed on May 30, 2017. http://docs.wbcsd.org/2017/CE/CaseStudy_Unilever_Sachets_final.pdf.
8 Steve Hanley. 2017. "Mercedes & Audi Pushed & Pulled To Accelerate Electric Car Plans". Cleantechnica. Posted on March 30, 2017. https://cleantechnica.com/2017/03/30/mercedes-audi-pushed-pulled-accelerate-electric-car-plans/.

Bibliography

Ansoff, H. Igor. 1965. *Corporate Strategy: An Analytical Approach to Business Policy for Growth and Expansion*. New York, NY: McGraw-Hill.

Bartlett, Christopher A., and Sumantra Ghoshal. 1994. "Changing the Role of Top Management: Beyond Strategy to Purpose." *Harvard Business Review* 72 (6): 79–88.

Cristoni, Nicolò and Marcello Tonelli. 2018. "Perceptions of Firms Participating in a Circular Economy." *European Journal of Sustainable Development* 7 (4): 105–18. doi: 10.14207/ejsd.2018.v7n4p105.

Dutton, Jane E., and Robert B. Duncan. 1987. "The Influence of the Strategic Planning Process on Strategic Change." *Strategic Management Journal* 8 (2): 103–116.

Harrison, E. Frank. 1996 "A Process Perspective on Strategic Decision Making." *Management Decision* 34 (1): 46–53.

Hofer, Charles W., and Dan Schendel. 1978. *Strategy Formulation: Analytical Concepts*. St. Paul: West Publishing.

Kim, Yoon Hee, Fabian J. Sting, and Christoph H. Loch. 2014. "Top-Down, Bottom-Up, or Both? Toward an Integrative Perspective on Operations Strategy Formation." *Journal of Operations Management* 32 (7–8): 462–74.

Lacy, Peter, and Jakob Rutqvist. 2015. *Waste to Wealth. The Circular Economy Advantage*. New York, NY: Palgrave Macmillan.

Mintzberg, Henry. 1978. "Patterns in Strategy Formation." *Management Science* 24 (9): 934–49.

Mintzberg, Henry, and James A. Waters. 1985. "Of Strategies, Deliberate and Emergent." *Strategic Management Journal* 6 (3): 257–72.

Skinner, Wickham. 1969. "Manufacturing – Missing Link in Corporate Strategy." *Harvard Business Review* 47: 136–45.

Wheel Wright, Steven C. 1984. "Manufacturing Strategy: Defining the Missing Link." *Strategic Management Journal* 5 (1): 77–91.

Witcher, Barry J., and Rosemary Butterworth. 2001. "Hoshin Kanri: Policy Management in Japanese-Owned UK Subsidiaries." *Journal of Management Studies* 38 (5): 651–74.

World Business Council for Sustainable Development. n.d. UNILEVER CreaSolv® process. Accessed on May 30, 2017. http://docs.wbcsd.org/2017/CE/CaseStudy_Unilever_Sachets_final.pdf.

Part IV

CE @ 360°

To fully support the formulation and planning of their CE strategies, organizations can use a variety of approaches that help them attain a more precise quantification of the environmental impacts of a product or service. In addition to this set of tools that operate at a micro level (company), a different family of methodologies is also valuable to measure a firm's contribution towards a true large-scale CE (economic sector, region or country level of analysis). While mastering the micro-level tools is going to be more and more important for businesses to make competitive CE decisions, at least a basic understanding of the macro-level tools is advisable to stay up to date on the trends shaping policies, laws, regulations, and standards, both nationally and internationally.

The tools presented in Chapters 11 and 12 cover different physical dimensions (e.g. product level, regional value chains, flows of materials, and substances within a national economic system) and rely on distinct kinds of indicators (monetary costs, environmental impacts, resources use, etc.). Yet, the linkages and connections between them are increasingly evident as the complexity of the information and data needed to devise, implement, and monitor CE strategies at both micro and macro levels urges for an integration of multiple tools, thus creating holistic approaches that can embrace apparently incompatible metrics.

11 Tools for CE Analysis at a Micro Level

11.1 Introduction

The various steps of the CE strategic management process have repeatedly highlighted the importance of working with accurate information and to implement effective systems for data gathering, monitoring, and assessment. Inaccurately estimating a CE strategic gap can be dangerous and result in formulating a strategy that is not achievable, thus leading to a failed implementation regardless of the planning approach or investments made. For these reasons, companies should be aware of and select the product-related tools most relevant for their situation. While there is a wider range of methods available, we limit our assessment to the three more fitting from a CE perspective: Life Cycle Assessment (LCA); Life Cycle Costing (LCC); and Material Input per Unit of Service (MIPS). They all serve a purpose in the evaluation of resource use and environmental impacts/costs throughout a product life cycle, with the aim of identifying possible risks and inefficiencies in connection with design and production systems (Ness et al. 2007). These tools shall not be looked in isolation, but rather as different sub-elements of a broader approach to evaluate and improve product circularity in line with the defined CE strategy. Therefore, these tools shall ideally be integrated together, a task that is more easily achieved by organizations if intra- as well as extra-company collaboration is fostered. In fact, with specific regards to new product development, collaboration across departments (and even between companies) allows to detect a higher number of solutions for sustainable product innovation (Gmeling and Seuring 2014).

11.2 Life Cycle Assessment (LCA)

The most studied and adopted of the product-related tools is undoubtedly LCA, a methodological approach used to identify and measure all the environmental impacts (resource and energy consumption, emissions, and waste) associated with a product or service along its entire life cycle (i.e. from cradle – raw material extraction – to grave – the disposal stage). As such, LCA is useful to compare different alternatives, as well as evaluate what is already on the market. Since 1997, the LCA method has been formalized by the International Organization for Standardization through a series of documents (the so-called "ISO 14040 family of LCA standards") that have played a central role in consolidating the procedural process, generating widespread acceptance by the international community (Finkbeiner et al. 2006). Over the last decades, LCA has served the evaluation of products and services in a variety of industries, like automotive (Arena et al. 2013; Traverso et al. 2015), pulp and paper (Lopes et al. 2003; M'hamdi et al. 2017), construction (Ortiz et al. 2009), waste management (Wittmaier et al. 2009), and food (Poritosh et al. 2009; Ruini et al. 2013).

The process of LCA develops along four phases.[1] It commences with a definition of the aim and boundaries of the study (Phase 1: Scope and goals definition), aspects that will guide the development of the assessment until results can be drawn and communicated to all interested parties. This stage also determines "the functional unit" of analysis, i.e. the product reference to which inputs/outputs and impacts will be related to (e.g. 1 kg of coffee, 1 litre of beer, etc.). The next phase is about identifying relevant inputs and outputs (Phase 2: Inventory analysis). Inputs include all natural resources (water, energy, and raw materials) consumed to produce, use, and dispose of the functional unit. Outputs refer to emissions generated throughout the product/service life cycle and absorbed by air, water, and soil. The third phase is about evaluating the potential environmental and health implications linked to those emissions as well as resource use (Phase 3: Impact assessment). This is accomplished by translating the results of the previous phase into a set of indicators linked to selected impact categories (e.g. global warming, ozone depletion, etc.). Finally, results are interpreted to derive conclusions, limitations, and recommendations that will form a solid base for discussion about ways in which the product's ecological footprint can be mitigated through direct interventions along the value chain, or by choosing alternative solutions (Phase 4: Interpretation). It has been argued (Millet et al. 2007) that the specific traits of the LCA process make this method more suitable for products that are relatively simple, whose design concept has already been finalized, and to compare alternatives that show similar functionalities. Additional limitations of the LCA approach have been found with respect to the availability and quality of input data for the assessment, the inherent complexity and long-term perspective of the study, and the use of assumptions to exclude some elements from the assessment (De Benedetto and Klemes 2009).

With specific regard to formulating and implementing a CE strategy, an LCA study can be useful at two distinct points in time:

- **Ex ante analysis**: LCA can help identify the potential environmental impacts of a product or service that is still at the concept phase.

In 2014, car manufacturer BMW conducted in-depth LCA studies to understand the environmental consequences of its concept electric car – the BMW i3 model. The results informed what measures needed to be taken for the life cycle of the car to have lower CO_2 emissions compared to conventional vehicles of similar size and performance.[2] In the food and beverage industry, circular innovation in packaging solutions has been a top priority, with the Italian brand Barilla being a leading player in this respect. The company has adopted a dedicated tool, the "LCA Pack Design", to support its R&D department compare the environmental performance of different packaging solutions.[3] Another LCA pioneer is Carlsberg, known worldwide for its beer products. The Danish company used proprietary LCA software to come up with new concepts for its packaging. In 2017, by operationalizing the tool with sustainability performance data on materials used, the company launched "DraughtMaster", an innovative packaging for its draught beer, which required recycled plastic instead of steel, significantly reducing carbon emissions and water usage.[4] Prior to that, in 2015, Carlsberg had announced plans to develop the world's first fully biodegradable wood fibre beer bottle. After a three-year project with packaging company ecoXpac, the "Green Fibre Bottles" are now promoted on the company website.[5] Carlsberg's examples confirm that businesses can benefit greatly from combining the potential of C2C design with LCA. The two approaches can in fact be extremely complementary, with the first challenging designers to re-invent traditional approaches to product design and development, and the second harnessed to perform environmentally oriented reality checks on the novel solutions identified (Bakker et al. 2009).

- **Ex post analysis**: LCA can also help identify the most significant environmental impacts of a product or service already on the market, thereby helping decisions concerning a redirection of the current framework of operations. In the food industry, Barilla is once again a shining example of this approach. Back in 2000, the company started using LCA to develop environmental metrics for its strategic decision-making processes and to include sustainability goals at the very heart of its business strategy.[6] By investigating the impacts (mainly CO_2 and water related) linked to each phase of its products' value chain, the company was able to address areas of major concern, with specific projects aimed at lowering the environmental footprint of its foods. For example, after finding out that cultivation was one of the most environmentally impactful phases of durum wheat pasta (one of the first LCA studies conducted), the firm launched a dedicated programme for sustainable cropping (Ruini et al. 2013).

But the application of LCA is not limited to products. It can also help compare standard business operations with circular alternatives, thus enabling a company to innovate quicker and allocate investments more effectively. With this purpose, LCA can significantly reduce the chances of losing money and resources in the pursuit of CE business strategies that are poorly relevant or not effective. In the carpet sector, Interface has been using LCA since 2001 to integrate circular solutions in its business operations. The company has, for example, replaced traditional flooring adhesives, that contributed greatly to emissions of volatile organic compounds (VOCs), with innovative adhesive "TacTiles" which have no VOC emissions.[7] At the raw material level, the company took action after LCA revealed that virgin nylon, a key component of carpet manufacturing, was contributing severely to the overall environmental footprint of the company. As a result, Interface embarked on an ambitious project with external suppliers to replace virgin fibres with recycled nylon, which is significantly less environmentally damaging.[8]

In recent times, LCA has been widely used in the public sector as well, with applications in resource and waste management at a country level.[9] With specific regard to waste management, studies have recently attempted to examine the potential benefits of implementing waste biorefinery solutions in developing countries (Nizami et al. 2017), given their capacity to use biomass waste from a variety of industries (like forestry, agriculture, pulp and paper, and food) to produce transportation biofuels, power, and chemicals. In such a context, LCA has been proposed as a valuable decision support tool to identify the most suitable biorefinery technology (e.g. fermentation, anaerobic digestion, pyrolysis, incineration, or gasification). The European Union has traditionally been at the forefront of LCA applications, particularly since 2005 with the release of two key strategic documents for the realization of its sustainability objectives: the "thematic strategy on the sustainable use of natural resources" and the "thematic strategy on prevention and recycling of waste".[10] The Life Cycle in Practice (LCiP) project targets SMEs in France, Belgium, Portugal, and Spain, and represents a good example of EU initiative aimed at fostering LCA adoption. The project is centred on reducing the environmental impacts of products and services in building and construction, waste management, and energy equipment. So far, 32 SMEs have undergone a product life cycle investigation, conducted an LCA assessment, and tailored strategic plans to embed circular solutions in their operations.[11]

11.3 Life Cycle Costing (LCC)

LCC helps to calculate the total costs of a product or service along its entire life cycle. Although it originated as a tool for financial analysis in neoclassical economics (Gluch and Baumann 2004), more recently LCC has proved a valuable resource to support the integration of green solutions at the design stage of product development (Bradley et al. 2018) as well as during procurement. Environmental LCC can in fact be used to calculate the whole spectrum of costs associated with managing the ecological impact of a product, from the acquisition of licences and permits to waste management costs, from charges for product/material disposal to even the investments made to set up a dedicated EMS or conduct LCA studies.

The real value of LCC consists in its ability to include the widest possible range of environment-related costs, including those not directly bore by the manufacturer. Total Costs of Ownership (TCO) – consisting of purchase price, operating costs (including energy and water use), and end-of-life expenses – can be accounted for, as well the societal costs (e.g. pollution, waste, health damages, etc.) linked to the environmental externalities produced by the product or service (ISO 20400:2017). In other words, it is an approach that transcends levels of analysis, allowing for a comprehensive picture inclusive of the costs produced by all stakeholders: manufacturer, user, and society at large (Asiedu and Gu 1998) (Figure 11.1).

Similarly to LCA, an environmental LCC analysis is also guided by the identification of a functional unit and system boundaries (Kloepffer 2008). In addition to that, the definition of cost categories is a crucial task in LCC, for it provides a framework to systematically classify all the possible costs associated with the life cycle of the product. For example, in a study investigating how to improve the sustainability of Norwegian fishing vessels (Utne 2009), five macro-categories of costs were identified, three of which were representative of the direct costs of building (capital expenditure associated with all the activities needed

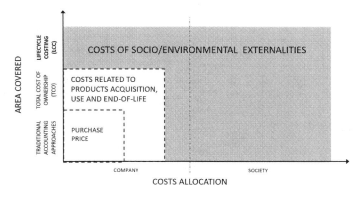

Figure 11.1 The LCC Approach Compared to Other Accounting Tools.[12]

to design and construction), using (operational expenditure linked to operations and maintenance costs), and disposing of the vessel (decommissioning-related costs). The remaining two categories for the calculation of LCC referred to indirect costs: risk (insurance, and the costs of fatalities and injuries that are bore by society and which could be inferred from national or industry statistics) and environmental costs (linked to GHGs emissions and water acidification caused by fuel consumption of the fishing vessels). So, the steps an organization needs to follow for an LCC assessment involve: mapping out all environmental costs along the entire lifespan of the product while trying to calculate their economic value; identifying the LCC categories to which each cost will be allocated; analysing cost frequency (monthly, yearly, etc.) and possible recurrence; and assigning the unitary cost to the LCC cost categories.

When performed in tandem with LCA, LCC can overcome some of its major pitfalls such as being monetary-centred and the dependency on subjective assumptions due to a lack of reliable data (Glouch and Baumann 2004). At the same time, LCC gives LCA the cost considerations it is usually missing, adding value to the capabilities of this decision support tool (De Benedetto and Klemes 2009). The results of an integrated LCA–LCC approach can best be used at the design stage to assess both economic and environmental performances of product ideas, to identify their trade-off (Norris 2001), and ultimately to inform how and when to intervene to lower environmental impacts and costs – possibly through circular solutions. Evidently, reducing costs can help sustainable alternatives compete in the market (Kloepffer 2008) as production becomes more efficient and users enjoy spending less in the running, maintenance, and replacement of products. Notwithstanding all that, thus far these two tools have seldom been integrated into a unified holistic approach to life cycle analysis (Swarr et al. 2011). Examples of studies outlining integrated LCA–LCC approaches can be found in waste management at a municipal level (Reich 2005) and in manufacturing (Palousis et al. 2008). In the latter case, attempts have been made to integrate an economic-LCC approach with additional dimensions of LCA-based environmental impacts and sustainability risks (physical, regulatory, litigation, competitive, reputational, and supply-chain-related) specific to a product's life cycle characteristics. In another engineering study, environmental data from LCA and cost considerations from LCC have been combined with quality criteria to define a process for sustainable product development aimed at improving quality while concurrently reducing both costs and environmental impacts (Zhang 2010). The concept has been applied to evaluate engine filters for heavy-duty trucks along the three steps of: technical requirement identification, product concept generation, and product/process design.

11.4 Material Input per Unit of Service (MIPS)

The core idea behind MIPS is that (natural) raw materials' utilization is the primary indicator of product environmental impacts. Initially devised in Germany at the Wuppertal Institute for Climate, Environment and Energy (Schmidt-Bleek 1995), MIPS is an input-oriented tool that measures the resource efficiency of any product by assessing the total amount of natural resources (called Materials Input, or "MI") required for its manufacture, use, recycling, and/or disposal. Thus, the MIPS allows to unveil what has been called the "ecological rucksack" (or ER) of a product, i.e. the sum of all the natural inputs used to produce, use, recycle, and dispose of it, minus the mass of the product itself (Spangenberg et al. 1999). Measuring the ecological rucksack of products can alone be the reason to conduct MIPS studies. For example, an assessment of the ecological rucksacks of three types of food (wheat, rice, and citrus-based products) was performed to identify policy interventions to enhance the sustainability of food farming in Italy (Mancini 2012). The MI is given by the ER and the weight of the product, and is expressed through five different resource categories: abiotic (non-renewable), like minerals and fossil fuel; biotic (renewable), like biomass from agriculture and wild harvest; air (for combustion or as a component for chemical/physical transformation); water; and Earth movements in terms of consumption (erosion) and alteration through farming and forestry.[13] MIPS is then calculated dividing the MI by the unit of delivered service (S) or product function.

MIPS (Material Input Per unit of Service) = MI (material inputs)/ S (service unit).

The service unit must allow for easy comparison between products' alternatives and embed all the most relevant aspects associated with the use of a product (Ritthoff et al. 2002). For example, the passenger kilometre[14] indicator can be used as the service unit to compare different transport vehicles.

Because the calculation of primary data can be a lengthy and complex process, MIPS can be computed using average MI factors for substances and materials that have already been calculated and made available by the Wuppertal Institute on its website.[15] There is clearly a close connection between MIPS and the development of CE strategies in the private sector for it provides robust information on where to intervene to reduce the environmental impact of the solution being assessed. MIPS can in fact be lowered either by decreasing material inputs for a given S or by increasing the value of the service unit at a fixed rate of resources used. The first goal is achievable through innovative design focused on dematerialization, the latter through business solutions aimed at extending the life and utilization of the product, such as asset sharing and re-use.

11.5 Conclusions

Once CE decisions have been made about corporate goals, preferred business model, and feasible alternative actions, companies can still rely on several techniques to measure and compare the economic and environmental benefits of the various options at a product/service level. It is recommended to carry out this sort of micro-level testing before making a long-term financial commitment, but also to decide the most appropriate pilot project.

The tools presented in this chapter address product/service sustainability at different levels. LCA and LCC both follow a life cycle approach and can help organizations not only make more informed product decisions, but also, and perhaps most importantly, gradually forge a new company culture based on accountability for the environmental impacts caused by products and services during their entire life cycle. Also, data from life cycle studies can help an organization when devising CE alternative solutions, both in terms of product design and to communicate the socio-environmental advantages. The same assumption holds true with respect to MIPS, particularly when the CE alternative is highly efficient from a resource perspective. For this reason, despite the application of LCA to date hugely outweighs that of the other two approaches (not least because a family of ISO standards has been devoted to the methodology), we envision LCC and MIPS to be progressively leveraged by organizations either as stand-alone assessments or in tandem with LCA.

In Chapter 12, we will move away from the micro perspective of LCA, LCC, and MIPS to investigate a different family of tools: those attempting to define sustainability and circular indicators at a macro level (region, country, world, etc.). As we will see, the linkages between these two groups of methodologies are manifold, relating on the one hand to the use of company-level assessments as a source of valuable inputs to understand broader environmental impacts at industry or regional levels; but on the other hand, also to use the information derived from broader approaches to substantiate the CE hotspots that companies identify when investigating their external environments.

Notes

1 International Organization for Standardization (ISO). "ISO 14040:2006. Environmental Management — Life Cycle Assessment — Principles and Framework".
2 Elizabeth Gasiorowski Denis. 2014. "BMW Gears up Clean Cars with ISO Standards". International Organization for Standardization (ISO). Accessed February 3, 2018. www.iso.org/news/2014/07/Ref1864.html.
3 Barilla. 2016. "Barilla's Principles for Sustainable Packaging". Posted on May 25, 2016. www.barillagroup.com/en/groups-position/barilla-principles-sustainable-packaging.

4 Carlsberg. n.d. "DraughtMaster". Accessed on January 20, 2018. www.draughtmaster.com/#System.
5 Ecopax. n.d. "Green Fiber Bottle". Accessed on February 25, 2018. www.ecoxpac.dk/green-fiber-bottle/.
6 EPD International AB. n.d. "Declaring the Impact of Pasta". Accessed November 20, 2017. www.environdec.com/Articles/EPD/Declaring-the-impact-of-pasta/.
7 Thinkstep. n.d. "Using LCA to Guide Their Sustainability Journey". Accessed on February 15, 2018. www.thinkstep.com/case-study/interface.
8 Thinkstep. n.d. "Using LCA to Guide Their Sustainability Journey". Accessed on February 15, 2018. www.thinkstep.com/case-study/interface.
9 European Commission. 2016. "European Platform on Life Cycle Assessment (LCA)". Posted on June 8, 2016. http://ec.europa.eu/environment/ipp/lca.htm.
10 European Commission. 2016. "European Platform on Life Cycle Assessment (LCA)". Posted on June 8, 2016. http://ec.europa.eu/environment/ipp/lca.htm.
11 Life Cycle in Practice (LCiP). n.d. "About the Project". Accessed on March 2, 2018. www.lifelcip.eu/EN/ABOUT-THE-PROJECT-7.html.
12 Adapted from ISO20400:2017.
13 https://epub.wupperinst.org/frontdoor/deliver/index/docId/1577/file/WS27e.pdf.
14 Passenger Kilometre (Pkm) is given by multiplying the number of passengers transported by a vehicle by the number of kilometres covered by the vehicle itself.
15 The list of MI factors spans across different materials, fuel, transport services, and foods. It is continually brought up to date and expanded. https://wupperinst.org/en/a/wi/a/s/ad/365/.

Bibliography

Arena, Marika, Giovanni Azzone, and Antonio Conte. 2013. "A Streamlined LCA Framework to Support Early Decision Making in Vehicle Development." *Journal of Cleaner Production* 41: 105–13. doi:10.1016/j.jclepro.2012.09.031.

Asiedu, Y., and P. Gu. 1998. "Product Life Cycle Cost Analysis: State of the Art Review." *International Journal of Production Research* 36 (4): 883–908. doi:10.1080/002075498193444.

Barilla. 2016. "Barilla's Principles for Sustainable Packaging." Posted on May 25, 2016. www.barillagroup.com/en/groups-position/barilla-principles-sustainable-packaging.

Bakker, C. A., R. Wever, Ch. Teoh, and S. De Clercq. 2009. "Designing Cradle-to-cradle Products: A Reality Check." *International Journal of Sustainable Engineering* 3 (1): 2–8. doi:10.1080/19397030903395166.

Bradley, Ryan, I. S. Jawahir, Fazleena Badurdeen, and Keith Rouch. 2018. "A Total Life Cycle Cost Model (TLCCM) for the Circular Economy and Its Application to Post-Recovery Resource Allocation." *Resources, Conservation and Recycling* 135: 141–49. doi:10.1016/j.resconrec.2018.01.017.

Carlsberg. n.d. "DraughtMaster." Accessed on January 20, 2018. www.draughtmaster.com/#System.

De Benedetto, Luca, and Jiří Klemes. 2009. "The Environmental Performance Strategy Map: An Integrated LCA Approach to Support the Strategic

Decision-Making Process." *Journal of Cleaner Production* 17 (10): 900–906. doi:10.1016/j.jclepro.2009.02.012.

Ecopax. n.d. "Green Fiber Bottle." Accessed on February 25, 2018. www.ecox pac.dk/green-fiber-bottle/.

EPD International AB. n.d. "Declaring the Impact of Pasta." Accessed on November 20, 2017. www.environdec.com/Articles/EPD/Declaring-the-impact-of-pasta/.

European Commission. 2016. "European Platform on Life Cycle Assessment (LCA)." Posted on June 8, 2016. http://ec.europa.eu/environment/ipp/lca.htm.

European Topic Centre on Sustainable Consumption and Production. n.d. "Life-Cycle Assessment and Life-Cycle Thinking in Resource and Waste Management." Accessed on January 10, 2017. http://scp.eionet.europa.eu/themes/lca.

Finkbeiner, Matthias, Atsushi Inaba, Reginald B.H. Tan, Kim Christiansen, and Hans-Jürgen Klüppel. 2006. "The New International Standards for Life Cycle Assessment: ISO 14040 and ISO 14044." *The International Journal of Life Cycle Assessment* 11 (2): 80–85. doi:10.1065/lca2006.02.002.

Gasiorowski Denis, Elizabeth. 2014. "BMW Gears up Clean Cars with ISO Standards." *International Organization for Standardization (ISO)*. Accessed on February 3, 2018. www.iso.org/news/2014/07/Ref1864.html.

Glouch, Pernilla, and Henrikke Baumann. 2004. "The Life Cycle Costing (LCC) Approach: A Conceptual Discussion of Its Usefulness for Environmental Decision-Making." *Building and Environment* 39 (5): 571–80. doi:10.1016/j.buildenv.2003.10.008.

Gmelin, Harald, and Stefan Seuring. 2014. "Determinants of a Sustainable New Product Development." *Journal of Cleaner Production* 69: 1–9. doi:10.1016/j.jclepro.2014.01.053.

International Organization for Standardization (ISO). 2006. "ISO 14040:2006. Environmental Management — Life Cycle Assessment — Principles and Framework."

International Organization for Standardization (ISO). 2017. "ISO 20400:2017 Sustainable Procurement — Guidance."

Kloepffer, Walter. 2008. "Life Cycle Sustainability Assessment of Products". *The International Journal of Life Cycle Assessment*, 13 (2): 89–95. http://dx.doi.org/10.1065/lca2008.02.376

Life Cycle in Practice (LCiP). n.d. "About the Project." Accessed on March 2, 2018. www.lifelcip.eu/EN/ABOUT-THE-PROJECT-7.html.

Lopes, E., A. Dias, L. Arroja, I. Capela, and F. Pereira. 2003. "Application of Life Cycle Assessment to the Portuguese Pulp and Paper Industry." *Journal of Cleaner Production* 11 (1): 51–59. doi:10.1016/S0959-6526(02)00005-7.

Mancini, Lucia, Michael Lettenmeier, Holger Rohn, and Christa Liedtke. 2012. "Application of the MIPS Method for Assessing the Sustainability of Production–Consumption Systems of Food." *Journal of Economic Behavior & Organization* 81 (3): 779–93. doi:10.1016/j.jebo.2010.12.023.

M'hamdi, Asmae Ismaili, Noureddine Idrissi Kandria, Abdelaziz Zeroualeb, Dagnija Blumbergac, and Julija Gusca. 2017. "Life Cycle Assessment of Paper Production from Treated Wood." *Energy Procedia* 128: 461–68. doi:10.1016/j.egypro.2017.09.031.

Millet, D., L. Bistagnino, C. Lanzavecchia, R. Camous, and Tiiu Poldma. 2007. "Does the Potential of the Use of LCA Match the Design Team Needs?" *Journal of Cleaner Production* 15: 335–46. doi:10.1016/j.jclepro.2005.07.016.

Ness, Barry, Evelin Urbel-Piirsalu, Stefan Anderberg, and Lennart Olsson. 2007. "Categorising Tools for Sustainability Assessment." *Ecological Economics* 60: 498–508. doi:10.1016/j.ecolecon.2006.07.023.

Nizami, A. S., M. Rehan, M. Waqas, M. Naqvi, O. K. M. Ouda, K. Shahzad, R. Miandad, et al. 2017. "Waste Biorefineries: Enabling Circular Economies in Developing Countries." *Bioresource Technology* 241: 1101–17. doi:10.1016/j.biortech.2017.05.097.

Norris, Gregory. 2001. "Integrating Life Cycle Cost Analysis and LCA." *The International Journal of Life Cycle Assessment* 6 (2): 118–20. doi:10.1007/BF02977849.

Ortiz, Oscar, Francesc Castells, and Guido Sonnemann. 2009. "Sustainability in the Construction Industry: A Review of Recent Developments Based on LCA." *Construction and Building Materials* 23: 28–39. doi:10.1016/j.conbuildmat.2007.11.012.

Palousis, N., L. Luong, and Kazem Abhary. 2008. "An Integrated LCA/LCC Framework for Assessing Product Sustainability Risk." *Risk Analysis VI: Simulation and Hazard Mitigation.* doi:10.2495/RISK080131.

Poritosh, Roy, Nei Daisuke, Orikasa Takahiro, Xu Qingyi, Okadome Hiroshi, Nakamura Nobutaka, and Shiina Takeo. 2009. "A Review of Life Cycle Assessment (LCA) on Some Food Products." *Journal of Food Engineering* 90: 1–10. doi:10.1016/j.jfoodeng.2008.06.016.

Reich, Marcus Carlsson. 2005. "Economic Assessment of Municipal Waste Management Systems—Case Studies Using a Combination of Life Cycle Assessment (LCA) and Life Cycle Costing (LCC)." *Journal of Cleaner Production* 13 (3): 253–63. doi:10.1016/j.jclepro.2004.02.015.

Ritthoff, Michael, Holger Rohn, and Christa Liedtke. 2002. "Calculating MIPS: Resource Productivity of Products and Services." *Wuppertal Spezial* No. 27e. Wuppertal. http://epub.wupperinst.org/frontdoor/index/index/docId/1577.

Ruini, Luca, Laura Marchelli, and Assunta Filareto. 2013. "LCA Methodology from Analysis to Actions: Examples of Barilla's Improvement Projects." The 6th International Conference on Life Cycle Management in Gothenburg 2013. http://conferences.chalmers.se/index.php/LCM/LCM2013/paper/viewFile/576/177.

Ruini, L., M. Marino, S. Pignatelli, F. Laio, and L. Ridolfi. 2013. "Water Footprint of a Large-Sized Food Company: The Case of Barilla Pasta Production." *Water Resources and Industry* 1–2: 7–24. doi:10.1016/j.wri.2013.04.002.

Schmidt-Bleek, Friedrich. 1995. "Increasing Resource Productivity on the Way to Sustainability." *Industry and Environment* 18 (4): 8–12.

Spangenberg, Joachim H., Friedrich Hinterberger, Stephan Moll, and Helmut Schutz. 1999. "Material Flow Analysis, TMR and the MIPS Concept: A Contribution to the Development of Indicators for Measuring Changes in Consumption and Production Patterns." *International Journal of Sustainable Development* 2 (4): 491–505. doi:10.1504/IJSD.1999.004339.

Swarr, Thomas E., David Hunkeler, Walter Klöpffer, Hanna-Leena Pesonen, Andreas Ciroth, Alan C. Brent, and Robert Pagan. 2011. "Environmental Life-Cycle Costing: A Code of Practice." *The International Journal of Life Cycle Assessment* 16 (5): 389–91. doi:10.1007/s11367-011-0287-5.

Thinkstep. n.d. "Using LCA to Guide Their Sustainability Journey." Accessed on February 15, 2018. www.thinkstep.com/case-study/interface.

Traverso Marzia., Patrick Kim, Stefan Brattig, and Wagner Volkmar. 2015. "Managing Life Cycle Sustainability Aspects in the Automotive Industry." In: Sonnemann Guido and Manuele Margni (eds) *Life Cycle Management. LCA Compendium – The Complete World of Life Cycle Assessment*, pp. 331–339. Dordrecht: Springer. doi.org/10.1007/978-94-017-7221-1_24

Utne, Ingrid Bouwer. 2009. "Life Cycle Cost (LCC) as a Tool for Improving Sustainability in the Norwegian Fishing Fleet." *Journal of Cleaner Production* 17 (3): 335–44. doi:10.1016/j.jclepro.2008.08.009.

Wittmaier, M., Langer, S., and Sawilla, B. 2009. "Possibilities and Limitations of Life Cycle Assessment (LCA) in the Development of Waste Utilization Systems — Applied Examples for a Region in Northern Germany." *Waste Management* 29: 1732–38. doi:10.1016/j.wasman.2008.11.004.

Zhang Y. 2010. "Green QFD-II: A Life Cycle Approach for Environmentally Conscious Manufacturing by Integrating LCA and LCC into QFD Matrices." *International Journal of Production Research* 37 (5): 1075–91. doi:10.1080/002075499191418.

12 Tools for a CE Analysis at a Macro Level

12.1 Introduction

Throughout the world, governing bodies at local, regional, and national levels[1] are increasingly embedding circular principles in their development plans and territorial strategies to become more sustainable and eventually break away from a spiral of environmental degradation that is suffocating them. In some cases, specific environmental and circular targets define new policies and laws. In Australia, for example, the State of Victoria has recently passed a law explicitly targeting a 40% use of renewable energy by 2025.[2] The decision-making processes in the public sector, over sustainability issues, are being supported by increasingly solid data, derived from the application of tools that quantify and compare material flows and/or the environmental footprint of societies, projects, programmes, and plans. These tools, although all built around the same rationale (i.e. allow for more informed and environmentally conscious decisions), can nonetheless differ greatly in terms of both the object being assessed and the method used to perform the assessment: some focus largely on procedures, while others are more analytical; some are descriptive, while others are change-oriented; some include economic aspects, while others focus exclusively on resources used and environmental impacts.

Given the complexity and interconnectedness of Nature as a system, the study of a company can be conducted in isolation only to a certain extent and for very specific purposes. More generally, our investigations necessarily concern the linkages and implications of the entity under study with policies, regions, and material elements. For example, a policy may restrict the use of a substance in a product within a specific region of the world (Finnveden and Moberg 2005). For these reasons, a basic understanding of macro-level tools is advisable for any firm in the process of making CE decisions as they inform how the environment behaves, thus allowing for more precision and awareness in estimating the CE strategic gap between current and desired company's positions. A strategy formulated on solid data that gets regularly updated will facilitate a process of continuous CE improvement. In this chapter, we will briefly introduce a selection of the methodologies available to date: MFA, VCA, EIOA, LCA, EF, EMC, LEAC, HANPP, EIA, SEA, CBA, and CEA.

12.2 Material Flow Analysis (MFA)

Developing a thorough understanding of how substances, nutrients, materials, and products flow across sites, regional industrial clusters, or even entire sectors is paramount to make a CE possible. MFA is a family of different methodologies that include Total Material Requirement (TMR), Material Intensity Per Unit Service (MIPS), and Substance Flow Analysis (SFA), all techniques to assess material flows in a certain spatially and temporally defined system (Brunner and Rechberger 2004; Finnveden and Moberg 2005). MFA has been used in different fields like medicine and urban metabolism, and it is increasingly applied to industrial ecology (Allesch and Brunner 2015), especially at a regional level (Ness et al. 2007). At a macro level, MFA is leveraged to "enhance the understanding of the material basis of the economy and the associated economic supply and demand issues and helps identify inefficient use of natural resources, energy and materials in process chains or the economy at large that would go undetected in conventional monitoring systems. It achieves this by using already available production, consumption and trade data in combination with environment statistics, and by improving modelling capacities" (OECD 2008, p. 11). Hence, MFA can help public institutions at various levels: to identify and further engage those players managing the flows of materials that require an intervention at a policy level (Kalmykova et al. 2018); to adjust resource and waste management programmes to establish recycling and closed-loop processes, given the approach can provide essential information about the characteristics of waste streams (Brunner and Rechberger 2004); or even to analyse the decoupling of economic growth from use of materials – in this case, MFA will be used as a single indicator and compared with GDP (Kleijn 2001).

At a national level, the Economy-wide MFA (EW-MFA) developed by Eurostat represents the primary and most standardized measurement tool to track (whole, grouped, or individual) flows of materials entering and leaving a country's economy, with its results potentially defining the baseline for future circular programmes. These assessments, performed for purposes like in-depth analysis, modelling, or to define material-specific indicators (OECD 2008), use data from economy-wide material flow accounts (EWMFAcc) that are processed across three main categories: input, output, and consumption (Ness et al. 2007). The potential of MFA to provide detailed information about the release into the environment of harmful materials is deemed of great support in crafting more informed CE decisions and strategies that address specific aspects of environmental protection, pollution prevention, resource conservation, and material as well as waste management.[3] As an example, in 2003 the Japanese Government established a plan for a sound material-cycle society[4] with explicit targets on resource productivity and waste management based on MFA indicators.

SFA is a method that is sometimes used interchangeably with MFA (Brunner and Rechberger 2004). However, it has its own specific purpose when applied to inform policymaking (OECD 2008) through the monitoring of production/consumption flows of chemicals that can cause concern for human health and/or the environment (like cadmium, lead, zinc, mercury, nitrogen, etc.). Given that phasing out toxic and dangerous chemicals from the production system is a key pillar of the CE paradigm, SFA assessments play a central role in supporting decision makers to identify substance-level hotspots for the implementation of CE policies.

12.3 Value Chain Analysis (VCA)

VCA is an assessment method that explores how economic sectors and activities are linked to each other, both economically and in terms of material flows. The scope of a VCA study is the value chain of a product or service within the economy, which is analysed in depth to pinpoint its inefficiencies. This is done by developing a supply chain structure map inclusive not only of the companies involved in the chain and their processes, but also the main connections between them, i.e. what processes link one company to the others (Taylor 2005). The mapping exercise leads to identify a number of opportunities to improve physical and information flows, as well as actions concerning the setup, control, and management of the value chain itself (Taylor 2005). Recent developments in VCA (Fearne et al. 2012) increasingly point to the need of broadening the scope of these assessments, by integrating social and environmental considerations to identify improvement actions that are not limited to an economic nature, but also encompass health, poverty, environmental degradation, etc. The addition of sustainability-related considerations should occur along three dimensions: boundary of analysis (shifting the focus on inter-firm relationships and including end-of-life product management within the material flows), scope of value (the need to look not only at the value generated for the single consumer but also the impacts caused to the society as a whole, including environmental externalities), and governance (including the collaboration channels, in terms of resources and competences, within the value chain) (Soosay et al. 2012).

More recently, a city-level VCA has been commissioned by the Municipality of Amsterdam to detect CE opportunities within the most important value chains operating in the territory (Circle Economy 2016). The world's first "City Circle Scan" assessment initially included the ten most significant industry-wide value chains operating locally, later narrowed down to two flows of production activities (construction and organic residual streams), for they showed the highest economic and ecological impacts, as well as the highest value retention and potential for transition to circularity. The final report included six recommendations to help the municipality further improve the circularity of the two activities.[5]

12.4 Environmental Input–Output Analysis (EIOA)

Input–Output Analysis (IOA) is a macroeconomic method originally developed to determine the economic transactions flowing between industry sectors in an economic system, generally at a country level. The interdependencies identified by IOA studies usually draw from the input–output tables (IOTs)[6] that cover a country's entire economy using accurate government statistics (Suh and Nakamura 2007) and providing monetary values (including imports from other countries). IOTs, hence, unpack a national economy in terms of the added value provided by each industrial sector. Such tables have been thoroughly addressed by the United Nations in a series of handbooks and guidelines that set the principles for undertaking these kinds of analysis.[7] But despite the ability to provide information on complex dynamics occurring within an economic system, IOA calculations might carry a number of limitations and biases relating, for example, to sectoral aggregation, price variations, and assumptions concerning international trade (Huang et al. 2009).

In terms of CE potential, the scope of IOA assessments has gradually expanded to include flows of materials and energy, as they link industrial to ecological systems (Bailey et al. 2004a, 2004b). More specifically, EIOA adds the physical flows of natural resource use and emissions to the traditional economic IOTs, either by replacing monetary data with matrices covering physical flows, or, more simply, by adding emission coefficients (Jeswani et al. 2010). Hence, an EIOA study seeks to link material flows with environmental variables to assess the footprint that a certain economic sector is leaving on natural ecosystems, particularly in terms of resource use, pollution, and emissions (e.g. GHGs). These environmental impacts are followed through the entire supply chain in order to reach a deeper understanding of how and when damage occurs. Once identified, environmentally impactful sectors and products can be ranked, compared, and prioritized for further sustainability actions (Finocchiaro et al. 2009). Governments have also made use of EIOA to calculate emissions of greenhouse gases and pollutants (e.g. CO_2, SO_2, and NO_x) as part of long-term national strategies or to assess emission levels of different goods traded within the economy (Huang et al. 2009). EIOA has been appraised for its flexibility and compatibility with LCA (Cicas et al. 2007; Yi et al. 2007), as well as for being a reliable tool (insofar as valid data are available for calculation): EIOA identifies critical areas, which then undergo further LCA analysis before specific policies can be planned.[8]

12.5 Life Cycle Assessment (LCA)

At the macro level, LCA has thus far found wide application in the field of resource and waste management, particularly for its potential to provide reliable data on the likely environmental impacts of a given resource as well as assessing the environmental burdens associated with the different waste management options available, like recycling, incineration, or landfilling. In this respect, LCA focuses specifically on the end-of-life stage of a product, rather than its entire life cycle.[9]

Apart from its integration with EIOA analyses, LCA can also be successfully combined with MFA to provide more accurate estimations of the environmental externalities associated with the production and consumption patterns of large-scale products. An MFA+LCA (or Hybrid MFA–LCA) approach has already been tested in various contexts, but most notably in urban environments and by the European Commission. As far as the former is concerned, the methodology was used to assess the environmental footprint of urban areas using certain representative products as proxies (Lavers et al. 2017). Thanks to the availability of data concerning the consumption of thousands of products at the urban level, the environmental life cycle impacts of the selected goods were profiled using LCA data coming from both public and private databases. In 2012, the Joint Research Centre of the European Commission published two reports outlining the MFA–LCA process, which led to estimate a range of waste management and resource life cycle indicators for monitoring the environmental impacts of member states (Joint Research Centre of the European Commission, 2012a; Joint Research Centre of the European Commission, 2012b).

12.6 Ecological Footprint (EF)

The EF is an estimation of the amount of land consumed to cover the needs of the human enterprise at different levels: country, region, economic sector, company, or even individual. Since 2003, the EF approach has been operationalized and further expanded by the Global Footprint Network, an international non-profit organization that developed a resource accounting calculator to assess the ecological assets (cropland, grazing land, fishing grounds, built-up land, forest area, and carbon demand on land) required by an entity (i.e. country, city, individual, etc.) to produce the natural resources necessary for its own existence. EF has been calculated for many materials, services (e.g. transport), waste treatment, and infrastructural processes with results showing their respective footprint to be in the majority of cases dominated by the consumption of non-renewable energy. Exceptions are for biomass energy, hydro energy, paper and cardboard, and agricultural products which, on the other hand, require a higher contribution of direct land occupation (Huijbregts et al. 2008).

According to the most recent data, presently +80% of the world's population lives in areas that exhibit an "ecological deficit", meaning these societies are depleting resources faster than the time it takes for natural ecosystems to regenerate them.[10] To date, countries like Belgium, Ecuador, France, Germany, Indonesia, Luxembourg, Spain, Switzerland, and the United Arab Emirates have adopted EF to calculate their national footprint and prioritize actions based on identified hotspots. In terms of its predisposition for a combination with other methodologies, EF relates closely to MFA and may serve as a screening indicator for environmental performance.

12.7 Environmentally weighted Material Consumption (EMC)

EMC is an attempt to define an indicator for the environmental impacts relating to the use of one certain resource. This is done by multiplying the amount of each resource used by a factor (the environmental impact indicator) thought to represent the overall environmental burden it causes. The impact factors attached to the different materials being assessed can be derived from LCA databases (Giljum et al. 2011), while resource use would come from material flow data. EMC can best express its full potential when used regularly over time, for its sequential data can show if a separation between economic growth and environmental damage is taking place within a certain economic system (Reisinger et al. 2009) – for example, because of the adoption or specific circular policies or programmes.

12.8 Land and Ecosystem Accounts (LEAC)

LEAC has been promoted by the Environmental European Agency (EEA) as a means to provide reliable information to policymakers regarding how different land areas are being used for economic activities, hence inform environmental policies or conduct advanced assessments and analytical modelling (Romanowicz et al. 2006). LEAC assessments have already been performed in 24 European countries and the results have been published by EEA.[11] To help assessing the impact of human activities on ecosystems and biodiversity, EEA released in 2005 the LEAC Methodological Guidebook (Gómez and Ferran 2005), prompting other scholars to suggest the type of information that should be fed into the LEAC database: remote-sensed (satellite) data, data on net primary production (NPP), demographics, and spatially distributed economic data (Reisinger et al. 2009).

12.9 Human Appropriation of Net Primary Production (HANPP)

HANPP is another approach to estimate man-made land appropriation and use intensity which provides insights into the pressure exerted by human activities on natural ecosystems. HANPP assessments are fed with data coming from agricultural and forestry statistics and inventories, land use statistics, and geographic information systems (GIS) technology (Reisinger et al. 2009) to measure the amount of NPP – the organic matter produced by vegetation cover – captured by economic activities and thus no longer available to natural processes. HANPP assessments are conducted on delimited spatial areas, requiring three categories of data: the NPP of the vegetation assuming no interference by humans, the current NPP, and the human harvest of NPP (Haberl et al. 2001).

12.10 Environmental Impact Assessment (EIA) and Strategic Environmental Assessment (SEA)

According to the International Association for Impact Assessment (IAIA), EIA is the "process of identifying, predicting and mitigating the biophysical, social and other relevant effects of development proposals prior to major decisions being taken and commitments made[12]" (IAIA 1996, p. 2). EIA applies to all (macro) development projects – like the construction of roads or dams – that can have a significant effect upon the environment and must be undertaken at the project's planning phase to effectively influence design and further execution. The EIA process comprises a set of sequential stages, going from an initial screening of the project to evaluate whether or not a complete EIA is necessary, through to the assessment of potential impacts and mitigation measures, and up to the final approval/rejection by the authority of the solution presented by the developer (Figure 12.1).

SEA operates at policy, plan, or programme level, and – like EIA – aims at ensuring that environmental consequences are comprehensively included and fully addressed in the decision-making process of new developments. Below, the key stages of a typical SEA assessment are represented (OECD 2006) (Figure 12.2). By embedding CE considerations in both EIA and SEA, organizations and public institutions alike can identify opportunities to boost circular practices and promote closed-loop

Figure 12.1 The Stages of an EIA.

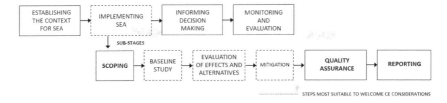

Figure 12.2 The Stages of a SEA.

processes. The inclusion of circular indicators and metrics can occur at the following stages of EIA and SEA processes (Yijun et al. 2011):

- *Baseline study*: the purpose of this stage is to comprehensively measure and evaluate the status of the environment as it is, before the new development being implemented. Currently, this means taking stock of both the quantity and quality of environmental factors like biodiversity, water, air, and soil. Adding circular indicators would imply the inclusion of evaluations on the status of key resources for the CE like rare-Earth elements (REEs), water reuse, and renewable energy sources. The assessment should measure not only the availability of these resources, but also other important indexes like total utilization volumes and utilization efficiency (Yijun et al. 2011).
- *EIA of the proposed development*: mirroring the enhanced spectrum of data sought in the baseline evaluation, the impact evaluation stage would also broaden its scope to identify and measure the likely impacts on the CE factors identified earlier.
- *Mitigation*: this stage is possibly the most suited to welcome CE principles, particularly in contexts where end-of-pipe solutions[13] have traditionally been prioritized for environmental protection. Alternative measures, like establishing closed-loop processes, adopting renewable energy sources, or replacing chemicals with bio-based products could in fact play an important role in reducing the overall environmental impact of a new development.

12.11 Cost–Benefit Analysis (CBA) and Cost-Effectiveness Analysis (CEA)

CBA is a decision support tool widely used by the public administration to establish whether to undertake a certain development project like airports or highways. In CBA, all costs and benefits are identified (including those bound to manifest overtime), converted into a one-dimensional measure (money), and then evaluated following a methodology that allows to estimate their present value. As such, both indicators (costs "C" and benefits "B") can be narrowed down to a single number, so that the action is worth pursuing only if B>C. Sometimes however, CBA is inadequate to grasp the entire complexity of a policy scenario (e.g. pollution control measures for which a minimum/maximum safety threshold must be established) or to monetize certain effects (e.g. over health). In those cases, CEA can prove a more useful option as it aims at identifying the cheapest means for achieving the desired environmental target. At the current stage of a transition towards CE, public institutions may decide to undertake the earlier analyses to evaluate, for example, different alternatives with respect to recycling, refurbishing, asset sharing, etc.

12.12 Conclusions

The tools presented in this chapter deal with the identification and collection of environmental information and data at a macro level to inform sustainability decisions as well as monitoring the progress towards a CE system. The information collected by these tools is clearly of great relevance for all private organizations, whose strategies are constantly influenced by local as well as global environmental regulations, trends, and standards. Similarly, to the methods discussed in the previous chapter, the macro-level tools of chapter 12 can be used either separately or in combination. Their different scope makes them at times suitable to complement each other, especially since their linkages and connections are becoming increasingly evident to companies in the pursuit of holistic approaches capable of embracing apparently incompatible metrics. Among the dimensions to be considered when evaluating if two or more approaches are compatible with each other are: time horizon, system boundaries, and data type (Finnveden and Moberg 2005).

The extent to which these tools are already being leveraged to support circular decisions in the public sector varies greatly by geographical area and type of tool. While in fact the application of EIA, SEA, and CBA is still theoretical regarding CE, other tools have already been tested successfully (e.g. MFA–LCA and VCA). Looking ahead, most (if not all) of these macro-level methodologies will prove useful in identifying hotspots for CE interventions and in defining specific CE targets (e.g. MFA and EIOA) or assessing whether eco-economic decoupling is occurring as a result of CE policies adoption (e.g. EMC, LEAC, and HANPP).

Notes

1 As reported in Chapter 2, examples of circularity at a territorial level cover different sizes, ranging from cities (London's "Advance London" project) to States (the tax breaks on repair activities introduced by the Swedish government in 2017) and even entire continents (the EU Action Plan for the Circular Economy).

2 Wahlquist Calla. 2017. "Victoria Moves to Become First State to Enshrine Renewable Energy Targets in Law." *The Guardian*. August 23, 2017. www.theguardian.com/australia-news/2017/aug/23/victoria-moves-to-become-first-state-to-enshrine-renewable-energy-targets-in-law.

3 The Organization for Economic Cooperation and Development (OECD). 2008. "Measuring Material Flows and Resource Productivity. Volume I: The OECD Guide." Accessed on March 10, 2018. www.oecd.org/env/indicators-modelling-outlooks/MFA-Synthesis.pdf.

4 Ministry of the Environment, Government of Japan. 2003. "Fundamental Plan for Establishing a Sound Material-Cycle Society." Accessed January 10, 2018. www.env.go.jp/en/recycle/smcs/f_plan.pdf.

5 Circle Economy. 2016. "Circular Amsterdam. A Vision and Action Agenda for the City and Metropolitan Area." Accessed on February 13, 2018. www.circle-economy.com/wp-content/uploads/2016/04/Circular-Amsterdam-EN-small-210316.pdf?submission=364946456.

6 Input–output tables are integrated at the country level into the economic national accounts that, in turn, are used to elaborate statistics such as the Gross Domestic Product (GDP). Such calculations are made following the United Nations 1993 System of National Accounts, the international standard for the compilation, and reporting of national economic statistics that allow for easy comparison of data between countries.

7 The United Nations Statistics Division. 2010. "Handbook of National Accounting—Input-Output Table Compilation and Analysis." Accessed on March 10, 2018. https://unstats.un.org/unsd/EconStatKB/Knowledgebase Article10053.aspx.

8 Policy Design Lab. n.d. "Environmental Input-Output Analysis / Environmentally Extended Input-Output." Accessed on April 10, 2018. http://policy-design.org/wiki/policy-formulation-2/formulation-tools-in-support-of-life-cycle-assessment-lca/environmental-input-output-analysis-environmentally-extended-input-output/.

9 European Topic Centre on Sustainable Consumption and Production. n.d. "Life-Cycle Assessment and Life-Cycle Thinking in Resource and Waste Management." Accessed on January 10, 2017. http://scp.eionet.europa.eu/themes/lca.

10 Global Footprint Network. n.d. "Country Work." Accessed on February 2, 2018. www.footprintnetwork.org/our-work/countries/.

11 European Environmental Agency (EEA). 2006 "Land Accounts for Europe 1990–2000. Towards Integrated Land and Ecosystem Accounting." *EEA Report No 11/2006*. Accessed on March 15, 2018. www.eea.europa.eu/publications/eea_report_2006_11.

12 International Association for Impact Assessment (IAIA). 1996. "Principles of Environmental Impact Assessment Best Practice." Accessed on February 13, 2018. www.iaia.org/uploads/pdf/principlesEA_1.pdf.

13 "End-of-pipe solution" is an approach to pollution control which concentrates on effluent treatment or filtration prior to discharge into the environment, as opposed to making changes in the process generating waste (Source: www.eionet.europa.eu/gemet/en/concept/2707).

Bibliography

Allesch, Astrid, and Paul H Brunner. 2015. "Material Flow Analysis as a Decision Support Tool for Waste Management: A Literature Review." *Journal of Industrial Ecology* 19: 753–764.

Bailey, Reid, Janet K. Allen, and Bert Bras. 2004a. "Applying Ecological Input-Output Flow Analysis to Material Flows in Industrial Systems: Part I: Tracing Flows." *Journal of Industrial Ecology* 8: 45–68. doi:10.1162/10881980 41269346.

Bailey, Reid, Bert Bras, and Janet K. Allen. 2004b. "Applying Input-Output Flow Analysis to Material Flows in Industrial Systems, Part 2: Flow Metrics." *Journal of Industrial Ecology* 8(1–2): 69–91.

Brunner, Paul H., and Helmut Rechberger. 2004. *Practical Handbook of Material Flow Analysis.* Boca Raton, FL: CRC Press.

Cicas, Gyorgyi, Chris T. Hendrickson, Arpad Horvath, and H. Scott Matthews. 2007. "A Regional Version of a U.S. Economic Input-Output Life-Cycle Assessment Model." *The International Journal of Life Cycle Assessment* 12 (6): 365–372. doi:10.1065/lca2007.04.318.

Circle Economy. 2016. "Circular Amsterdam. A Vision and Action Agenda for the City and Metropolitan Area." Accessed on February 13, 2018. www.circle-economy.com/wp-content/uploads/2016/04/Circular-Amsterdam-EN-small-210316.pdf?submission=364946456.

European Environmental Agency (EEA). 2006 "Land Accounts for Europe 1990–2000. Towards Integrated Land and Ecosystem Accounting." *EEA Report No 11/2006.* Accessed on March 15, 2018. www.eea.europa.eu/publications/eea_report_2006_11.

European Topic Centre on Sustainable Consumption and Production. n.d. "Life-Cycle Assessment and Life-Cycle Thinking in Resource and Waste Management." Accessed on January 10, 2017. http://scp.eionet.europa.eu/themes/lca.

Fearne, Andrew, Marian Garcia Martinez, and Benjamin Dent. 2012. "Dimensions of Sustainable Value Chains: Implications for Value Chain Analysis." *Supply Chain Management: An International Journal* 17 (6): 575–581. https://doi.org/10.1108/13598541211269193.

Finnveden, Göran, and Åsa Moberg. 2005. "Environmental Systems Analysis Tools—An Overview." *Journal of Cleaner Production* 13 (12): 1165–1173. https://doi.org/10.1016/j.jclepro.2004.06.004.

Giljum, Stefan, Eva Burger, Friedrich Hinterberger, Stephan Lutter, and Martin Bruckner. 2011. "A Comprehensive Set of Resource Use Indicators from the Micro to the Macro Level." *Resources, Conservation and Recycling* 55 (3): 300–308. https://doi.org/10.1016/j.resconrec.2010.09.009.

Global Footprint Network. n.d. "Country Work." Accessed on February 2, 2018. www.footprintnetwork.org/our-work/countries/.

Gómez, Oscar, and Paramo Ferran. 2005. "Land and Ecosystem Accounts (LEAC). Methodological Guidebook: Data Processing of Land Cover Flows." Universitat Antònoma de Barcelona, European Environment Agency.

Haberl, Helmut, Karl-Heinz Erb, and Krausmann Fridolin. 2007. "Human Appropriation of Net Primary Production (HANPP)." *Entry Prepared for the Internet Encyclopaedia of Ecological Economics.* www.researchgate.net/publication/11307431_Human_Appropriation_of_Net_Primary_Production.

Huang, Y. Anny, Manfred Lenzen, Christopher L. Weber, Joy Murray, and H. Scott Matthews. 2009. "The Role of Input–Output Analysis for the Screening of Corporate Carbon Footprints." *Economic Systems Research* 21 (3): 217–242. https://doi.org/10.1080/09535310903541348.

Huijbregts, Mark AJ, Stefanie Hellweg, Rolf Frischknecht, Konrad Hunger-bühler, and A. Jan Hendriks. 2008. "Ecological Footprint Accounting in the Life Cycle Assessment of Products." *Ecological Economics* 64 (4): 798–807.

International Association for Impact Assessment (IAIA). 1996. "Principles of Environmental Impact Assessment Best Practice." Accessed on February 13, 2018. www.iaia.org/uploads/pdf/principlesEA_1.pdf.

Jeswani, Harish Kumar, Adisa Azapagic, Philipp Schepelmann, and Michael Ritthoff. 2010. "Options for Broadening and Deepening the LCA Approaches." *Journal of Cleaner Production* 18 (2): 120–127. https://doi.org/10.1016/j.jclepro.2009.09.023.

Joint Research Centre of the European Commission. 2012a. "Life Cycle Indicators for Resources, Products and Waste: Waste Management." *Publications Office of the European Union*. doi:10.2788/50351.

Joint Research Centre of the European Commission. 2012b. "Life Cycle Indicators for Resources, Products and Waste: Resources, Resource-Efficiency, Decoupling." *Publications Office of the European Union*. doi:10.2788/49877.

Kalmykova, Yuliya, Madumita Sadagopan, and Leonardo Rosado. 2018. "Circular Economy—From Review of Theories and Practices to Development of Implementation Tools." *Resources, Conservation and Recycling* 135 (2018): 190–201. https://doi.org/10.1016/j.resconrec.2017.10.034.

Kleijn, René. 2001. "Adding It All Up. The Sense and Non-Sense of Bulk-MFA." *Journal of Industrial Ecology* 4 (2), 7–8. https://doi.org/10.1162/108819800569762.

Lavers, Alexandra, Yuliya Kalmykova, Leonardo Rosado, Felipe Oliveira, and Rafael Laurenti. "Selecting representative products for quantifying environmental impacts of consumption in urban areas." *Journal of Cleaner Production* 162 (2017): 34–44.

Ministry of the Environment, Government of Japan. 2003. "Fundamental Plan for Establishing a Sound Material-Cycle Society." Accessed on January 10, 2018. www.env.go.jp/en/recycle/smcs/f_plan.pdf.

Ness, Barry, Evelin Urbel-Piirsalu, Stefan Anderberg, and Lennart Olsson. 2007. "Categorising Tools for Sustainability Assessment." *Ecological Economics* 60 (2007): 498–508. https://doi.org/10.1016/j.ecolecon.2006.07.023.

Policy Design Lab. n.d. "Environmental Input-Output Analysis / Environmentally Extended Input-Output." Accessed on April 10, 2018. http://policy-design.org/wiki/policy-formulation-2/formulation-tools-in-support-of-life-cycle-assessment-lca/environmental-input-output-analysis-environmentally-extended-input-output/.

Reisinger, Hubert, Nina Eisenmenger, John Ferguson, Judit Kanthak, Giovanni Finocchiaro, Graham Donachie, Cathy Maguire, Iñaki Arto, and Christoph Rotzetter. 2009. Material Flow Analysis (MFA) for Resource Policy Decision Support. Position Paper of the Interest Group on the Sustainable Use of Natural Resources on the Needs for Further Development of MFA Based Indicators." Accessed on January 23, 2018. http://epanet.pbe.eea.europa.eu/fol249409/our-publications/MFA_for_Resources_Paper_IG_Resources_090911_final.pdf/download/en/1/MFA_for_Resources_Paper_IG_Resources_090911_final.pdf.

Romanowicz, A., F. Daffner, R. Uhel, and J. L. Weber. 2006. "European Environment Agency Developments of Land and Ecosystem Accounts: General

Overview." *Systemics, Cybernetics and Informatics* 6 (2). www.iiisci.org/journal/CV$/sci/pdfs/M567EH.pdf.

Soosay, Claudine, Andrew Fearne, and Benjamin Dent. 2012. "Sustainable Value Chain Analysis—A Case Study of Oxford Landing from "vine to dine"". *Supply Chain Management: An International Journal* 17 (1): 68–77. doi:10.1108/13598541211212212.

Suh, Sangwon, and Shinichiro Nakamura. 2007. "Five Years in the Area of Input-Output and Hybrid LCA." *The International Journal of Life Cycle Assessment* 12: 351. https://doi.org/10.1065/lca2007.08.358.

Taylor, David H. 2005. "Value Chain Analysis: An Approach to Supply Chain Improvement in Agri-Food Chains." *International Journal of Physical Distribution & Logistics Management* 35 (10): 744–761. doi:10.1108/096000 30510634599.

The Organization for Economic Cooperation and Development (OECD). 2006. "Applying Strategic Environmental Assessment. Good Practice Guidance for Development Co-Operation." *DAC Guidelines and Reference Series.* Accessed on April 15, 2018. www.oecd.org/environment/environment-development/37353858.pdf.

The Organization for Economic Cooperation and Development (OECD). 2008. "Measuring Material Flows and Resource Productivity. Volume I: The OECD Guide." Accessed on March 10, 2018. www.oecd.org/env/indicators-modelling-outlooks/MFA-Synthesis.pdf.

The United Nations Statistics Division. 2010. "Handbook of National Accounting—Input-Output Table Compilation and Analysis." Accessed on March 10, 2018. https://unstats.un.org/unsd/EconStatKB/KnowledgebaseArticle10053.aspx.

Wahlquist, Calla. 2017. "Victoria Moves to Become First State to Enshrine Renewable Energy Targets in Law." *The Guardian*, August 23, 2017. www.theguardian.com/australia-news/2017/aug/23/victoria-moves-to-become-first-state-to-enshrine-renewable-energy-targets-in-law.

Yi, Ilseuk, Norihiro Itsubo, Atsushi Inaba, and Kanji Matsumoto. 2007. "Development of the Interregional I/O Based LCA Method Considering Region Specifics of Indirect Effects in Regional Evaluation." *International Journal of Life Cycle Assessment* 12 (6), 353–364. doi:10.1065/lca2007.06.3.

Yijun, Ji, He Ying, and Sun Xuhong. 2011. "Applying Circular Economy Theory in Environmental Impact Assessment." *Energy Procedia* 11: 4013–4018.

13 Conclusions

Time is running out! The future is set! We cannot go back! Alarming and devious statements that can yet represent business opportunities never seen before. The devastating environmental truths behind the unprecedented and steady growth in material wealth that has experienced humanity since the Second Industrial Revolution can no longer be argued or ignored. The reality in which we live gives firms two options: take notice but do not act and instead go with the flow until externally forced to change (due to depletion or prohibitive prices of raw materials, customers' boycotts, environmental regulations, etc.), or take charge of the situation and rethink their business models from top to bottom.

The linear system of production or take-make-waste paradigm, where natural resources are extracted from the Earth, processed, and transformed into usable objects that eventually (and rather quickly) get incinerated or discarded in landfills, brought the Earth on the brink of destruction. By decoupling environmental degradation from economic prosperity, the CE model offers a new framework for achieving a development "that meets the needs of the present without compromising the ability of future generations to meet their own needs" (Brundtland 1987, pp.11). The fit between CE and Brundtland's embryonic definition of sustainable development seems even more adequate under the Planetary Boundaries (PB) perspective, which sets the limits for conducting human activities so that the ability of future generations to meet their own needs will no longer be in danger. PB in fact do not provide any guidance on how to create an economic system capable of respecting the safe operating space it proposes, and the CE model stands out as the missing link for operationalizing, at an actionable level, those scientific findings.

CE embraces all stages of the value chain to retain the full worth of both biosphere and technosphere products. It applies to all industries (non-manufacturing included) in terms of their products, services, and processes across departments, markets, and geographies. This all-inclusiveness makes the paradigm valid for a world economy, while its focus on profitability makes it appealing and pragmatic. But the will to change how we do business is not just a consequence of economic interests or environmental pressures. A favourable alignment of technological, regulatory, and social factors is also contributing to the exponential interest towards CE. Regarding high-tech, companies can now choose from a sizable range of enabling solutions when defining their circular strategies, which can be broadly divided into digital and design/engineering technologies. Among the former are IoT, trace and return systems, mobile apps, digital sharing platforms, big data, and digital substitutes like cloud computing. Primary technologies for design and engineering include green chemistry, open source, 3D printing, and advanced recycling solutions. When adopting such technologies in line with CE principles, the results for firms are innovative business models and novel approaches of product design, material management, and value retention to continually circulate flows of products, components, and materials at their highest utility, thus creating value-creation systems that are decoupled from natural resource exploitation and environmental pollution.

CE is an elegantly simple and straightforward concept but, at the same time, a rather complex melting pot of principles and ideas derived from a variety of philosophies and approaches to environmental sustainability – like Cradle to Cradle, Biomimicry, Regenerative Design, Natural Capitalism, Blue Economy, Industrial Ecology, and Permaculture. There is no one-size-fits-all solution for CE adoption in the private sector, as the many facets of the paradigm need to be acknowledged and investigated before a new array of core competencies can be envisaged: one based on specific resources and capabilities moulded with circularity in mind. As we cannot expect and would be disastrous for companies to radically change their business models and processes overnight, we wanted to give managers a CE-actionable framework to learn about circular thinking and its opportunities. The strategic management process presented in this book is a structured roadmap filled with the typical tools and methodologies that companies have been applying to their businesses for decades (e.g. VRIE, Five Forces, PEST, and SWOT), but here calibrated for a CE assessment that investigates internal, industry, and external settings.

The tools we selected support a comprehensive strategic decision-making process, but the list was not meant to be exhaustive. Other tools for strategic management exist and their "usual" application could theoretically be reconsidered in light of CE considerations. Growth is a major theme in business, and when sought, it is important to establish its direction. Important tools of growth and corporate strategy include: the "Strategy Direction Matrix" of product vs market, with its options of specialization, vertical integration, economies of scope, economies of search, or unrelated diversification (Ansoff and McDonnell 1988); the 3 × 3 GE-McKinsey matrix to assess business strength vs industry attractiveness (Coyne 2008); or the BCG matrix of market share vs industry growth rate (Morrison and Wensley 1991). Also, the Kraljic portfolio matrix (1983) to optimize the use of capabilities of different suppliers, and thus managing them most effectively, could find great applications under a strategic CE perspective. During strategy implementation – an aspect of the strategic management process barely touched in this book – the Balanced Scorecard is definitely a tool that could be worth a mention, especially for communication purposes and its ability to link strategic statements with tangible actions (Kaplan and Norton 1992).

With regard to implementation – and quantification/monitoring activities – a full set of (accounting) tools is already available to practitioners. They can be broadly divided into two families – for micro- and macro-level studies – although the possible units of analysis (substance, material, product, individual, company, conglomerate, supply chain, industry, community, country, and region) do not really allow for such a neat separation and some tools find application at multiple points of this continuum. What is true is that the extensive number and characteristics of these instruments attest the pervasive nature of environmental sustainability, and consequently CE applications. In this book, we have limited ourselves to mention some of the main concepts of environmental accounting in an effort to introduce the reader to the vast potential already available in the quantification of environmental sustainability. Beside what is already at our disposal in terms of methods, indicators, and indices, there is continuous development in the field with most findings being the result of very recent research activities. The level of fervour, of course, causes multiple overlaps, duplications, and sometimes modest propositions, but good approaches are already available, well-tested, and perhaps even more importantly converging towards a level of integration that will allow for comprehensive as well as solidly grounded analyses. This trend is of particular interest to firms, for at least three reasons: (1) they are positioned in the centre of value chains which can greatly influence or control; (2) they represent a unit of analysis also meaningful for extrapolation or interpolation in the running of simulations; and (3) they generally are – or could be – a great source of primary data, useful in benchmarking or to negotiate active roles in open-source projects.

Digitalization and globalization forces have guided changes in the global economy since the turn of the century. A look into the future and we can easily imagine an industrial organization and social structure monopolized by business ecosystems and megacities. As these macro systems develop, it seems reasonable to also envisage a virtuous self-reinforcing loop between these organizational forms and CE best practices. In the private sector, large MNCs – arguably the promoters and engines of business ecosystems – are all already active in developing CE competencies and forging partnerships with like-minded entities when these cannot be internalized, often breaking the sectorial boundaries typical of business as usual. As a consequence, also SMEs and start-ups, wishing to be part of future economic transactions (especially in B2B), will be forced to be circular and bring specific CE-oriented resources and capabilities to the ecosystem. Similarly, in the public sector, megacities that are CE-efficient will attract and favour businesses whose offering, in terms of products and services, is compliant with the CE principles of the urban settlement.

Bibliography

Ansoff, H. Igor, and Edward J. McDonnell. 1988. *The New Corporate Strategy.* New York, NY: John Wiley & Sons.

Brundtland Commission. 1987. *Our Common Future: Report of the World Commission on Environment and Development.* Oxford, UK: Oxford University Press.

Coyne, Kevin. 2008 "Enduring Ideas: The GE-McKinsey Nine-Box Matrix." *McKinsey Quarterly* (Sep).

Kaplan, Robert S., and David P. Norton. 1992. "The Balanced Scorecard: Measures That Drive Performance." *Harvard Business Review* 70 (Jan–Feb): 71–79.

Kraljic, Peter. 1983. "Purchasing Must Become Supply Management." *Harvard Business Review* 61 (5): 109–17.

Morrison, Alan, and Robin Wensley. 1991. "Boxing up or Boxed In? A Short History of the Boston Consulting Group Share/Growth Matrix." *Journal of Marketing Management* 7 (2): 105–29.

Index

Note: **Boldface** page numbers refer to tables; *italic* page numbers refer to figures; page numbers followed by "n" denote endnotes

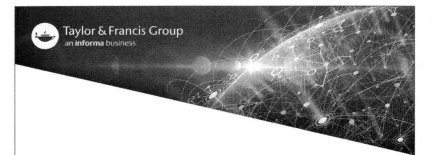